Andy Harper is a high school physical education teacher by qualification, a professional footballer by passion and a football commentator by fortune. During his fifteen-year NSL playing career he has worked in football coaching and development and served on the executive of the Australian Professional Footballers' Association. He has regularly appeared on SBS's football programs (including their France '98 World Cup coverage) and is part of Channel Nine's Korea/Japan 2002 World Cup Finals commentary team. Andy's business card reads, 'Football Odyssey—Enjoying the Journey' which sums up his worldview and his raison d'être.

Josh Whittington loves many sports but has always known that soccer (football) is the greatest of them all. Growing up, his sporting heroes were overseas footballers Diego Maradona, Marco Van Basten and Ruud Gullit. While working as a journalist, Josh completed a masters degree in sports media and as a result of his studies realises his childhood list of sporting heroes would have included Johnny Warren if Australian soccer had ever been given the credit it is due. Josh has played semi-professional football in the New South Wales Premier League and is now playing amateur football in England.

Sheilas, wogs & poofters

An incomplete biography of Johnny Warren and soccer in Australia

Johnny Warren

with Andy Harper & Josh Whittington

Random House Australia Pty Ltd
20 Alfred Street, Milsons Point, NSW 2061
http://www.randomhouse.com.au

Sydney   New York   Toronto
London   Auckland   Johannesburg

First published by Random House Australia 2002

Copyright © Johnny Warren 2002
Introduction, Chapters 15 and 18–20 and Epilogue
by Andy Harper and Johnny Warren
Chapters 1–16 by Josh Whittington and Johnny Warren
Chapter 17 by Andy Harper, Josh Whittington and Johnny Warren

All rights reserved. No part of this publication may be reproduced, stored in
a retrieval system, or transmitted in any form or by any means, electronic,
mechanical, photocopying, recording or otherwise, without the prior written
permission of the publisher.

National Library of Australia
Cataloguing-in-Publication Entry

   Warren Johnny, 1943-.
   Sheilas, wogs & poofters: an incomplete biography of Johnny
   Warren and soccer in Australia.

   ISBN 1 74051 121 2.

   1. Warren, Johnny, 1943-. 2. Socceroos (Soccer team). 3. Soccer
   players - Australia - Biography. 4. Soccer - Australia - History.
   I. Harper, Andy. II. Whittington, Josh. III. Title.

796.334092

Cover and internal design by Greendot Design
Cover photos and internal photos c/o Johnny Warren except
for picture of the Socceroos in 2001 © Getty Images
Typeset in 11.5/14 pt Garamond 3 by Bookhouse, Sydney
Printed and bound by Griffin Press, Netley, South Australia

10 9 8 7

This book is dedicated to the inventor of the round ball, the greatest and most pleasurable toy of mankind—can you imagine life without it? It is also dedicated to the true believers in Australia for their support of the greatest game of all. I would finally like to dedicate the book to my family, in particular to my late father Victor, my late nephew Timothy and my daughter Shannon.

Contents

Acknowledgments *ix*
Tribute *xi*
Sheilas, Wogs & Poofters: An Introduction *xiii*

1 Wog Warren's Early Years *1*
2 Canterbury Babes *18*
3 The 'Big' Move *40*
4 Australia's Sporting Gallipoli:
Our First World Cup Attempt *52*
5 My Coming of Age *60*
6 The Birth of the Socceroos: the Vietnam War *67*
7 The Mighty Saints *83*
8 The Curse on Australian Football *98*
9 Our Revenge *108*
10 The Dark Days *119*
11 Australia Makes It: The 1974 World Cup *133*
12 Goal of a Lifetime: A Dream Finish *166*
13 Football: The First Sport to Go National *176*
14 The New York Cosmos *198*
15 Australia's Best Coach: SBS *214*
16 My Latin Love Affair *225*
17 The Olympics *252*
18 The Mourning After *266*
19 The Young Guns *304*
20 Where to Now? *328*

Epilogue *344*

Acknowledgments

⚽ *Why don't you write a book about Australian soccer and your time in it?* is a question that has been put to me thousands of times over the years. It might sound easy but it's far from it. I set out to write my autobiography and history of Australian soccer and have, at best, come up with an incomplete insight into both.

This book would not be possible without my publishers, Random House Australia, who dared to go where other publishers would not with the bold and perhaps somewhat controversial title *Sheilas, Wogs & Poofters*. My stand was always that the book had to bear this title or otherwise there would be no book. I lost other publishers on that basis so I thank Random House, in particular Jeanne Ryckmans, for having the balls to back us. A special word of thanks goes to Jo Butler for her patience and expertise and, like Jeanne, for her support and enthusiasm.

Having an attention span of three seconds, I needed people to put my thoughts down on paper and, in this respect, Josh Whittington and Andy Harper were fabulous teammates on this exciting mission. Josh, a university graduate and young player recovering from knee reconstruction surgery, and Andy, a highly educated student of the game and player in his own right at the highest level in this country, are both true believers. They pushed me and supported me during the tough times. Andy, whose contribution to this book has been outstanding, worked with me at SBS for three years until he moved to Channel Nine for the World Cup 2002 coverage, is a true pro and is representative of the army of people at SBS who have put all their efforts into taking the world game to the Australian people.

In thanking everyone, I want to make particular mention of my SBS colleague and friend, and one of the network's great characters, Boucci Kowalenko, for her encouragement when the yards became harder and for her invaluable advice while reading the manuscript and listening to my thoughts. Also, a special thank you to colleague Lou Gautier, who I have known for forty years from the days when the national team first travelled in the early 1960s, for reading the final manuscript.

It has been impossible to mention everyone who has been involved in my life in football and in the writing of this book and I feel I haven't acknowledged many people I played with over my career and others who have been an influence on my life. You will know who you are and my thanks go out to you all.

Tribute

 'To think of football as 22 hirelings kicking a ball is to say that a violin is merely wood and catgut, that Hamlet is so much ink and paper.'

J. B. Priestley

In the symphony orchestra that is world sport, football (soccer) is the lead violin. While barely musical, Johnny Warren's philosophical ear has leaned towards the Stradivarius end of the sports' spectrum for decades. In this respect he is ahead of his time.

Johnny is a forward thinker, the quintessential big-picture man. For Johnny, his big picture has often borne the brunt of scandalous ignorance from those outside football and wanton disregard from those within. From his adolescent days, behind the veil of cloistered Cold War Australia, Australian-born Johnny Warren fell in love with the world game. And, as much as he could see football for what it was, equally were his parochial countrymen blinded. Perhaps it is our status as an island nation that makes us fearful of things dubbed foreign. Wrongly, football was considered one such thing. In many ways and on many occasions it would have been easier for him to leave Australia and live elsewhere. In almost any one of the world's countries where football is respected and adored; where it is both *lingua franca* and currency, Johnny Warren would have felt comfortable. But, unlike others of equal standing in their respective fields who, over the years, have left Australia for destinations friendlier to their professional sensibilities, Johnny Warren has stayed to fight—with dignity, determination and doggedness. His one great hope in life has been that Australia would share the world's love of football—and do so for its own good.

We live in a world and work in a sport that are both perennially suspicious of people's motives. However, since I have known him I have never suspected a Johnny Warren public postulation to be made out of selfish ambition or vain conceit. It is always for the sake of the game that he speaks out. For him, to gain is to see Australia embrace football and to see Australia embraced by the world, through football. Football is the visa that our nation's passport needs, particularly in these globalised times. Johnny cottoned on to that fact long ago and his work from then until now has been to open Australia's eyes to this reality.

His frustration comes from his impatience and that he doesn't think he will see Australia become a football country in his time. But there is a grand work definitely in progress and lying very close to its source is Johnny Warren. He has made his mark on Australia, and indelibly so. Let Australia's sports historians judge him reverently, for no less is deserved.

Thank you Johnny for inviting my contribution to your book. Thank you for including me in your mission.

Andy Harper, 2002

Sheilas, Wogs & Poofters:
An Introduction

⚽ THROUGHOUT MY LIFE, football has come to mean so much to me. It has made me more aware, it has awakened the world citizen inside me and it has alerted me to what the sport is capable of achieving for my own wonderful country, Australia. Football has been the vehicle as well as the window for that awakening. I want the same experience of awakening and awareness for Australia. No other sport reflects life more than football. Perhaps that is one of the reasons why it is so popular around the world. People relate intimately to the ninety minutes of drama that unfolds before them in a football match, because it is so often a metaphor of their own existence. Of course, the game is aesthetically beautiful too, but this is a more subjective thing. In half the games we see, the best team doesn't win, just as the best person doesn't always get the top job or the most deserving person isn't always rewarded. Soccer reflects all those injustices and it is the way people relate to football that brings the emotion into the game. It is the sport of the people of the world. It is physically, socially and financially democratic.

I am fascinated by soccer's story in Australia. It has been one of struggle; an incredible, relentless, frustrating and frequently unjust struggle. Soccer is a sport with a long history in this country, a sport which provided a vehicle for assimilation for new Australians, the sport of the people of the world and the national sport of the country which, historically, was so connected with Australia's national psyche—England. Yet, soccer in Australia still faces entrenched cultural and institutional resistance. One only has to scan the national newspapers to get the feeling that the editors consider the sport a minor one and not worthy of much coverage except, of course, for the occasional incident of crowd trouble when there is always a camera available and a reporter ready with pen poised. For the most part, Australians are fixated on what are relatively minor sports. The big news is rugby league or Aussie Rules. In world terms, who plays these sports? Yet, at the same time, we have our own Australian soccer players like Viduka and Kewell performing on the world's largest stages. Their exploits and triumphs scarcely feature at all in our mainstream media. Maradona, considered by many throughout the world as the greatest footballer of all time, was barely considered newsworthy in Australia (except at SBS) for the magnificent feats he performed on the football field until, of course, drugs and scandal took over his life and then he became front-page news. Local soccer, the NSL, faces the same predicament. There never seems to be footage of goals and games but the rare moment that there is any sort of crowd disturbance the cameras are there to capture the action and lead the news for that night. Why is this so?

Sheilas, Wogs & Poofters is really the story of my time in soccer in this country. It is a story of discrimination against the game and the individuals in it. I hope the title doesn't offend anyone—it's not meant to. And if it does offend in twenty-first century Australia then you can imagine what it was like fifty-odd years ago. 'Sheilas', 'wogs' and 'poofters' were considered the second-class citizens of the day and if you played soccer you were considered one of them. That's how soccer was regarded back then and, to some extent, still is today.

Understanding the social environment of Australia fifty-odd years ago offers some insight into the discrimination that, unfortunately in large part, has plagued Australian soccer and its players. The setting of my upbringing was classic postwar Sydney. Extended and close-knit families, sun-drenched summers playing cricket, grazed knees from tarred playing fields, 'six'n'out' and broken windows. A city rebalancing after the turmoil of the war, a society looking to redefine its mores and holding fast to what it knew to be true.

My brothers and I were products of people who had lived through the Depression. The Depression taught my parents not to take anything for granted and to always have a contingency or escape plan. They firmly believed that education and sport were an integral part of life. Like all Australian kids we played heaps of sport. Golf, cricket, swimming, tennis—you name it. When we played tennis we pretended we were tennis stars Lew Hoad and Ken Rosewall, when we played cricket we were Norm O'Neill, and when we played golf we were Peter Thomson. We played every sport we could and didn't specialise in one in particular. It is one of my favourite jibes that while Pelé is the world's most outstanding footballer, I'd bet he wasn't proficient in cricket, tennis, golf and swimming, the staple diet of many an Australian childhood.

But always superimposed over the playfulness and backyard test matches of my childhood was an understanding that we had to get a good education. Do well at school and graduate to university. Work hard and leave nothing to chance—a real White Anglo–Saxon Protestant worldview. My parents wanted us to have opportunities they were denied. Education was the gateway to a happy life. That was the culture of our time. The Second World War was still a fresh memory and the Cold War was upon us. There was an ever-present lack of certainty in society and the way to avoid the anxiety that resulted from this was to guarantee your future. Like all kids through the ages, though, these were the worries of adults. All we wanted to do was play sport.

On both sides of my family I am sixth-generation Australian. My mother's great-great-grandparents came out to this country from Leeds in England as a seventeen-year-old married couple in 1824, while my other forebears were from such places as East Perth in Scotland, Manchester and Liverpool in England, and Ireland. (It's amazing that Leeds is part of my heritage when this city is now the home to Australian players Harry Kewell, Mark Viduka, Jacob Burns, Shane Candsell-Sherriff, Danny Milosevic and Jamie McMaster.) So I am certainly from British stock and it is this background that always stamped me as a 'true-blue Aussie' during my soccer career. In fact, had soccer not taken over my life as it has, I would probably never, to this day, have had any real idea about the relationship between the old and the new Australia.

Position that Anglo–Australian social type against the post-war migrant boom. Europeans seconded to work the Snowy Hydro Scheme, migrants looking for a new economic opportunity, refugees fleeing the ravages of the world's most comprehensively destructive war. Boatloads of new Australians, the non-Anglo migrants often labelled in their new country as 'wogs', arriving to make a new home for themselves. I can only imagine what it was like for them.

How welcoming was this land to its new migrants? According to official policy, Australia was still for 'whites' only. The largely homogenous Anglo–Celtic culture was deep rooted, reinforced by the country's geographic isolation and island status. Australia was monolingual, narrow-minded, conservative, war-wounded and suspicious. We hankered for all things English; the place, its people, its games and its recognition.

Upon arrival, immigrants were herded into migrant camps or shuttled off to sponsored work programs. They would try and familiarise themselves with their new surroundings, attempting to lay some foundations. Their work was menial. They spoke little or no English. Their time at work was often extremely difficult; they were fobbed off as lesser people, as ignorant wogs. It was difficult for them to shop, to buy groceries, to communicate outside their language group. They came to rely heavily on their children to break down the barriers erected by Anglo–Australian society; barriers that were founded upon language and cultural difference. They were foreign; they looked and sounded different. Their food was strange, its aromas unfamiliar and they didn't eat bacon and eggs for breakfast. On top of all this, they loved this game—soccer. It was a game many Australians had perhaps seen but, for the most part, didn't know or understand. Soccer would turn out to be a key ingredient in the cocktail of marginalisation of Australia's new migrants.

It is a common misconception that it was the migrants who were responsible for soccer in Australia. One of the earliest football codes played in the colony of New South Wales was soccer. The first recorded soccer match in Australia was actually played in 1880. Australia was one of six countries to be part of the world governing body of soccer of the time. There are wonderful archives showing packed crowds and bona fide full houses at the Sydney Cricket Ground for soccer matches. Some of the oldest sporting clubs of any sport in this country are soccer clubs—for example, Wallsend and Adamstown in Newcastle, Balgownie and Corrimal in Wollongong.

That it was the King's School, the oldest school in Australia and bastion of society's establishment, that played in that first recorded soccer match against the Wanderers is both fascinating and ironic particularly since the Greater Public Schools (GPS) network has been one of the most dogged strongholds against soccer. Why wasn't soccer embraced in the same way that the GPS embraced rugby union, for example? All I know, and it might not be related, is that England is our fiercest sporting rival yet if we are not involved in competition with them then Aussies, by and large, support the Poms. It speaks to our entrenched Anglophilia. There is a frustrating reticence in Australian society to cut the chord and set ourselves free from Britain, as demonstrated by our fears of becoming a republic.

The greatest irony is that soccer is England's national sport. We are, in many ways, so English it's ridiculous that soccer isn't also our national sport. As I cast my historical eye around the place I notice that it is the countries that were former English colonies in which soccer hasn't become the national sport—for example, Australia, New Zealand, the subcontinent, the United States and Canada. Aside from this group of nations there aren't many countries in the world that aren't completely infatuated with soccer. I think it is fascinating, given the passion for football in England, that Australia is an Anglophile nation yet hasn't taken on the main sport of the English.

Despite football's Australian history, antagonists often point to the migrants as the sole reason for soccer in this country. Soccer did become a circuit breaker for new Australians. It was their weekend safe haven that followed a week of being a foreigner in a strange land. They would gather on weekends and play the game they loved. They would be transported, once a week, back home through the culture surrounding the game. It softened the blow from the hostilities of Anglo–Australians towards what was commonly perceived as the 'otherness' of the migrants.

The bulk of the migrants were young males, many of whom were accomplished footballers. Almost all of the migrants were at least familiar with football, but for many it was their life's passion. Almost as soon as they had settled, they began to congregate with football as their focal point. It was something common to all, regardless of language or cultural backgrounds. The evolution of the St George club is an example of the unifying qualities of soccer. Hungarian migrants, many fleeing the Russian tanks and the 1956 revolution, arrived with only the clothes on their backs and would meet in Rushcutters Bay or Rose Bay, in the eastern suburbs of Sydney, and play soccer. They formed a club, called it Ferencvaros and played in the New South Wales second division. They joined the breakaway football federation and won promotion and became Budapest. Then, it was Budapest St George followed by St George Budapest and finally St George. They moved their whole operation to the St George district and became a St George identity. Other migrant groups—Italians, Greeks, Maltese, Czechs, Macedonians, Dutch, Yugoslavs, Poles, Croatians, Germans—all followed a similar pattern forming their clubs.

The need for migrants to form their own clubs exposes some unwelcome realities of Australian society. Many soccer clubs already in existence—typical Aussie district clubs—refused access to some migrants. The measuring stick for determining suitability to join their club was, too often, proficiency in English. It is one of the ironies I have observed that people within soccer should discriminate in ways so similar to ways in which the game itself has been discriminated against by Australian society at large.

The wog clubs didn't inflict the discrimination which was their struggle. For them football was always the currency. It didn't matter to them what someone looked like. It only mattered that they could play football. The late Charlie Perkins told the story that the Greek and Croatian clubs in Adelaide, and later the Pan Hellenic club in Sydney, were the first Australians to recognise him as a person to be treated equally. Charlie's football career commenced before the 1967 referendum moved to include Aborigines as part of the 'official' population of Australia. The axiom of 'the enemy of my enemy is my friend' rang true and as such, both Charlie Perkins and non-English speaking migrants shared a bond through the common enemy of racism. Charlie became hugely popular in the migrant football communities primarily because he was a good footballer. To be finally accepted as an equal was a powerful social panacea for Dr Perkins. To achieve that sense of equality, on an individual level as well as on behalf of his people, was the summation of his life's mission. Football assuaged that passage for Charlie, from which point his charm took over and his relationship with the football community was forged—truly, madly and deeply, for life. Indeed, it was Pan Hellenic (now Olympic Sharks) who paid his way through university in return for his playing service and Charlie became only the second Aborigine to graduate from university in Australia. His education empowered him in his political undertakings, the embryonic expression of which were the freedom rides through the deep north-west of New South Wales. He did so much for so many people and that he was such a big part of football makes me very proud. Like all players, he loved the dressing room with its congregation of players. 'G'day champ' he would say; everyone was always 'champ'. Perkins was a champion—a real Ben Hur, smashing his way through Australia's race politics and football was his first chariot. Even until his recent sad passing, he would visit Olympic's home games as a guest of the club and be swamped with well wishers and warmth. He reciprocated too; the affection was mutual. I played against Charlie and admired him for what he was doing on and off the field. However, it wasn't until I moved to Canberra that I became really close with him through football. Our friendship was cemented through our association with the Canberra City club, of which he was president, through our Old Boys team which played for many years together from the late 1970s to the early 1990s, and through fighting causes together for football's rights in Australia. Charlie was the ideal type of person to lead Australian soccer's fight against discrimination, using the same principles as he did leading the Department of Aboriginal Affairs. He always told me he had three loves in his life—his family, Aboriginal Affairs and soccer. Notably, upon his death, Dr Perkins was reported as being a great sportsman, not a great footballer. Even in eulogising this great Australian, remembering the sporting love of his life, soccer, seemed too difficult for some.

In the environment my brothers and I grew up in soccer wasn't prominent and it certainly wasn't readily accessible to kids the way it is today. Instead, we were surrounded by Rabbitohmania. We grew up in Botany in the middle of South Sydney rugby league territory and it was the era of the great Clive Churchill and his all-conquering team. Despite the fact that I played a complete range of sports like most Aussie kids, my nickname at school was 'Wog Warren' because I also played soccer. Only sheilas, wogs and poofters played soccer, was the prevailing narrow-minded attitude. It was all a product of the area's working-class allegiances and roots—of being suspicious of anything new or difficult to understand and instead exalting the image of bronzed Aussie machismo and the physical demands of work and struggle, best epitomised by the brutality of rugby league. Sport was a natural extension of the working week. The league players were society's heroes. Rugby league neatly defined the way things were. It was an unsubtle game played at the end of a week of unsubtle work. Society and its sport, sharing and reinforcing each other's values. A man was defined by his work and his play, so of soccer players it would be asked, 'Why don't you play a man's game?'

I have a daunting image, still prominent in my memory. It was the occasion of a ticker tape parade for the Australian national team in 1969. I had taken my allotted place in one of the sports cars which had been organised for the event. The cavalcade was snaking its way through the streets and turned a corner. This one particular corner, like so many of its kind in Sydney, was adorned by a pub. Wooing the punters to drink from its kegs were pictures on its outer wall of rugby, cricket and horse racing. True-blue Aussie sports. Spilling out of the pub's doors were tank-topped, steel-cap-booted, tattooed workers quenching their thirst after the dust of the day's work. 'Fuckin' poofters,' some hooted at us. 'Dago bastards,' followed others. The odd projectile was hurled our way. Needless to say, I had, in my life, felt much safer than I did during that parade.

Australia has welcomed migrants as long as they have moved straight into Australian pursuits, or those accepted as so. The recent Sydney 2000 Olympics produced a great example where Tatiana Grigorieva, who left Russia a few years ago to pursue a pole-vaulting career in South Australia, was wholeheartedly embraced as one of ours. Good-looking, blonde and winner of an Olympic silver medal she is deemed one of us. Kostya Tszyu, super lightweight boxing champion is also embraced as one of us. Thinking back, there have been Barassi, Silvani, Koutoufides, Di Pierdomenico and Jesaulenko (Aussie Rules), Raudonikis, El Mazri, Sorridimi and Peponis (rugby league)— all 'one of us'—but Milan Ivanovic, Peter Raskopoulos, Atti Abonyi (Australian soccer players) too often are considered 'wogs'. There were huge declarations heralding Richard Chee Quee as the first person of Chinese origin to play first-class cricket in Australia, and pronouncements made about how his selection for the New South Wales cricket team represented the new Australia. All the while, one of Australia's best ever soccer players, Alan Davidson (who even has an 'Aussie' name), Australian-born of a Japanese mother, went totally unnoticed. Look at the cricket teams now and they are still ostensibly representative of the Anglo–Celtic culture of Australia. It is soccer that represents multicultural and twenty-first century Australia and in this sense no other sport comes close. While soccer has been representative of the many cultures that make up Australian life it remains to be seen how long it will take the bulk of Australian society and the media to take to it, en masse. The media often criticise Prime Minister John Howard for having a 1950s view of Australia but, in the way they treat soccer, the media are no more progressive.

SHEILAS, WOGS & POOFTERS: AN INTRODUCTION

It is amazing that a journey such as mine through the world of soccer could have started from underneath the umbrella that it did. I suppose I didn't at all expect what I got. I didn't yet know of the cultural struggles being endured by my new compatriots. I only knew that I was, in some way, one of them because I also played soccer. Football wasn't a television product and, as a result, we didn't see overseas football. Exposure to football was very limited. We used to have to go to the movies to watch a film clip. Back then, in pre-television days, you went to the movies to watch the prelude to the main feature—twenty minutes of news, which also included three minutes of the FA Cup Final. That's the only image we had of soccer. We were so transfixed by the football though, we even ignored the Jaffas rolling down the aisle.

Admittedly, soccer's coverage has been much better recently because at least nowadays there will be a page or so of soccer in the newspaper. There might be a big England report with a photo and a piece on the national league and down the side of one page a series of snippets from the leagues around the world. It seems to reflect the anti-'wog' attitude again because if you didn't know better, you would think that the English competition was the world's best which, to the fan, is debatable. What is undeniable is that the leagues of France, Italy, Germany and Spain are globally significant competitions but they are not reported as such in Australia. This even impacts on the reporting of Australian footballers playing for European clubs. We hear about the boys in England because England is acceptable to the media masses. Viduka scores against Spain's Real Madrid (arguably the biggest sporting club in the world) and we hear about it somewhere at the end of a news report. At the same time, Paul Agostino is scoring and playing well enough in the German league to prompt Silvio Berlusconi, Italian Prime Minister, television magnate and president of AC Milan football team, to offer huge amounts of money for his signature yet the Australian general public barely even knows who Agostino is because leading the news are stories about the netball, cricket, rugby union or rugby league 'world' champions.

I have been working with radio programs for a long time. I have very much enjoyed the work and the media have been good to me. To the sport, though, they haven't been so fair. I can't recall the number of occasions that air-time, which had been allocated for soccer, was expeditiously reduced because of other supposed imperatives. For instance, I might be doing a 'phoner' from the World Cup of a magnificent match at a crucial knockout stage of the world's biggest sporting event and I am told at the start of the interview to 'keep it brief, Johnny, there's a lot of "big" sport to get through today'. Or I will be telephoned for an interview and kept waiting on hold for half-an-hour and finally, at the last minute, will be welcomed onto the program to talk soccer 'for a quick minute or two because the news is approaching and time's up' on what has been a two-hour sports show. There is never any time to talk soccer. I don't understand this resistance to the game.

We know that Australians love winners. At least that is what we are told. We love a world champion. I mean no disrespect to other athletes or sports but to be the best cricket nation there are perhaps four or five contenders. It is the same for rugby union and rugby league, while Aussie Rules is completely parochial. It is easy to love the teams from these sports as winners because, quite simply, the competition is not as fierce as in football. To win the World Cup of Football we have to beat two hundred and three countries and in most of those countries football is the national sport, the religion of the people, the passion of the masses. This is not the case for any other sport that I can think of; athletics, swimming, tennis... whatever. So why, in Australia, don't we acknowledge the sport for what it is? Why don't institutions embrace the sport and undertake a concerted effort to push and promote football to take us onto that world stage? Why the resistance? Why this folly that 'soccer is a good game, it's really skilful, but Australians just don't play it'?

Statistics show that it is not the case that Australians don't play soccer. Soccer boasts huge participation rates in this country. That, in itself, has not been enough for power brokers to give the sport a more elevated place and profile. People will trot out the line that kids play soccer because mums and dads don't want their kids to get hurt and soccer is a soft sporting option. This is the sheilas and poofters mentality rearing its head again, not giving the game any credit and ignoring the fact that the kids may actually be enjoying the sport in the same way their counterparts around the world do. Soccer gives kids a good grounding for other sports, proper sports, manly sports, Aussie sports. That's about all the credit some will give soccer.

To the extent that soccer has cruelled itself by very poor administration I also wonder why more public scrutiny hasn't been placed on the sport. Why hasn't it been in the public and national interest to make the sport accountable? The participation rate amongst kids, the unisex appeal of the sport and its international significance all suggest to me that serious analyses should be undertaken of the sport. People in power have been prepared to leave soccer, and its proven propensity for dysfunctionality, on the periphery and as far as I am concerned it highlights further the institutionalised attitude that 'it is just those wogs having another stoush'. I don't think Australia can afford to have that attitude. Football is too important.

Football for me, apart from being a virtual lifelong love affair, has been a missionary job. I was an Aussie by accident who mixed all my life with those who chose to become Australians. There was also the task of converting those who called me a wog. My mates were petrified by football. They didn't know about it, it was foreign and it was played by people who spoke a different language and ate different food.

Football is certainly a game, but it is also a phenomenon. Indeed, Australia still doesn't fully understand exactly what it means for people when the national teams of Italy or Morocco or Paraguay play. It is something that Australia has not yet fully appreciated but must ultimately explore. It is football that gives the cross-cultural insight that international treaties and diplomatic ties could never achieve.

1
Wog Warren's Early Years

⚽ I'M LUCKY TO be here at all. In fact, I shouldn't be here. Two years before I was born, almost to the day, my parents had their third child, a son, tragically stillborn. Sticking to their plan of having three children my parents decided to have another child and I was the result. The recognition that I am particularly lucky to have been born at all has always been something that has made me put the events of my life in perspective and has made me appreciate how lucky I am just to be here.

I was born in the Sydney suburb of Randwick on 17 May 1943 as the youngest of three boys to Marjorie Bertha and Victor George Warren. My eldest brother Ross was six years older than me and my other brother Geoff was four years older. I have always thought it somewhat fitting that I emerged into the world at the very Greek-sounding Hellenie Hospital. I like to think that the close connection throughout my life with the Greek community in Australia started way back on that day in 1943.

I grew up in a very average suburban house in Edward Street, Botany in Sydney. Family, friends and neighbours seemed to be always around and there was a tangible sense of community. On Sundays the whole family would pack up and go out to the country for picnics with friends and all the kids would play muck-around sports games. Friends, uncles, aunties, cousins, grandparents, great-grandparents—everyone would come along. During the holidays, in particular, everyone from our community would get together on a regular basis or actually go away together. September school holidays were spent at my great-aunt's farm at Glennies Creek outside Singleton, where we would round up, crutch and earmark sheep with the shearers, bottle-feed lambs and milk cows. Our farm holidays were an enjoyable and educational part of my childhood. At Christmas we would always go camping on the Central Coast, mainly Terrigal. We would put up the tent on the first day of the school holidays and it wouldn't come down until the day before school started again. I wouldn't swap one night of camping at Terrigal for all the many five-star hotels and glamorous resorts to which I have travelled throughout my football career.

Other times we played all kinds of sport. At night, several families would get together and play cards and make our own fun. There was always something to do and I was never bored. In fact, Mum's greatest saying when the sun was shining was, 'Get out of the house!' I just loved being outdoors and would spend hours picking blackberries and mushrooms before trying to sell them by the side of the road—my entrepreneurial streak shining through at an early age. (The downside of living in the sun in the days before sunscreen, however, was skin cancer. Even though my dad was olive-skinned as opposed to Mum, who was red-haired with a freckly complexion, he not only suffered from skin cancer but also glaucoma, which eventually took his eyesight. His plight alerted all of us to these two dangers later on and after hundreds of skin operations on my face, neck, back and hands, my own skin cancer is under control and eyedrops that I've used for the past twenty years have stemmed my glaucoma.)

Dinner in our family was always at six o'clock and afterwards everyone would enjoy a cup of tea and a chat. There was never any alcohol or coffee in the house and the food was always very simple. Of course there was also no television back then. I'm sure the kids of today would go crazy in the same environment but for me life was good. I can remember in the summer holidays, there would be twenty people congregated around the radio in the living room, transfixed, listening to the Davis Cup or the Test cricket. The Boxing Day Test was always a major event in our household, as in many others across the country. I really think they were the good old days.

My dad, Victor, was a furniture maker. He ran his own business even though he never considered himself a businessman. First and foremost he was always an artisan and the things he built were all individually crafted and designed to last centuries. For most of his life he eschewed the growing trend towards mass production because it simply wasn't the way he had been brought up to do things. My dad was a very hard worker and he encouraged me to develop a strong work ethic from an early age, getting me to do odd jobs in his factory during the school holidays. I would tidy up, get lunches, sweep the offices, switch off the machines collect offcuts of wood to sell to the neighbourhood as firewood—pretty much anything that needed doing. It was a valuable experience for me, running around in the factory and observing the way my dad worked and his commitment to his craft.

Dad was the sort of person that had to have everything done perfectly. He would persist at a task until it was done properly because he thought there was no point doing it otherwise. Unfortunately, I simply never inherited his patience. The thing about Dad was that he would never let me or my brothers do any handiwork because he could always do it better. So in the end none of us ever really learned these skills.

We didn't mind but it has meant that the three of us now have trouble even driving a nail into the wall!

Dad was a fun-loving, easygoing, giving person, especially to kids. My only regret is that he didn't give me a clip across the ear when I deserved it. Neither of my parents ever laid a hand on us.

My mum, Marjorie, who is now over ninety years of age, is a strong, spirited woman—a typical Leo—and has always been an inspiration to me in everything that I do. Unlike Dad, who would never offend, Mum simply calls it as it is—no-nonsense, direct and mostly right. Like most women of that era, she was in charge of domestic duties. She was incredibly devoted to us and was determined to make sure we never wanted for anything. Both my parents had grown up in the Depression and they desperately wanted to make things easier for us and provide us with the opportunities they never had. As a result they were always supportive of whatever we did. My mum was constantly involved with the local mothers' club, organising social functions, helping out in the school tuckshop and, at one stage, even serving as the Secretary of our school's Parents and Citizens organisation. Throughout my childhood it seemed she was constantly organising a fundraising function for new boots or balls for one of our various sporting teams. She did all she possibly could to involve herself in our lives and to make sure her kids were happy.

Both my parents were very keen on sport. My dad played soccer at one stage and would regularly take my brothers and me to watch visiting teams, from as far afield as Austria, South Africa and even China. The game I most vividly remember was when I was a six year old on my father's shoulders at a packed Sydney Showground on 30 July 1949 and the visiting Yugoslavian team Hajduk Split beat Australia 3–2 (the famous Yugoslav goalkeeper Beara played for Hajduk that day). It was my first introduction to international football. I'm so grateful that my father was interested in soccer because it really wasn't considered a true-blue 'Aussie' sport in those days.

The Showground was, in fact, the centre of our life, and not just for football because Mum and Dad were members of the Royal Agricultural Society. Every Saturday night was spent at the speedway there, chasing the autographs of my idols— not soccer stars but superbike rider Lionel Levy and midget car champion Ray Revell. When the Royal Easter Show came around every year, we would spend most days and nights at the Showground, which stirred my love of the country, polo and rodeo.

The result of my parent's interest in sport was that my brothers and I were always involved in some sort of game or sporting activity. In the winter I would play soccer on Saturdays and in the summer it would be cricket. I was stronger at cricket than soccer in my early years and several of my childhood sporting heroes, such as Norm O'Neill, wore the baggy green cap for Australia. My dad was also a huge fan of cricket and was usually a manager or coach of my team. Another huge influence on my love affair with cricket at that time was the Chegwyn family, in particular John Chegwyn. (John and I were born ten days apart at the Hellenie Hospital and attended Botany Public and eventually the University of New South Wales together. His uncle, Jack Chegwyn, was heavily involved in cricket, being a New South Wales selector and, more significantly, heading the Jack Chegwyn XI which travelled Australia playing country teams and discovering young country talent to invite to join the big Sydney clubs. Doug Walters was among the most famous of these country kids. In his own field, John turned out to be a visionary in linking sport, tourism and events as a senior partner at Price Waterhouse. He has spent the last decade in Vietnam, putting projects together for Australian companies.) I played cricket right up into my teenage years and it's a sport I still love.

Both my parents were always there with the car to watch my brothers and me play. We could be playing anywhere in junior competitions throughout Sydney and it often required a great deal of travel. So, in the end, all the boys involved in the competition from our community would meet at the town hall and my dad and several other family friends would be designated drivers. Everyone would pile in amongst the picnic baskets and we would set off for the day. For my family it was always an all-day affair because it meant going to my game, then to Geoff's and finally to Ross's.

In summer there was always the beach. We would muck around playing games of tennis, golf and cricket on the sand, we would go swimming in the ocean and we would devour the food Mum had packed in the picnic basket. When we weren't at the beach, our backyard was the site of our sporting battles. It was usually cricket or football but we would play other games as well. My mum gave up on the garden in the end because we were always trampling it in search of a cricket or soccer ball.

There were four tennis courts opposite our house and in the holidays we would play tennis there in the morning before pulling the net down to play soccer in the afternoon. Some afternoons I would head down to the Botany Golf Course with my mates, John Chegwyn and Darryl Nelson, and we would wait for the course ranger to leave before sneaking on for a free game. We probably only had three or four golf clubs and a couple of balls between us but we always had a great time. Golf is a game I still play regularly now.

During my childhood I was particularly close to my maternal grandfather Herbert 'Bertie' Gobbe. (Mum tells me that one of the nicest things when she got married was that she no longer had to spell her last name, pronounced *Go-bee,* for people. Through her younger years she had to endure mispronounciations such as *Gabb, Gobb, Gabble* or *Gobble!*) Though he was born in New Zealand, Bert's family moved the family to the warmer climate of Sydney when he was very young. Bert, along with his brother Jack, was expelled from school—the same school I would later attend—at the tender age of eleven and he later told me it was because the teachers had been picking on him! Without the benefit of an education he alternated between working as a shearer and a wool classer.

It seems my family doesn't have the greatest track record in terms of schooling because my father also didn't last too long at school. He decided to leave high school after one day because he simply didn't like it. I think this rebellious streak has rubbed off on me because while I never had great problems at school, I have regularly clashed with authority over the years. One of my very first and most memorable clashes came when I was nearly expelled for organising a fight between two guys in a lane at the back of school when I was ten. The entire school found out about it and so many kids turned up to watch after school that the crowd spilled out onto Botany Road and stopped the traffic. I think boxing promoter Don King would have been proud of my effort but the school wasn't so thrilled. It was probably my first brush with trouble and, even though I still maintain that I was simply organising a legitimate sporting event, it certainly wasn't my last. I still blame my genes.

While I knew my other grandparents, I was closer with Bert because he spent much of his life living with us. He was a real character and was in many ways just like a mate to me. I spent so much time around him that he inevitably influenced me in a number of ways. I probably first learned to swear by helping him perform magic tricks. Although he was very much a part-time magician, and would often simply make up his own tricks, he would always be called upon to perform at a show at school or church functions. He would use rabbits and pigeons in his performances and was always entertaining even if his tricks didn't turn out as planned. But when he did muck them up he would let fly with a few expletives which would be considered very tame by modern standards but back then seemed very risqué to my innocent ears. Like any young kid, as soon as I heard them I would start putting them to good use myself.

One of his favourite tricks was to ask for a banknote (the equivalent of one hundred dollars today) from the audience. He'd write down the serial number on a blackboard for all to see then load the banknote into a rifle. I would be on the other side of the stage with an apple on my head—in the style of William Tell. With a flamboyant flourish he would aim the gun at me (his nervous grandson) and there would be a loud shot. He would then invite someone from the audience to take the apple off my head, inspect it for any signs of tampering and then cut it open. Hey presto—inside would be a banknote. The person would then compare the serial number with the one written on the blackboard which, of course, would magically be exactly the same. After Bert's magical influence, I now also perform amateur magical tricks on my grandnephew and even on my grandchildren.

I also have fond memories of going ferreting with my grandfather when our family went out to the country on picnics. I would help Bert cover all the rabbit holes we could find with nets and then we would put ferrets down one of the holes. The idea was that the ferrets would chase the rabbits out of their burrows and into the nets. It was a sound theory but even though we would spend a long time plugging all the holes there was always one that hadn't been covered. When the rabbits would come scurrying out the hole we had missed, my grandfather's language would turn slightly blue again! That wasn't the end of it though because there was also the problem of the ferrets refusing to come out of the holes. Bert's language would gradually worsen the longer they stayed underground. Many times he was eventually forced to smoke them out and although he would be cursing and muttering as he did it, I used to have a great time.

Like the rest of us my grandfather also loved his sport. He would always be at various games and events simply because he loved the atmosphere of a team or club environment with all the boys around. A great deal of his character rubbed off on me in that respect. In fact, it's only now, with the benefit of hindsight, that I can appreciate how important he was to my upbringing and how much he influenced my outlook on life.

In many respects they really were the good old days. It was a real community of parents, family and friends and everyone helped each other. My Uncle Hilton's (my father's brother) family and nearby families—the Watkisses, the Newmans and the Mortimers—became my own extended family. Sport played a big role in keeping that family together.

Like many members of my family before me, I was sent to Botany Public School. Unlike my grandfather though, my days there were happy ones. As with my life outside school, my time at Botany Public was also full of sport and recreation. I'm sure schoolwork was done but it's the sport that I remember. Recently I went back to the school to help celebrate its one hundred and fifty-year anniversary and it was such a great trip down memory lane that I now go back every year to present the school's sports awards.

My brothers and I also went to Sunday school in the area and we were soon invited to join a neighbourhood church youth club which met on Friday nights. I'm sure my parents were happy to get us out of their hair for a while as well. I can actually remember sitting around talking one night when the youth leader said, 'Why don't we play a team sport?' Everyone seemed immediately keen and so the only real question to resolve was which sport we should play.

In those days Botany was a dyed-in-the-wool rugby league area. It was the middle of the Clive Churchill era and the great reign of the South Sydney Rabbitohs and, while the church did have soccer teams in the older age groups, soccer wasn't a highly regarded activity among the wider community. I didn't realise it fully at the time but it was generally considered, especially at school, that only 'sheilas', 'wogs' and 'poofters' played soccer. It was something to do with the game not being 'manly' enough to suit the traditional rough-and-tumble Anglo-Australian culture and if you played soccer it meant that you were considered feminine or lacking in the necessary attributes to be considered a 'man'. Maybe the others weren't aware of this attitude either because the group ultimately chose soccer as the team sport we wanted to play. It was a strange decision given the sporting environment that surrounded us at the time and I still find it quite incredible to think that had the group chosen any other sport, as you would have expected, I would not be where I am today.

The next Friday night the group leader brought all the registration forms that were needed for us to sign up to the local competition. I was hanging around as usual and my brothers just grabbed my hand and signed me up. I was only five so they quite literally had to guide my hand across the page. We then went home to tell our parents that we were registered and I'm sure they wondered how I had managed to register myself when I could barely even write! But they were excited for all of us nonetheless and, in the end, one of the great defining moments of my life was very simple. I was officially registered in the Botany Methodists under-12s team in the Protestant Churches competition. My soccer career had begun.

My first goal in competitive soccer was scored playing as a five year old for the under-12s local team in a match at Haberfield. The field was extremely muddy and when the ball flew across the goal towards me, I automatically dived and hit it with the top of my head. Amazingly, it flew straight into the net and I can still remember the opposition's big goalkeeper—all the twelve year olds were giants to me in those days—fell right on top of me and squashed me into the mud. Scoring a goal was obviously a big thing but scoring one with your head was as rare as hens' teeth. Everyone hated heading the ball in those days because the ball was really heavy with big laces across the middle. It was nothing like the scientifically engineered balls of today and heading it was absolute agony if you didn't get it exactly right. It meant most kids simply avoided heading the ball wherever possible. Otherwise we just had to shut our eyes and hope for the best. So scoring my first goal with my head became a big deal.

This first goal was also exciting for my teammates and our supporters because I was so small. They were always encouraging me because they knew I was playing well beyond my weight division. While I probably didn't realise it at the time my teammates had a powerful influence on developing my sense of how the game should be played. It was always about helping your mate, encouraging everyone else and working hard for each other. It proved to be a great grounding in the game and was a philosophy I would take with me throughout my career.

Funnily enough, one of the players in the under-12s team was Brian Hambly, a good mate of my brother Ross. Though a good soccer player, Brian went on to play rugby league for South Sydney and for Australia. He lived in the same street as us—Edward Street, Botany—a street of around fifty houses which produced three Australian internationals: Brian Hambly, John Watkiss and myself. Not bad for a simple surburban street.

By the time I was ten, I was selected for the Protestant Churches state team which played off for the state championship. It was also particularly gratifying for me to be selected because I'd missed out on selection for my local under-12s team as a nine year old, the year before. Even though everyone believed I was good enough to play, the selectors told me I was too small and needed to go home and eat more porridge before coming back next year to try out!

The state championship was the major competition for all of us at that age because all the districts of New South Wales were represented. The competition was run at all age levels up from the under-12s and no team representing Protestant Churches had ever won the championship at any level.

The Protestant Churches team always viewed soccer as more of a social game than a competitive event and there was never any pressure on us to win. That was why everyone was so incredulous when my team actually did win. For the players it was like winning the World Cup. I didn't think it could get any better until I found out there was going to be a special presentation night at the Sydney Town Hall with all the teams invited.

Unfortunately, I never got to hold the trophy and I now look back on that competition more as a great lesson in life than as a momentous victory. The drama began when, on the eve of the presentation, officials discovered that one of the kids in our team, who didn't actually even play a game during the competition, was over twelve years of age. The officials informed us that we had broken the rules so would have to be disqualified. I was so young that I didn't really understand how they could take the title away from us after we'd played so hard and so well to win it. When I eventually realised that they were going to strip us of the title, I was desperately upset and I'm sure there were tears.

I can remember my dad trying to gently console me by explaining that nothing is yours in life until it is really yours; in other words, you can't assume anything before it actually happens. I hadn't really understood him at the time but I guess it made sense later down the track. It was only a minor incident in the scheme of things but it meant a great deal to me and, as such, turned out to be a great lesson about the vagaries of life. In many ways that is why I believe sport can be so important for children. It teaches you that life is sometimes unfair and it also teaches you that you have to just keep going in the face of adversity.

I wasn't so engrossed in soccer in those early days that it had become an all-consuming passion. I was still playing other sports but I had definitely developed a taste for soccer. When I look back I can't help but think about why those guys at the youth group chose to play soccer. It was such a strange choice for the times, considering our rugby league environs, and it had such an impact on my life that I always shake my head in wonder at how fortuitous such an impulsive decision was.

Remarkably, my daughter Shannon experienced a similar situation when she was growing up. She has always been a talented sportsperson but fell particularly in love with ice-skating. She became so involved in the sport that she eventually competed in and won state and national titles. She even spent several years travelling the world with the *Disney on Ice* skating program. I don't know why she chose ice-skating; it certainly wasn't any influence from me, but I could certainly appreciate how little recognition she received for her efforts in Australia. It was like my path into football because in many ways it was the wrong sport, in the wrong country at the wrong time.

Another seemingly random event that would steer me towards soccer came when a family from England moved into my street when I was about eight. The Watkiss family came from Wolverhampton in England. They still run the Wolverhampton Scrap Metals business in Marrickville—a reminder of their heritage. When the Watkiss family arrived in Australia they brought with them two things that would leave an indelible mark on my life: a young son and a love for soccer.

I first met John Watkiss at school in Botany and we immediately became friends. It wasn't long before I was spending nights down at his house reading the *Charles Buchan's Football Monthly* magazine. In those days it was *the* soccer magazine to read and the Watkiss family had a stack of them. They arranged for them to be sent over from England every month and reading them opened my eyes to a whole new world of soccer. The images of players and stadiums were like something from another world and the excitement and glamour of it all transfixed me.

John's father, Joe Watkiss, would further tantalise my imagination by telling me stories of the great Stanley Matthews and other big-name English players of that era. He would talk about how the game was played in England and how the crowds behaved and soon I was hooked on learning more about the game. In fact, going down to the Watkisses to read *Charles Buchan's Football Monthly* became the highlight of my week.

In many ways the Watkiss family was a great example of the wonderful contribution British migrants have made to soccer in Australia. Right back to the earliest days of the sport in Australia the British were critical in establishing the foundations of the round ball game. The influx of British migrants to the coal and steel areas of Newcastle and Wollongong for example, particularly in the Depression of the 1890s, firmly established a love of football in those areas, a love which still exists today. The role of British migrants in administering the game and coaching teams in these early years was also integral to the development of the game in Australia. Even on a personal level, my coach at the Botany Methodist club, Eddie Whittle, was an Englishman, originally from Preston. He was a huge football fan and gave everyone in the team a sound education in the game.

My family enjoyed the company of the Watkisses and they soon became part of my extended family. They would join us on picnics and holidays and although John was two years older than me, we became very close. The friendship even changed our weekend routine. Now on Saturdays we would go to my game and then John's game before heading off to see my brothers play. It was now a longer day but one that was even more enjoyable.

Joe Watkiss even coached my soccer team at one stage. His training sessions always centred around drills and exercises I had never experienced before and were always enlightening. Once a week, for the entire session, he made us train with tennis balls instead of soccer balls. Training with a smaller ball meant we had to concentrate harder as the ball was so much more difficult to control, so we really had to master the correct technique early on. I have seen a lot of soccer since those early days and yet the only time I can remember seeing a similar session was during the 1988 Bicentennial Gold Cup in Australia. I was at the Brazilian team's training session when coach Carlos Alberto da Silva brought out tennis balls and made the players train with them. It immediately sent my mind racing back to Joe Watkiss and made me realise what a progressive and innovative coach he must have been. Here were players like Romario, Jorghino, Muller and Branco in 1988 using the same training methods we had been using back in the early 1950s for the Botany Methodists.

Just like that fateful decision by the youth group at the Botany Protestant Church, I sometimes wonder about the fatefulness of the Watkiss family moving in down the road from me. When I was young I hadn't settled on soccer as the game upon which I would concentrate and it was certainly the proximity of the Watkisses that guided me away from other sports and closer to the round ball. They could have settled anywhere in Sydney and yet they moved in down the road from me. It makes my head spin.

I'm jumping ahead a few years but John went on to become one of the best soccer players Australia has ever produced. In fact, I believe he is *the* best player Australia has ever produced. I have seen some good ones during my time in and around the game but while John may not have been the best striker, best midfielder or the best defender, he was certainly the best *all-round* player. During his career he played every position on the field with success. I was playing for St George when he, as a striker for Apia, scored five goals against us in the 1964 grand final. I can remember him as an outstanding defender and as a dynamic player in the middle of the park at the international level. Although he didn't play goalkeeper I have a feeling he would have been sensational at that as well. In many ways he was the Di Stefano of Australia and it was really only a lack of opportunity in this country that prevented him getting the recognition he deserved. I feel fortunate that I was privileged enough to see him play all through his career.

At my fiftieth birthday celebrations some years ago my mum was kind enough to offer a few words about me to the family and friends that had gathered for the occasion. Her first words were, 'I can assure you John was born in a hurry and he has been in a hurry ever since.' Those words pretty much sum me up. I have always tried to live each day fitting in as much as I can. I value life so much and that's something for which I have my parents to thank. My parents gave all their children time, love and support for everything we did. I can't remember ever wanting for anything even though we weren't rich. Clothes, shoes, and sports gear were all passed down the line to me from my older brothers, teaching me a valuable lesson about the real necessities in life. People are always asking me now why I don't buy new clothes, a better car or a bigger house. The simple fact is that I don't need a bigger house or a new car; those things simply aren't important to me. One of my dad's favourite sayings was, 'I cried because I had no shoes until I saw a man who had no feet.' It's a philosophy by which I have lived my life. I thank my parents for instilling it in me because it has been a real blessing and has carried me through the more difficult moments in my life.

My dad passed away in 1992. He had been ill for a while and when I would go to visit him, he would tell me that he was upset because he was not leaving anything material behind for the family. I was incredulous that he thought that because both my parents gave us everything that they could. And more than that, they gave not only us but many other kids in the community things money simply can't buy. I wouldn't swap the love and support I received during my early years for material things. No way in the world.

Unfortunately, the most ironic thing about my childhood and all the support and opportunity I was given is that when my own daughter, Shannon, came along in 1975 I wasn't able to give her the same support. For many years I was so busy in the soccer world that I simply wasn't there for her because of my gypsy lifestyle, travelling around as a player and coach. As a young teenager Shannon told me, 'Dad, you were never here when I wanted you'—very sobering stuff for me to hear. It is only now that I am starting to become close to my daughter and I enjoy spending as much time with her, and my two young grandchildren, Riley (born July 1999) and Natasha (born September 2000), as I can. I'm hoping to make up for lost time.

2

Canterbury Babes

⚽ IN MY LAST season in the Botany Methodist Soccer Club, my under-14s team played the entire eighteen-game season without losing. In the process we racked up one hundred and sixteen goals and remarkably didn't concede even one. When the finals series came around we scored another nineteen goals, again without letting one into our own net. I managed to find the back of the net fifty-one times that season, including seven in one match. Not a bad tally when you consider I wasn't even playing as a striker! My position in those days was called 'inside right', which I guess would be seen as an attacking midfielder these days. In any case, I was doing pretty well and having a great old time. The game seemed to come relatively easily to me.

However, even though I was showing some talent, there simply wasn't a career path to senior football where I was living. The situation wasn't anything like today where young players are scouted to talent identification programs from all over the country at a very young age. I certainly wasn't being invited to an academy or sports institute to hone my talents.

If you wanted to play at a senior level in those days you had to find yourself a team and prove yourself. It was just lucky for me that I had two older brothers and John Watkiss to blaze a trail for me to follow. They quite literally did all the hard work in getting me to a senior level. I can never pay tribute enough to them for doing so. I was also reasonably lucky that there were revolutionary things happening in Australian soccer when I was in my teenage years. The 1950s proved to be a time of great activity in Australian soccer as the post-Second World War migrant boom transformed the game, and I was able to slip into the top level at a perfect time.

My journey towards a career in soccer was kickstarted at the presentation night for the Protestant Churches teams in 1955 when my parents were introduced to former Canterbury player and noted coach Bernard 'Tugger' Bryant. After talking to my parents, he invited John Watkiss, my brothers and me to a coaching clinic at Arlington Oval—the ground where the Canterbury senior side played their matches in the New South Wales state competition. The Canterbury side of that era was quickly emerging as a team of bright, young talent. Bernard Bryant, who was the team's coach at the time, was somewhat of a football visionary because he was one of the first people to try to introduce passing football to Australia. In fact, he was one of the first real 'coaches' in Australian soccer, in the sense that he actually offered players more than mere physical training. Bernard could see the talent in the young, local Australian kids and was intent on schooling them in the tactics and methods of the game to develop their skill.

Bernard was also trying to set up a youth structure at Canterbury in the mid-1950s because, while the club had a very old and famous history in Australian soccer, he recognised a new era of soccer was fast approaching with the arrival of so many talented European migrants to Australia. He wanted to ensure the 'Australian' youth weren't left behind by the skills the soccer-loving migrants brought to the game and the money they poured into soccer to develop these. So he was intent on giving young soccer players like Jimmy Moore, Bruce Young, Ray 'Whoopee' Neal, Geoff Campbell, Eddie Jones, Ron Brown, Tommy North and Don Brown a chance.

When John Watkiss, my brothers and I went along to his coaching session, we obviously showed some promise because we were invited to another clinic, this time at St George soccer stadium. (The stadium, believe it or not, was on the Princes Highway right where the St George rugby league club now stands. The St George Soccer Association later took shares in the club in return for handing over the land.) Soon after the clinic my brothers were invited to join the Canterbury senior squad. John Watkiss was still a bit young so he went to play for a junior team called Earlwood Wanderers that also played in the Canterbury district. The Earlwood junior team was seen as a stepping stone to the Canterbury senior side.

A bloke called Cec Barlow used to scout talent for the senior Canterbury club in those days and he immediately recognised John Watkiss as something special. Cec was a legendary figure in the Canterbury district and I reckon he would be a millionaire today as a talent scout. His record in spotting young talent was amazing and he was invaluable to Canterbury in ensuring a continuous flow of talented young players. Cec made sure John went to Canterbury and, as a result for me, there was now little doubt about the path I would follow.

I went to Earlwood Wanderers in 1958 and was lucky enough to make the district representative team in the same year. In that team was my cousin Keith who was a very good player but abandoned his soccer career to become an apprentice in his chosen trade, winning Apprentice of the Year during his training. The district representative team was a particularly good one and we won the under-16s New South Wales championship. What's more, this time the title wasn't away from us, as in the case of my under-12s team several years previously. From Earlwood I was chosen to go into the third-grade senior team at Canterbury in 1959, along with quite a few other players from the same junior team. One of those players was a young goalkeeper called Ron Corry, who would go on to play for Australia and coach the Wollongong Wolves in their victorious 2001 National Soccer League championship season.

Before I knew it I was playing alongside my brother Geoff and John Watkiss in the first-grade side under the renowned coach 'Uncle' Joe Vlasits. I played one of my first matches in the senior side against Auburn in 1959 and scored right near the end of the match. My first goal in the senior competition was a big thrill for a sixteen year old. Things just seemed to be going from strength to strength in terms of my football.

The senior team at Canterbury at that time was so young that we were given the nickname the 'Canterbury Babes'. It was a fitting nickname because at one stage the average age of the team was only eighteen. That's why the club was such a great place for me to start because it really tried to give kids a chance. Another club might not have started me at such a young age but the guiding philosophy at Canterbury was that if you were good enough, you were old enough. In a way, Canterbury was the 'true-blue' Australian club in the increasingly multicultural world of soccer in Australia. While most of the emerging European migrant-based clubs were intent on having a winning team by buying the best players, Canterbury realised the importance of developing a junior production line of local talent that would ensure the future of the game in Australia. They were pioneers in that regard.

A big part of this attitude was due to coach Uncle Joe. He was very much a father figure to the team. Sometimes we would poke fun at him, as young lads tend to do, because of his broken English but we all really loved and admired him and his approach to the game. His willingness to trial young Australian players was so important to the careers of many of us from that era. In fact, John Watkiss, my brothers and I couldn't have chosen a better club or a better coach to play for at that time.

At the same time I had been making my way into a new soccer environment I had also entered a new educational environment. Because my parents remained so intent on giving my brothers and me the opportunities they didn't have, they wanted to send us to one of New South Wales's most elite private high schools, Sydney Grammar School. My mum was so determined that we should go there that she folded wire in a factory at night to make extra money to pay the fees. She would leave home when we went to bed and come home from work in the morning to make us breakfast. I still don't know how she managed such a load.

Unfortunately, my brothers weren't suited to Sydney Grammar at all. They had to wear a hat, wear long socks, participate in the cadets program and go away on camps. All the extra-curricular activities that private schools offered outside the classroom simply weren't what my brothers were looking for. Worst of all, they couldn't play soccer at Sydney Grammar. At private schools in New South Wales in those days you had to play rugby union. It was as simple as that. So, in the end, my brothers had a tough time and their negative experiences had a marked impact on me.

When my time came to go to high school I simply refused to go to Sydney Grammar. Of course, it was never going to be that simple and I had some huge arguments with my mum especially about it. Eventually, my parents realised that sending me there was pointless if I really didn't want to go. When I look back I was lucky they were willing to listen to me and didn't force me to attend Sydney Grammar because things would have turned out so differently for me.

As it was, I ended up going straight from Botany Primary School into the high school for our area, Cleveland Street High School. I still have bad memories of my mum making me wear a hat on the first day of school as a result of the school's instructions that students should wear a hat and long socks. Unfortunately, when I arrived at the school I quickly discovered that I was the only one wearing a hat and, as you would expect, my classmates showed me no mercy. My hat lasted exactly one day.

Once I had my uniform worked out though, Cleveland Street, or 'Clevo' as we called it, turned out to be a great school for me. I was lucky to be blessed, particularly in fourth and fifth year, with teachers who were true sports lovers. Many of the guys in my year were full of admiration for some of our teachers because of the way they would teach us 'normal' subjects and then take us for sport as well. Teachers like Ken Kirkness, Reg Harrison, Jim Lowe, John Henry, Elwyn Lynn and Jock Fraser made us want to succeed at both sport and at study. Largely because of them I experienced a wonderful all-round education at Cleveland Street.

I also made some excellent lifelong friends. At that time students at Cleveland Street High came from the western and southern suburbs of Sydney, right down to Botany where I lived. The result was that the school had a very multicultural mix of students, with kids from all sorts of different backgrounds attending. It was this mini 'melting pot' of cultures that provided me with valuable lessons about the existence and importance of other cultures and ways of life.

Of course, my parents had always encouraged me to treat everyone as an equal and to value other cultures. I can remember my father taking on a young Greek boy as an apprentice while I was growing up. His name was Con Harsas and he was from a newly arrived migrant family. Con's family was so thankful when my dad decided to give him a chance in their new country that they invited us to all their social events to express their gratitude. I can remember being spoilt rotten by the Harsas family and friends and having a great time. I was often even mistaken for a Greek kid. This early introduction to a different cultural environment gave me a first-hand glimpse of the benefits that a multicultural community offers.

Ever since my early association with the Harsas family, the Greek influence in my life has been quite considerable. I became really good mates with a young Australian-born Greek kid called John Economos when I went to Cleveland Street High School and I spent a great deal of time with his family. John was a passionate rugby league fan, mad about the Western Suburbs team and players of that era like Kel O'Shea and Darcy Henry. We soon developed a friendship which has lasted some forty-five years. For over twenty years John has been heavily involved in soccer. He now writes for a Greek community newspaper and compiles *Australian Soccer Weekly*. He has been a great friend and we still laugh about the old days—Clevo, being on the hill at the SCG for all the test matches, and our experiences on the stockmarket in which we disastrously sold our Poseidon shares the day before they took off, a decision that cost us the chance of becoming overnight millionaires in our early twenties.

Also, while I was growing up, I was close to the Panaretos family and similarly, my Greek affinity was further entrenched when I moved to Canberra in the late 1970s to coach the Canberra team in the Philips National Soccer League and was virtually adopted by the Moulis family. Theo Moulis is a well-known restaurateur in Canberra and his son Danny, who played in my team at just sixteen years of age, was for a time the chairman of the Canberra Cosmos. I'm not sure what it is about the Greek community; maybe it was being born at the Hellenic Hospital, but I have always had a special place for it in my life. I guess it was the welcoming and fair-minded attitude of my parents that I should thank for the connection I feel for other cultures.

During the first four years I spent at Cleveland Street I was involved in all sorts of sport. I was captain of the school soccer team and a member of the Combined High Schools side. I was also vice-captain of the first XI cricket team and a member of the athletics team. Strangely though, when I entered my final year in 1960 there was no school senior soccer team. I still had to play a sport, it was just that soccer was no longer an option. It was indicative of soccer's lowly status and it meant that I was forced to play another sport.

I was more familiar with rugby league than rugby union at the time but all my mates were union players so I was swayed to give the rah-rah game a go. I obviously wasn't too familiar with the rules though because the first time I went down with the ball in a tackle I forgot to release it. (It is mandatory in rugby union, as opposed to rugby league, to release the ball once tackled.) In a flash it seemed like the entire group of players had jumped on top of me! I think it was a good way to learn the game because I made sure that was the only time it happened.

Before my first game of rugby union I had decided to make sure the coach knew I had never played before. I can remember saying to him very directly, 'I can't play rugby union,' before getting the reply, 'Well, you can kick, can't you?' I couldn't really argue with that given my soccer background. When I did play everyone was just amazed that I could kick the ball off both feet. Of course it was natural for me, having played soccer for most of my life, but it certainly appeared to be a big deal to everyone else. I was put in at fullback with the instructions to kick the ball out when I got it and so that's exactly what I did. Needless to say, I was an instant hit and before I knew it I was playing in the first XV.

A couple of times I was forced to volley the ball into touch straight from a line-out just so I wouldn't get absolutely flattened. Everyone seemed amazed at that as well. I certainly wasn't trying to show off but I was definitely interested in self-preservation because outside of school I was playing soccer for Canterbury and wasn't really interested in getting hurt through playing rugby. Can you imagine today's Harry Kewell having to play competitive rugby union the day before he had to play soccer? It makes me laugh thinking about it. Having said that, playing union is not something I regretted. In fact

I'm glad I did play because it was a nice diversion for me and made me realise how great a game soccer is. Moreover, it was just how the soccer scene was in those days. I was a member of one of the top soccer clubs in the country, I was playing rugby union at the same time and no one thought anything of it because soccer wasn't considered a serious sport by the bulk of Australian society.

It was a great thrill for me to be appointed vice-captain of Cleveland Street High in my final year but to this day I blame Australian cricket great Norm O'Neill for costing me the captaincy. O'Neill was one of my boyhood heroes and was part of the great Australian side of that era captained by Richie Benaud. I grew up listening to the radio commentary of their matches and occasionally watching them play. I was completely in awe of them. They had so much all-round depth that a player like Frank Misson, who used to open the batting for New South Wales, batted down at number eleven! Players like Richie Benaud, Alan Davidson, Ron Archer, Johnny Martin, Ken Mackay, Brian Booth, Neil Harvey, Bobby Simpson and Peter Burge were all amazing players that would have been brilliant in any era. But for me, elevated over them all was Norm O'Neill. He was something special and I loved watching him bat. In today's playing terms he was probably a bit like Mark Waugh. I thought he was so good that I would have rather witnessed him getting twenty runs than watch some other cricketers scoring a hundred. So, when I heard he was batting for Australia down at the Sydney Cricket Ground one summer's day during my fourth year at Cleveland Street High, my mind started racing.

I can remember the school janitor—Ike Harvey, a former boxer who was a favourite of all the kids at school and who used to regale us with tales of the old days of boxing and rugby league—giving me an update of the Test match Australia was playing while I'd been in class. It was lunch, Australia was batting and O'Neill was not out. After weighing up my options, school suddenly didn't seem so high on my list of priorities. I knew school would still be there tomorrow but I wasn't sure Norm O'Neill would be. I also knew it was only a three-kilometre walk that would be made more pleasant by the beautiful sunshine. The decision wasn't a difficult one in the end. I took myself off from school to watch my hero bat.

Unfortunately, on that afternoon the school held its elections for house captains. When the name 'Warren' came up all my mates decided to have some fun and cheekily started saying things like, 'Well, I'm sure he was here this morning, Sir' and 'Yeah, he was definitely here earlier'. I'm sure I would have been making the very same smart comments if one of them had gone to watch the cricket and left me at school but that didn't make me feel much better the next day when I was told to visit the headmaster's office. I probably should have come up with a better excuse but all I could say when I was questioned about my absence from school was, 'Norm O'Neill was batting, Sir'. I certainly thought it was a good enough reason anyway. For me it was like saying Pelé was playing down at the Sydney Football Stadium. How could you possibly stay in school? Headmasters don't seem to share such views though and I knew I was in trouble.

I wasn't punished in any immediate sense for my day at the cricket but the headmaster made it clear that it would cost me later on down the track. As it was coming up to the time to vote for next year's school captain I was pretty sure what he was hinting at. Many years later I saw Norm at a ceremony for the Walk of Honour at the SCG and told him the story. We both had a good laugh about it and I made sure that I told him that I have never regretted my decision. I can't remember how many runs he made that day but watching him bat was inspiring.

The thing that has always struck me about that episode, and maybe will also strike other people as odd, is that it doesn't concern soccer whatsoever. It wasn't a soccer match or a soccer player I was so enthralled by. I had snuck away from school to see my cricketing hero, not my soccer hero. It shows how gradual my path towards fully embracing soccer actually was because throughout my school years I was always involved in all sorts of different sports. I was never set on concentrating on soccer, let alone making a career out of it.

Many post-war migrants in Australia at this time were young men with an enthusiasm for football. Getting together on the weekend to mix with people from their own country and play football was an opportunity they relished and for many it was an escape from the racism they often experienced in Australia. Most European migrants couldn't speak English and struggled to adapt to the nuances of their new society. Australia had been a very isolated, Anglocentric nation up until this point and the local population often treated their new compatriots as second-class citizens. The changing cultural mix was as much a shock for the Australians as the newcomers and there was fear and distrust on both sides.

It was in this often unforgiving environment that soccer provided an escape. Migrants gained some comfort and some memories of home by getting together on the weekend and playing football. Soon the various migrant communities embraced the opportunity to form clubs and further cement this tangible link to their heritage. Many good players had arrived in Australia during the post-war influx, even though they went largely unrecognised by the Australian local community, and the quality of some of the new clubs that they formed was very high. In many cases the players were refugees who had been forced to leave their native countries and they still quite naturally wanted to play soccer at the highest level they could.

Trouble quickly developed when the governing body of football, the Australian Soccer Association, and its affiliated association in New South Wales, would not allow these new ethnic clubs into the first division competition. Any attempts by the new migrant clubs to compete against the established district clubs like Canterbury, Auburn, Bankstown, Granville, Cessnock, Adamstown, Balgownie and Corrimal were continually rebuffed. The 'wogs', as they were colloquially and patronisingly known, were only allowed to play in the second division even though they were usually of a good enough standard to play at the top level. The ethnic clubs were passionate about the game, they had good players and they were attracting strong and loyal crowds. How could they be left out? Many of the best migrant players would have been good enough to have become top players in their own countries if they had not had to flee from their homelands, so a potential drawcard for the sport in Australia was being wasted. What's more, the migrant clubs and their administrators were very innovative and progressive in their plans for the game. They wanted to take the game forward and, perhaps more importantly, they were people who put their money where their mouths were.

Eventually, several of these migrant clubs tired of the situation and decided, in 1957, to break away and form their own competition and their own governing body—the New South Wales Soccer Federation (NSWSF) which included teams such as Sydney Austral, Prague, Polonia and Apia. More established teams like Canterbury and Auburn could see the potential of the players at these clubs and were also convinced to join the new competition. The Australian Soccer Association responded by lodging a complaint with the Fédération Internationale de Football Association (FIFA) and, in a very short time, the new migrant-based Australian Soccer Federation had been outlawed by the world governing body.

While the FIFA ban meant the teams involved in the new NSWSF competition couldn't play matches against international opposition it also meant that the clubs could bring players in from overseas without a transfer fee. In fact, the ban was a blessing in disguise. By October 1962 there were more than thirty footballers playing in Australia without proper releases from their former overseas clubs or associations and the exclusion from FIFA turned out to be a major coup for the new competition, leading to one of the most exciting times in the history of club soccer in Australia. It not only lifted the standard of the competition but, by doing so, it created unprecedented interest and enthusiasm in the Australian public about the sport.

The two teams which epitomised this period better than any others were Prague and Canterbury. Prague was a Czechoslovakian-based club and it had brought over a host of players from Austria, many who were full internationals, to bolster its playing list. Players like the wonderful Leo Baumgartner, Walter Tamandl, Eric Schwarz, Stuart Sherwin and Erwin and Herbert Ninaus were tremendous exponents of the game and they all turned out in the New South Wales competition. Les Scheinflug, who later became the Australian youth team coach, also arrived and began playing for Prague as a left midfielder during this time. To bring so many quality players to Australia would simply have not been possible without the FIFA ban being put in place.

Apart from these overseas internationals Prague also secured the crème de la crème of the Australian players. One of the great goalkeepers of Australian soccer, Ronnie Lord, played for the team, as did former stars Kevin O'Neil and Ken Hiron. It was this mixture of players that made Prague the glamour team of the period.

Canterbury was different from Prague in that it had a policy of giving young players a go and taking a gamble on 'green' Australian talent. It meant that young players, such as myself, were given the opportunity to play against international standard players on a regular basis. The club and our team became known as the 'Canterbury Babes' for this very reason.

During my last year at Cleveland Street, Canterbury was in the news because Leo Baumgartner had joined the club. He was the biggest name in Australian soccer at the time and the spotlight followed him wherever he went. He was a real showman and people used to call him Sabrina, after a well-endowed movie star of the time, because of the way he ran with his chest out. The crowds used to love him because he was tremendously gifted with the ball and he would always try to keep them entertained in return. Of course he was a striker and loved scoring goals. He came to Canterbury from Prague, a club well known for its one-touch style of football. Leo drew people to the game and so his signing for Canterbury was a big deal.

When Leo came to the club he would usually train by himself. He would turn up, put our youth team goalkeeper Ron Corry in the goals and would fire long-range shots at him all night. That was all he would do. I had never come across anyone like him; I guess he was my first real taste of the European mentality of football which was so different from the style to which I was accustomed. Leo never liked running much and always demanded the ball be played to his feet. While I was used to people making the effort to retrieve a slightly mis-hit pass, Leo simply didn't move. It had to be played to his feet. Because of this attitude he wasn't the easiest person to play with on the field but at the same time he made everyone lift their own game and improve some of our weaknesses.

His arrival at the club represented a departure from Canterbury's traditional policy towards players. The club had always prided itself on its commitment to developing outstanding young players yet here it was bringing in probably the biggest star in Australian soccer. There had obviously been a change in mindset. The theory behind the decision was that the young players in the team would learn a great deal more, and a great deal more quickly, by playing with someone of

Leo's calibre every week. And, in the short term, the philosophy worked.

It quickly became a golden period to be involved in the sport in any shape or form. The people in charge of the soccer administration back then were among the best the game has ever seen because they were truly passionate and wanted the game to establish foundations and develop. They introduced innovations that were unheard of in any sport in Australia, such as playing matches under floodlights in the evening. Not many people would realise it but soccer also became the first sport in Australia to play a pre-season competition and the first to play matches on Sundays. For the first time the game was marketed and promoted to the public, attracting record crowds thereby giving the sport a profile it had never enjoyed before. Indeed, at that stage, there was a general belief that soccer would take over as Australia's number one sport over the next ten years. But I guess everyone has heard that one before. One thing was for certain though; the migrant influx had shaken up soccer in Australia.

With Leo in our team, Canterbury finished third in the league and progressed through to a final against Apia. It was my first finals series and there was a good deal of media interest in the match because of our team's youthfulness and Leo's high profile. At the time, the *Sun* newspaper described me as 'the tall, slightly built youth—with the freckled features and the ready smile looks as if he would be blown away in a strong wind—how wrong this impression is, every defender in Sydney can tell you'. I can't remember if there was a strong wind about for the final against Apia but it proved to be a memorable day nonetheless. We won the game 3–2 in extra time and I scored two goals. Unfortunately, my pride in my efforts was somewhat soured by an injury to my right knee.

The injury put me in hospital for around two weeks and meant I missed out on playing in the grand final. The knee needed to be aspirated but fortunately the doctors allowed me out of hospital to watch the team play Prague in the grand final. It was a great match. More than seventeen thousand people turned up to see the 'Canterbury Babes' stage a huge upset by trouncing Prague 5–2. Quite amazingly, all of the team's forwards scored goals. Joe Amigo, Brian Smith, Leo Baumgartner, Barry Salisbury and my brother Geoff all found the back of the net. Everyone was obviously in the mood to celebrate but I was forced to head straight back to hospital. Little did I know at the time that it was only the start of my troubles with knee injuries.

The excitement of playing in the finals and being in hospital for a prolonged period was very disruptive to my study. I had been in the limelight a lot more than I was used to and my mind was in several places at once. I'm certainly not making excuses, and my marks weren't bad in any case, but I'm sure my soccer affected my high school Leaving results.

I actually won the school's Conway Prize which was awarded for an outstanding combination of sporting and academic achievement. It was a great honour because it reflected the school's ambition to strive for both academic and sporting goals. I also won prizes for economics, accounting and geography (which I suppose ties in with football!) at various stages during my time at Clevo and in my end-of-school report, the headmaster wrote:

> John has distinguished himself in study, in sport, and in the field of school citizenship. He is an honest, reliable, stable well-balanced person, with the potential for leadership ... In soccer he was shown superior ability—competing against men of greater maturity and experience.

While I had done quite well at school, I guess, like most people, in hindsight I feel I should have done a bit better. At the time I really didn't have the luxury of thinking about pursuing soccer as a career. There was no Australian team to aspire to, no lucrative local professional competition and no television to spark dreams of making it in the football world overseas. All I knew was that I had to go to university and get a job. The theory was that you got an education, got a job and lived happily ever after.

I was so serious about finding the right career after finishing school that I went to the Australian Institute of Industrial Psychology and had a psychological profile prepared to help me figure out the career to which I was most suited. Its conclusion that I should concentrate on being a journalist 'later specialising in sports journalism' still makes me laugh when I look at it now and realise how prophetic it was.

At the time though I was happy when I was awarded a commercial traineeship with BHP that enabled me to go to university to study economics. The company initially sent me up to Newcastle to get some experience but I only lasted a week. I simply couldn't stand being away from the environment I was used to. I had moved away from home, I had been forced to leave Canterbury and the wrench away from my family was just too much. Luckily, the company was flexible and agreed to transfer me to Commonwealth Steel in Sydney.

I remember there was a young guy working for BHP at the time who used to look after all the trainees. He would regularly check up on how we were progressing at work, how we were going at university and how we were faring in general. One day he took another trainee called Phil Hawthorne and me aside and told us that we had to realise that our future was at BHP and not in sport. Phil must have paid as little attention to the advice as I did because he went on to become a famous rugby union and rugby league international.

When I bumped into the same trainee officer many years later he had completely changed his tune. This time he took me aside and said, 'Remember that advice I gave you? Well, I regret it. I'm sitting in an office while you are working in a field you love and travelling the world.' He was actually quite apologetic about trying to push me away from sport for my own good. I'm positive that at the time he thought he was doing the right thing by us and, for the times, it was probably sensible advice. I just think it demonstrates how far-fetched a career in sport was considered in those days and how lucky Phil and I were to make it in our chosen sports.

Commonwealth Steel gave me two afternoons off a week to go to university and I trained with Canterbury for the other three nights of the week. Not surprisingly I didn't have a great social life in those days because it was usually just football and work. I didn't even have my first drink until I was twenty-two. When I told a friend of mine that I didn't particularly enjoy my first beer, he wisely predicted that I would develop a taste for it. Of course he was right but I really didn't have time to be out drinking and socialising in those days. Work and soccer occupied all of my time.

I was particularly glad to be back playing at Canterbury after my brief stay in Newcastle because the team was playing really well. While Leo had now left the club we still managed to finish second in the league in 1961. I scored eleven goals to finish second highest goal scorer behind my mate John Watkiss and the entire team's fame was starting to grow. One of the newspapers even nicknamed us the 'killer kids'.

Unfortunately, we lost the 1961 grand final against Hakoah. We had gone in red-hot favourites but they completely outplayed us on the day and won 4–1. They had some great players, including the Israeli internationals Gerry Chaldi and Rafi Levi. Chaldi would later go on to coach Sydney City to win the first Philips National Soccer League championship in 1977 but back then he was a top-class player with a great deal of experience. In fact, their entire team was too experienced for us on that day. Many of our players were still learning the game and that match was a particularly harsh lesson.

But that was the great thing about Canterbury. They were consciously choosing to develop young Australian kids by giving them the opportunity to play big matches and they stuck to their guns. We were so young we actually knew very little about the guys we were playing against and looking back now, if I had actually known how good some of the players were that we were playing against, I probably would have been scared about matching up to them. But, as it was, I knew nothing about them and so I just went out and played. I'm sure it was the same for everyone else. In the end we learned a great deal from just being thrown in against them as if in a gladitorial battle. It was sink or swim and everyone quickly learnt to swim.

One of my strongest memories of playing for Canterbury is the shock of being thrown into a team of men as a young teenager. At least, compared to me they were men. I was always shocked and amazed at the stuff the older guys would talk about in the dressing rooms. Girls, drinking, going out, working and 'the wife' were all things that I hadn't discovered yet and knew little about. As a result, I would just sit there in wonderment, trying desperately to digest what was being said.

Once I got on the field though I was fine. Playing 'above my weight' was a constant for me during my early career, going right back to playing as a five year old in the under-12s at Botany Methodists. I had also been the youngest of three boys and although my brothers were never particularly rough on me, being the smallest can't help but toughen you up. I guess the same principle applied with my soccer in that being a boy amongst men made me a better player at a younger age. I progressed faster and improved at a greater rate than I would have if I had been playing against kids my own age. Unfortunately there were some painful implications that stemmed from my youthfulness and naïveté.

I never really got rubdowns in my teenage days at Canterbury but the massage guys at the club stick in my memory because they were real characters. The things that would come out of their mouths used to constantly shock me. Whenever one of the older guys in the team used to play badly or complain about being a bit tired or sore, one of the massage guys would always say, 'what you need to get you going is this liniment that you put on your balls'. I must have heard that saying a hundred times and it made a real impression on me because years later when I was playing for the University of New South Wales I actually tried it.

It was the only game I played for university because of all my other commitments but it certainly proved to be a memorable one. The match was in Armidale and after a long drive I was tired when I arrived at the ground. I must have remembered the rubdown tip because when I saw the liniment—Sloans Liniment it was called—among our team's gear I thought it might give me a lift. As soon as I began rubbing it in to the tender region where the rubdown guys had said it would help, I realised I had made a major mistake.

It didn't take long before my nether regions felt so inflamed that I could hardly walk. I literally felt like I was on fire. I was in so much pain that I certainly couldn't concentrate on the match and I'm still amazed I got through it at all. The real problem was that it wasn't simply a case of the heat burning for several minutes and then dissipating. It not only lasted the entire match but for days later! All I can say to anyone else thinking of trying it is that it certainly didn't help my game.

I think that episode perfectly illustrates how great the gap between myself and the guys in the Canterbury team was. They were men just kidding around and I obviously innocently believed whatever they had to say and took their bluffing at face value. It wasn't like today where there isn't so much of a gap between the generations. Then, I was quite literally a boy amongst men.

Canterbury's golden period came to an end when money entered the football equation. By the mid-1960s many of the migrants who had arrived in Australia in the post-World War II immigration influx had increased the size of their disposable income and much of this money was being spent on new migrant soccer clubs. This, in turn, meant that the old clubs began to struggle to compete.

A club like Canterbury paid its players what it could but it was never great money. We were on three pounds for a win, two pounds for a draw and one pound for a loss during my time there. That was pretty good money for most of us because we were all quite young. I was still only a teenager and was reasonably content with earning three quid a week to play a sport I enjoyed. But the situation inevitably changed when our eyes were opened to the tremendous amount of money being paid to players at other clubs. We were regularly beating these other clubs and it was only natural that we started asking ourselves, why the players on other teams were earning up to eighty pounds a game when we were beating them each week and only earning three pounds. It was probably the arrival of Leo that made the realisation really sink in. Canterbury was like any other old-fashioned Aussie club in that everyone knew what was going on around the place and word about Leo's pay-packet soon got around. Suddenly money became a concern. We had already found out that guys we were playing against and beating were being paid around twenty-five times what we were receiving but to discover that someone in our own team was getting paid a lot of money was a different matter altogether.

Of course, soon people from other clubs also began realising that we weren't being paid much for our success. They didn't hesitate to begin offering us lucrative deals to leave. When Uncle Joe left to coach St George in 1962 it really signalled the beginning of the end of Canterbury as I had known it. Players that had been there for years started to leave. My good mate John Watkiss went to Apia, Barry Salisbury went to South Coast, my brother Geoff left and Brian Smith went to Pan Hellenic. Most of the moves were successful for the players involved and members of the Greek community still rave about Brian Smith when I talk to them today. But the deals being made were all very secretive at the time and nobody openly discussed them, even though everyone was aware of exactly what was going on.

In my situation the idea of earning enough money from football to go to university full time became a very appealing one. The 1962 season was disappointing and Canterbury finished second last, only two points from the bottom of the table. It was a big turnaround from finishing second the year before and I'm sure it was all because of the distracting influence of money. Everyone's minds were elsewhere. This made my own decision to leave that much easier. Although the club wasn't happy about letting me go they received a good offer from St George Budapest and there was no acrimony.

Unfortunately, Canterbury never quite recovered from the simultaneous departure of so many good young players. It decimated the team and the club. It was a shame because no other club was focused on youth development like Canterbury at that time. It was a great club and we had had a wonderful team. I'm sure the money being offered by other clubs ultimately destroyed Canterbury. It was, in effect, a new era in Australian football and although Canterbury was quite progressive in terms of its promotion of young talent, it was also old-fashioned when it came to money and administration. It always relied solely on gate-money and fund-raising activities to keep the players paid and the club running. When the new migrant-based clubs began springing up across New South Wales in the 1950s, Canterbury was simply left behind. These new clubs were well supported and financed by businessmen who could see soccer's potential. There was simply a mismatch that saw the new guard of Australian soccer overwhelm the old guard.

3

The 'Big' Move

IN 1962, CONFECTIONERY company Scanlens created a series of eighteen football cards featuring Australian soccer players. The player cards were sold with a piece of chewing gum and were quite popular with local kids, who could enjoy their gum and either keep or trade the card. I was one of the players chosen to appear on a card and on it I was described as a 'devastating centre forward or inside forward, a soccer natural'. I'm not sure if I was 'devastating' but by that stage I had managed to get a bit of a name for myself in the New South Wales competition and other clubs had begun to pay attention to me. The first serious offer I entertained from another club came from St George Budapest in 1963. A committee member called Ziggy Bordacs, who was the brother of club president Les Bordacs and well connected with the club, approached me. I immediately took notice when he told me that the club was very keen to bring me over.

I would later discover that Les Bordacs was, alongside Alex Pongrass, the very heart and soul of St George Budapest in those days and a great administrator. He was so well regarded that he would later co-manage the Australian national team for a period of time. The offer that Les and the club eventually put on the table in front of me came at a time when Canterbury had lost many of its best players and at a period in my life when I was hoping to begin earning enough money from soccer to attend university full-time. The timing seemed perfect and the offer was one I simply couldn't refuse.

The transfer fee agreed upon by the two clubs was fifteen hundred pounds, a reasonable sum of money in those days. What's more, the deal was sweetened for Canterbury by the part exchange of St George Budapest captain Alan Hetherington so the club certainly wasn't shortchanged. Personally, I received a sign-on fee of three hundred pounds and would be paid a weekly wage of fifteen pounds for a win, seven pounds ten shillings for a draw and three pounds for a loss. It was obviously substantially more than the three pounds for a win and one pound for a loss that I was being paid at Canterbury and it was enough for me to live on while I went to university full-time.

I also distinctly recall receiving a big box full of sausages and salamis from St George as well as two new suits. In those days many Hungarians were in the rag trade and the delicatessen business so it was a payment in kind. Someone recently joked with me that they must have been good suits because it looked like I was still wearing one of them today. While the sausages and the suits certainly weren't part of the contract they made me feel that I was being welcomed into the entire Hungarian community that supported St George. It was a wonderful gesture and I immediately felt like I had made the right decision to switch clubs.

My link to St George Budapest actually went further back than my transfer in 1963 because my brother Ross had joined the club in 1961. By the time I started there he had already left to play for Concord but he still tells an amusing story about his brief time there.

When Ross arrived at Budapest he was still fairly young so he played a lot of his football for the reserve-grade team, where he earned his stripes. But as more and more matches passed without him being given a chance in the top team, Ross started to get the feeling he wasn't really wanted at the club. Hungarians dominated it at that stage and Ross felt he might not fit into the club's plans. There was certainly no hostility or even tension, it was just a case of Ross perceiving he was not being given a chance to prove himself.

When the first-grade fullback was injured one weekend, Ross really thought his chance had come. He trained all week thinking he would be a certainty for the first grade team and would finally have the opportunity to show what he could do. In those days they used to write the team for the weekend on the board in the dressing sheds after training on a Thursday night and so Ross hurried in after training to see if his name was recorded for the first-grade team. But he couldn't see it and was so annoyed and disappointed that he decided then and there that he wasn't going to play for St George Budapest any more.

As he stormed out of the training sheds, some of the supporters (hundreds of supporters used to come to training in those days), realised he was upset and stopped him. When they asked him what was wrong he told them he wasn't in the team and had decided to leave. 'No Ross, you are in the team,' they all assured him. They quickly led him back into the sheds and pointed to the board, 'There you are—Voron.' Ross initially couldn't work out what they were talking about but it soon clicked. They had spelt his name V-o-r-o-n! Ross had just completely overlooked that fact that people from a European background often tend to change a 'w' to a 'v' when they speak English. The story still makes me laugh because I was called Johnny 'Voron' all throughout my career. I can remember that the popular *Soccer World* newspaper was always laughingly referred to as 'Soccer Vorld' among the soccer community for this very reason. I still recall the old guys who used to wander around selling the newspaper at the grounds yelling out 'Soccer Vorld, Soccer Vorld'.

In the end, it was lucky for both Ross and me that the supporters stopped him before he left training in a huff. Otherwise the Warren name, or the Voron name, might not have already been established at St George Budapest by the time I arrived.

I soon learned that St George Budapest was a club very proud of its Hungarian tradition. It held firm views on the game that would irrevocably influence my philosophy on how soccer should be played. Much like the Brazilians of yesteryear, St George believed it was not enough to simply win the game. The club believed in what the Brazilians call the 'jogo bonito', or the beautiful game. Brazil might win but everyone involved would still be upset if the team played without beauty. The St George club embraced a similar outlook. The team might win but the club would be miserable because we were expected to win with style, to play like the great Hungarian team of the Puskas era. I remember the club officials used to urge the players to 'give it some pepper', meaning that the game had to transcend the technical aspects of play; the players had to give it some spice. It was the guiding ethos of the club and it was one that I came to wholeheartedly embrace.

When I arrived at St George Budapest, the club had just experienced a disastrous 1962 season. There had even been a player revolt, sparked by money, which had erupted just before the team played in the Australia Cup final. The dispute between the players and officials obviously affected the team and they were thrashed in the final. It was a terrible situation for such a proud club and the board decided that the only available course of action was to wipe the slate clean and bring in a new group of players, both from the local scene and from overseas.

While this new group of players would eventually become a potent mix on the field, the first year under former Barcelona star Miklos Szegedi was disappointing. One of the major difficulties was communication. Szegedi was from Romania and was quite linguistically talented because he could also speak Spanish, Hungarian and German. Unfortunately one of the holes in his language skills was English. Meanwhile, the South Americans in the team spoke Spanish, the Hungarians spoke mainly Hungarian and the Yugoslavs only spoke Serbian. I, of course, only spoke English. On match day or at training, Szegedi would speak to the South American players in Spanish and the Hungarians in Hungarian. He would also converse easily with my teammates Herbert Stegbauer and Manfred Schaefer because of their German-speaking backgrounds. But his messages needed to be translated for the Yugoslavs in the team and for the English-speaking Australians in the team, such as myself, Dave Buchanan and Neil Brisby. It meant the team talks would often take an hour because it was like a meeting of the United Nations! But that was very much how Australian soccer was in those days. It was a true coming together of cultures, languages, customs and playing styles, even if communication was sometimes difficult.

The club was slightly disappointed to finish sixth that year and when the 1964 season didn't start so well either, it brought in Laurie Hegyes as the new coach and decided to name me as the captain. I was only nineteen so the club was taking a bit of a gamble on me but I felt I could handle my new role. I was actually quite excited because I knew we had a good team. All the while though I realised that my appointment was also an example of St George's attempts to 'Australianise' the club. They wanted to use me as the 'Aussie' front that the public would recognise in association with the club. The officials could see that down the track they would have to become a club with a district behind it and they knew I was the stereotypical 'true-blue Aussie kid' that could help that transition. I was quite happy to play the role and I have always thought the club were very forward thinking in their approach. St George was a real melting pot of different cultures in those days and I wasn't too concerned if some viewed me as the token Aussie in amongst it all.

The year I joined the club they decided to bring the first four South American imports to Australia. Four Argentine players, Victor Fernandez, Hugo Rodriguez, Lorenco Heredia and Salvador Isaac, travelled by bus from Buenos Aires to Cartagena in Colombia before boarding a boat and sailing to Brisbane. When they finally arrived in Australia they were probably mortified to discover that they then had to drive for over twelve hours down to Sydney. But while it took an age for them to arrive here they were certainly worth it once they arrived. Not just for St George but also for me.

At the time, most Australians only watched English football on television and even these broadcasts were limited. The aggressive style of British football was, in many ways, mirrored in the approach taken to Australian Rules football and rugby league in Australia. Sport in Australia was based on aggression, toughness and the 'have a go' mentality. It was the arrival of these Argentines and my contact with other players from countries such as Poland, Greece, Hungary, Yugoslavia, Austria, Italy, Germany and Holland that opened my eyes to a different approach to sport.

There were some top-class players at St George during that time; players who had international pedigree, such as Julius Gergely, Erno Grosz, Petar Banicevic, Joe Csardas, John Galambos, Les Schauman, Joe Pompor, Herbert Stegbauer, Manfred Schaefer, Theo Tsombaras, Joe Vasvari, Mladen Krgin, George Kovac, Charlie Kangyar, Tivor Zuckerman and Joe and Frank Lang. (Little did I know when joining St George that Manfred Schaefer and I would become roommates and close friends for the next ten years playing in Europe, the Americas, Asia, Oceania and Africa—finishing our international careers together at the World Cup in West Germany in 1974. Manfred was a self-made player, not blessed with silky skills but a marvellous competitor who marked some of the great strikers out of games. As his roommate I can tell you that Manfred sulked for hours if he lost a five-a-side training game and if there was a cross-country run, Manfred *had* to win it. He was the type of competitive player every team needs.) Our coach Laurie Hegyes had played for the famous Ferencvaros club in Budapest while Mladen Krgin had played a major part in a European Cup victory over Italian giants AC Milan. Spanish player Eduardo Massey, who came to the club after playing professionally in Spain and Portugal, and Galantay Balint, who came to the club after arriving in Australia as a wrestler with the 1956 Hungarian Olympic team, were also from top-notch football backgrounds.

Many of the Hungarian players in the team had fled Hungary as refugees from the revolution in 1956. I can remember a conversation with Andrew Dettre, in my view the best soccer writer in Australia, who was himself of Hungarian descent, several years ago in which he told me that players like Galambos, who sadly died of cancer at thirty-three, and Schauman would have been stars in their own right back in Hungary if the revolution had not intervened. He even compared them to one of the great Hungarian stars of the 1970s, Florian Albert. That's how highly some of these players, who played for St George, were rated so it was an incredible combination of players who were associated with the club and who brought a magnificent style of soccer to the Australian public.

Watching, training and playing with these quality players was a marvellous experience and a wonderful, if belated, football education for me. Just watching the way the South Americans passed the ball was an education in itself. They could flick the ball with the outside of the foot, they could play it first time, they could touch it that way or bend it the other way. I had never seen anything quite like it. I was quickly taught the importance of skill and, even though I was aware then that my skill level wouldn't ever be all that it could have been had I been trained properly as a kid, I soon realised that it could be much better.

The truly multicultural nature of St George during my early years at the club was probably the most beneficial aspect of my time there. As well as having a different way of playing football they also had different views on life, different ideas about cuisine and music—differences that fascinated an Anglo-Aussie guy such as myself. There were also a lot of young Australian players, such as Neil Brisby and Dave Buchanan, complementing the migrant mix. It turned out to be not only an invaluable education, it also enabled me to gain a better understanding of the world and gave me a better respect for other people. These early encounters with players from overseas and their subsequent influence as teammates not only had an impact on my football, it also had a major bearing on my life. The early influence of players from South America and Europe is probably another reason behind my outlook on life. I was taught that football involved more than the British style that I had grown up with, more than simply winning games at whatever cost. I was shown another way of looking at the game—which I believe is a superior outlook—that emphasised soccer's beauty and style.

I feel very fortunate that my football education was broadened to look at the sport outside the narrow conception of British football that was dominant in Australia in those days. I soon realised that the mentality that conceived the English league as the best in the world was ill founded. It was in South America and Europe that a more beautiful approach to the game could be found.

I soon became very close with the South Americans in the team. They used to call me 'Concha' and I can remember being so pleased that they had given me a nickname because I felt more a part of their crowd. Although they took a while to settle into Australia, they were very funny guys and real personalities. I guess they were even rogues in a sense and I soaked up their views on the game and life. It wasn't until much later that I found out what 'Concha' actually meant and for those who don't know, I can only say it wasn't what I had thought and is actually a very rude term referring to a part of the female anatomy! I should have guessed really that they'd have a bit of a laugh at their impressionable Aussie friend's expense.

I always enjoyed the company of my South American teammates at St George because they always seemed so laid back and so happy to be alive. They made me realise that life didn't need to be completely serious every minute of the day. We used to just pile in a car when we weren't training and drive up to the Blue Mountains for the day to have a picnic. The guys really loved having big barbecues and Vic always used to bring his dog, who was called Pulga, along for the trip. Vic had spent hours training Pulga to play with a football and the dog was constantly amazing us with his tricks; he could run with the ball, juggle the ball and even sort of head the ball. Whenever we would start mucking around with the ball, little Pulga would always come over to join in. I would spend hours with the guys just kicking the ball around, laughing and having a good time. They were such vibrant people that I spent as much time as I could with them.

Although the 1964 season began poorly the team really came together under Laurie Hegyes towards the end of the season. We finished second in the league before progressing through to the grand final. Unfortunately my old mate John Watkiss scored five goals for Apia against us in the grand final and we were handed a 7–2 thrashing. John was on fire that day and although his performance will always stand out in my memory, I will also always remember that particular final series for a different reason. Almost as amazing as scoring five goals in a grand final, I was able to get soccer on the front page of the *Sydney Morning Herald,* an amazing feat in those days and, indeed, today.

The headline of the article which appeared in the *Sydney Morning Herald* on 6 September 1964 read: 'Hypnosis beats soccer nerves'. It had come about because I had decided to go under hypnosis before the semi-final against Apia. I did it for a number of reasons but mainly because I wanted to try and mentally prepare myself for the match so as not to be overwhelmed by nerves or the atmosphere. The first few paragraphs of the newspaper article read:

> A soccer player who was hypnotised last Thursday scored two goals in yesterday's premiership semi-final at the Sports Ground. He's Budapest St George's inside forward John Warren, whose team beat Apia 3–0. Warren said after the match he was placed under hypnosis on Thursday by a hypnotist.
>
> *'He put me under and spoke to my subconscious mind about getting over my nerves and not worrying about the match. I believe it did not take very long. It really helped out there on the ground, I'm not saying it made me play better, but it really helped me forget about the atmosphere and the big crowd. I will certainly go under hypnosis before the grand final.'*

I had been previously hypnotised when I was studying for university and I thought it could work successfully with my soccer performance as well. I'm sure people probably thought I was crazy at the time but in the end it worked for me and I scored two goals in the semi-final. Not surprisingly though, when Apia won their way into the grand final against us two weeks later, all the publicity and the previews in the newspapers were focused on my visit to the hypnotist. There were headlines like: 'We'll hypnotise them in the final: Apia', 'Apia says no to hypnotist' and 'Don't fall asleep today Johnny Warren'. I certainly copped a bit of flak over it and the situation didn't ease when we got walloped 7–2. But I never wavered in my belief in the benefits of hypnotism as part of a sports psychology approach to the game.

I have since used hypnosis with my own teams, particularly in 1974 with St George. Hypnosis and any sort of sports psychology was simply not accepted in those days and I was laughed at, as the headlines in the paper show, for using it. Nonetheless, I believed, and still believe, that there is so little between winning and losing in sport that if something has the potential to help the team it should be used, even if it is unconventional. I think the tremendous focus on the mental side of sport in modern competition only justifies my stance.

Losing to Apia in the grand final really hurt the club because they were seen as our nemesis during my time at St George. There was always fierce rivalry between us because we were both constantly near the top. On most occasions though Apia had the wood on us. Even when we did finish above them on the ladder in 1965 we were pipped into second place by the South Coast on goal difference. Then, to rub salt into the wounds, Apia made it through to the grand final and beat us again. This time the score was a little closer, 2–0, but it didn't make losing any easier.

When we finished third behind Apia and Hakoah in 1966 it seemed like we would never win the championship. I'm not sure whether this was on my mind when I was approached by St George's other bitter rivals Hakoah about switching camps. At that time leaving St George for Hakoah would have been like leaving Real Madrid to go to Barcelona—it just wasn't done—but I was still only young and I agreed to go and meet with the Hakoah board in town. It was a mistake on my part because I was too inexperienced to go to that sort of meeting by myself.

I ended up in a room with a number of high-powered, successful businessmen and I was completely overwhelmed. They coaxed and cajoled me and eventually I agreed to play for them. To be fair, they were offering me three times what I was currently being paid and it was a good deal. But I wasn't experienced enough to handle my own contractual negotiations and I was silly to attend that meeting by myself. The guys I was dealing with were experienced in contracts, business deals and negotiations, but it was my first time. I didn't realise that I should have gone away and sought some advice before agreeing to the deal. These days, player agents handle all contract negotiations and my story illustrates the important role these people assume on behalf of players, because I was pushed into agreeing to something almost immediately that I should have spent more time considering.

The next day I rang St George boss Alex Pongrass—in many ways, my mentor and as hard as nails but, in the end, always fair and someone who contributed so much to Australian football—to tell him the news. He was not very happy to say the least! He told me that there was no way that I was going over to Hakoah and that was that. I didn't know how to respond but I had the feeling Alex would be true to his word. Soon a big stoush developed between the two clubs over my services and I felt I was to blame for the entire matter because of the foolhardy way I had rushed into agreeing to play for Hakoah.

I'm not sure exactly what went on behind the scenes between St George and Hakoah but Alex was true to his word and I was back playing at St George in 1967. He made it clear to me that my future was with St George for the long haul.

4

Australia's Sporting Gallipoli: Our First World Cup Attempt

⚽ WHILE THE FIFA ban on the Australia Soccer Federation had been good for the local game it had the less positive consequence of stopping Australia from fielding an international team. The result was that during my early years in the sport there was simply no Australian team to aspire to. It was obviously not a great situation for Australia to be in and it was a relief when the ASF finally managed to wrest control of the game away from the Australian Soccer Association. It immediately agreed to comply with FIFA regulations and, after paying a compensation fee for its previous attitude, the international playing ban was lifted in 1963.

It was a crucial moment for Australian soccer because it reopened the world of international football. High-profile teams, such as Chelsea and Roma, began touring the nation and drawing big crowds. English heavyweights Everton drew nearly two hundred thousand spectators during an eight-match tour in 1964 while Scotland and Manchester United proved major successes in 1967. More importantly though, the lifting of the international ban meant Australia could enter a national team in the prestigious World Cup competition for the first time.

I still remember receiving the telegram that confirmed my selection in the first Australian squad chosen to try to qualify for the World Cup in England in 1966. I pulled it from the letterbox, read it and went into the bathroom to cry my eyes out. I'm not ashamed to admit it because being selected for Australia was the ultimate dream for me. The way that sportspeople of that era were brought up meant that playing for your country was the highest honour to which you could possibly aspire.

There was only one spot in the World Cup allotted to the African and Asian zones (Australia was part of the Asian zone, as deemed by FIFA) in those days and so we were expecting a tough route to England. But, as it turned out, every other eligible team withdrew from qualification for economic and political reasons. North Korea was the only other team left standing out of the two zones. The competition had not even begun and it was already down to two teams, North Korea and us. North Korea represented the only barrier to our participation in the World Cup finals. If we could beat them we were on our way to England to match up against the best players and best teams in the world. The team was understandably excited at the prospect of playing at a World Cup against the best players in the world.

Yugoslavian coach Tiko Jelisavcic was placed in charge of our squad and when he found out that the two-legged series against the North Koreans would be played in the supposedly neutral venue of Phnom Penh he decided to fly the team up to tropical Cairns for a month to prepare for the hot and humid conditions in Cambodia. The national team set-up wasn't anything like the situation the players find themselves in today. In fact Tiko wasn't even given an assistant. Training was completely his responsibility alone. It seems quite amazing when you think of the staff and resources that modern-day coaches have at their disposal but back then no one thought much about the lack of resources. It was just the way it was.

However, the team did have two managers—Jim Bayutti and Ian Brusasco. Jim was a very successful businessman, a leader in the Italian community and founder of the Apia club—and a soccer fanatic. He loved the game, knew a great deal about it and was well liked among the players because he always treated us properly. Jim had been a key figure in establishing the breakaway NSWSF so was also particularly keen to see the team do well. Ian was in charge of the administrative duties of our qualification campaign and he was also a great bloke to have around in camp. He went on to become chairman of the ASF and contribute a great deal to the game in Australia. Back then we were just so grateful for his ability to organise everything that needed to be done.

We also had masseur Lou Lazzari to give us rubdowns. He was a giant of a man with absolutely massive hands and he was an expert at his job. He turned out to be more than just a masseur though; he became a father figure to the players because of the warmth of his character. Lou had a heart of gold and the boys would often go around to his room just to sit and talk with him. Even though he wasn't playing he very quickly became an integral part of the squad.

Soccer journalist Lou Gautier, who is now the researcher for SBS soccer and an integral part of the SBS team, also joined the squad. He was the editor of the national soccer newspaper *Soccer World* and was the only journalist who made the trip with us. The lack of media interest was another sign of the times of soccer being treated as a second-class sport, so it was encouraging to have Lou along. Les Scheinflug was named as captain of the team and I was fortunate enough to be named as one of two vice-captains. At twenty-two years of age it was quite an honour for me. I knew I wasn't likely to play in any of the qualification matches because management did not want to risk such a youngster playing (anyone under twenty-three was considered young in those days), but I was excited anyway because I had been told that I was being groomed as a future captain of Australia.

In Cairns we stayed at a YMCA facility and trained three times a day, every day, for four weeks. It was absolute murder. We were paid a compensation fee of five dollars a day so we certainly weren't in it for the money. Despite training hard, the team played only one match during that four-week period and even that was only a 'friendly' match against local side Ingham so by the time we left camp the team was in no way match hardened. After four weeks of gruelling training, we still left Australia unprepared for the task that lay ahead.

Because of Australia's isolation, most of the team, myself included, had little idea about how people in other parts of the world, except the English, played the game. The only television coverage of soccer available in Australia arrived from England and there was no SBS television like today to provide action from all over the world and demonstrate the playing techniques of the various countries. As a result, our knowledge of the football world was mostly based on word of mouth. We had never seen North Korea play so they were very much an unknown quantity.

Despite this though, for the whole four weeks in the training camp and even during the trip over to Cambodia I can remember all the boys talking about what they were going to do after the World Cup in England; where they would holiday, what they would go and see, who they would go with. Everyone seemed to think it was a mere formality to go and beat the North Koreans, even though we knew nothing about how they played the game.

The culture shock when we first arrived in Phnom Penh was incredible. This was not only Australia's first venture towards the World Cup, it was also the first time this squad had been away as a national team. I'm always reminded of the Anzacs when I think of the trip because we travelled to a foreign place with no idea of what to expect; we were totally unprepared for what awaited us and we were thrown into the deep end and expected to come out on top. It just wasn't like today where people regularly travel overseas and know more of what to expect in different countries and different cultures.

When we arrived in Cambodia it was literally like landing on another planet. The situation became even more alien when our team and the North Korean teams were both paraded through the streets in a big bus. Thousands of people had lined the streets to have a close look at us and the North Koreans. I certainly hadn't expected this sort of public response in what was officially a neutral venue. It was so far from what we were used to back in Australia with our very modest fan base. Here were thousands of people turning out just to look at us, never mind the match itself!

I was given my first personal insight into the North Korean team when we were given a brief opportunity to watch them train. They immediately appeared very fast and very skilful and any worries I may have already felt were further heightened when I saw the program for the first match. Most of the Koreans players had up to sixty or seventy international caps under their belts and all of them were full-time soccer players and army personnel. We, on the other hand, were very much part-time players. I knew quite well that our team was largely inexperienced at international level and it was now becoming clear that the opposition was not the pushover we were expecting.

To make matters worse, not long after we arrived, several members of the team started getting sick. Our guys simply weren't used to foreign places where everything routine was suddenly very different and many of us were caught out. The team was simply unaware of all the health hazards posed by the Cambodian drinking water and food and by the time of the first match, illness was a serious problem in our ranks.

When the referee blew the whistle to start the first match on 21 November I was still awestruck by the amazing scene of a full house of sixty thousand spectators. The Cambodian crowd immediately made it known that they were far from neutral as they began cheering wildly for North Korea straight after the kick-off. They had plenty to cheer about because the Koreans were simply unbelievable players. They were a magnificent team and were simply too good for us from the outset. We were completely out of our depth. Despite our training camp we were totally unprepared for the two matches. We hadn't known our opponent and we weren't properly match fit. In short, we simply weren't ready for the challenge awaiting us. North Korea were such a good team that it was hard to see us winning under any circumstances.

Although our boys tried hard, the match finished in a 6–1 thrashing, dashing any hopes we held of qualifying for the World Cup. Pulling back a five-goal deficit was practically impossible and, what's more, it was like a war zone in our dressing sheds after the match. Players were injured, some were sick and most of the team was just stunned. The only positive to be taken from the match was Les scoring Australia's first goal back in international football following the years when we'd been banned by FIFA. Other than that it was a matter of just licking our wounds.

The team managed to slightly recover from its shell shock to put up a good show in the second match, some three days later. Although we lost again, this time 3–1. Les scored a goal again and it was a far better all-round performance. However, the team was simply not used to dealing with the huge crowd, the conditions and the atmosphere of the stadium. In many ways it was again like the Anzac troops—we had walked straight into an ambush.

The North Koreans had been skilful, disciplined and, above all, professional. They were both full-time players and full-time army personnel while we were only part-time players. They had given us a startling and revelatory eye-opener into the quality and depth of international football. Their eventual performance at the 1966 World Cup, where they knocked out Italy in the group stages, demonstrated how strong they actually were. In the quarter-final of the World Cup they were even leading Portugal 3–0 before the great Eusebio scored four goals to lead Portugal to a 5–3 win. Everyone in the Australian squad knew we would have to improve considerably to match the level of the top teams.

In retrospect, it is amazing that the ASF planned our trip so that we played a series of 'friendlies' *after* the World Cup qualifiers against North Korea, and not before, as should have been planned, so that we would be better prepared for our battle against North Korea. The friendly matches were played to offset the costs of Australia's World Cup effort. This decision illustrated the ASF's total lack of experience dealing with soccer on an international level. The team had only assembled to play the Ingham team in North Queensland before leaving for the World Cup qualifiers so the games against North Korea were our first together in a very long time. Had the friendlies with Cambodia, Malaysia and Hong Kong been held *before* the World Cup, the team would naturally have been more prepared and would have performed better.

I had sat on the bench for the two qualifying matches so I was yet to make my debut for Australia after the North Korea disaster. However, it wasn't long before I was on the field playing against Cambodia on 26 November in front of a crowd of around twenty thousand people. It was a special day for me even though we could only manage a 0–0 draw because it was my first time wearing the green and gold for Australia. It's one thing being in the squad but it's another experience all together running out on to the field and representing your country. I had been given a taste of being an international player and already knew I wanted more.

Our team went on to win three out of four games against Hong Kong and Malaysia before we returned home. The second match against Hong Kong was particularly memorable because of the violence that erupted in the crowd. We had won the match 3–1 but were pelted with stones from the crowd, who were obviously unhappy with the result, as we left the field. Later we were locked in the dressing sheds for a couple of hours as the authorities attempted to control the situation. It was a very tense situation for a while because the police simply couldn't get their vans in past the angry mob to get us out and although no one was hurt, the dressing sheds were badly damaged and the windows were smashed. Unfortunately, our pride was in much the same state when we arrived back in Australia.

5

My Coming of Age

⚽ HAVING AVERTED MY move to Hakoah, Alex Pongrass made it clear that he had long-term plans for me at St George. He wanted to train me to become both the football and club manager. He also wanted the club operations to be brought together under one umbrella. After the Hakoah debacle died down, he hired me to work full-time at the newly opened St George club as a public relations and marketing officer. I started visiting schools in the area, organising social events, holding coaching clinics for players, coaches and parents within the club, working with junior clubs and performing a whole host of other public relations activities. I was, in effect, the link between the club—a club with an ethnic background that wanted to broaden its base in the St George area—and the mainstream community.

In many ways Alex was a mentor to me. He was also a great negotiator and sometimes I felt he took advantage of my relative inexperience. Every time a contract came up, not only a football contract but also a work contract, I was really a kid coming up against a great businessman. It was a clear mismatch. Alex always had a great line that he would say to me: 'Johnny, money's not everything. You have job satisfaction. Money can never buy you that.' I'm not criticising Alex for the way he dealt with me because he always had my interests at heart. Nevertheless, I always knew I was out of my depth when we had to negotiate and I felt railroaded on occasion.

While I was committing myself to working at the club off the field, on the field I was still playing and captaining the team and we were scoring goal after goal. We won the 1967 Ampol Cup, ironically beating Hakoah—the club to which I'd almost transferred—in the final and amassed a record 8–2 victory over Cumberland along the way. From there the season only got better and we eventually beat our great nemesis Apia in the grand final. After trailing 2–1 at half-time, we played like men inspired in the second half to win 5–2. That season has since gone down in the club's history as one of its greatest.

The grand final victory was even sweeter because a couple of weeks previously the new St George social club had opened in Mortdale. It was a huge milestone in the club's history and I had been called in to help with the licensing application because it was considered so important to the future of the club. When we were awarded the licence it was like winning the lottery. For our St George social club to have its own licensed premises meant the financial future of the club was assured. It was a momentous occasion because it meant the club was now firmly established in the community and could promote soccer more effectively to the general public.

St George had never been flush with money but the club always prided itself on paying the players their due. In fact, St George never missed one week of paying the players in the entire time I was there, even though it was a constant struggle for them to do so. If the club didn't have enough money to pay the players on any given week then a hat would be passed around the supporters. If there still wasn't enough money when the hat was returned, it would be passed around the crowd again. Having a social club meant the financial strain was taken off the soccer club and it no longer had to figuratively beg, borrow and steal just to survive.

On a personal level, winning the McDowells Sports Star of the Year Award in 1967 topped off my year. The award was presented to the top sportsperson in the St George district, selected from athletes of all sports. Winning was not only an honour for me but it was also recognition of soccer's improving stature in Australia, especially considering the rich pedigree in the St George area of more mainstream sports such as rugby league and cricket.

I could not have been happier with how 1967 turned out in terms of my football. The ASF had decided to activate the national team again, following the disaster of trying to qualify for the 1966 World Cup and had also arranged for Manchester United and Scotland to tour Australia. I had settled in at St George, been involved in establishing the social club, won the grand final and had won a prestigious sports award.

1967 was also the year when the Australian team was transformed into a team of young, talented Aussie kids; players who had grown up in Australia, whether they were Anglo–Australians or migrants, and who had learned their football here rather than overseas. The lead-up to this point was that the failed attempt to make the 1966 World Cup had starkly illustrated the importance of being able to play against international opposition as often as possible. Those in charge realised we obviously needed more experience playing against top-class international opposition if we wanted to make the next World Cup. So, in 1967, it was arranged that the Scottish national team would tour Australia and play three international fixtures. I was again selected to play, this time under new coach Dr Joe Venglos.

Venglos was only a young coach in his early thirties when he arrived in Australia from Czechoslovakia. But he was a former international who had played club football with the Czech first division side Slovan Bratislava so he was not inexperienced in a playing sense. He had also completed a doctorate of physical education and several coaching courses after leaving the playing arena so, in terms of Australian football, he was exceedingly qualified. In Czechoslovakia, players didn't proceed from playing to coaching in the space of a week like they did in Australia. Former players were expected to study and complete several coaching courses before they were given coaching positions and even then they were usually sent to another country for three years to give them plenty of time to practise their methods before they were 'let loose' on Czech teams.

It just so happened that Joe came to Australia to coach Prague in the New South Wales competition to hone his coaching skills. He was almost immediately a revelation to Australian soccer because of his knowledge and appreciation of the game. While he wasn't actually much older than most of the players he always held everyone's total respect and admiration. The sad thing was that all of Joe's educational and football qualifications from Czechoslovakia were never recognised in Australia and he couldn't even get a job as a sports teacher at a high school in his early days here. At one stage he was working as a factory hand. It's quite amazing to think, although it never really surprised me, that he went on to an illustrious coaching career in Europe, including coaching the Czech national team to victory in the European championships in 1980 and taking them to the World Cup in the United States in 1994. He now holds the prestigious position of head of the Union of European Football Association's technical committee. To think he was working as a factory hand in Australia and not properly recognised for his expertise makes my mind boggle.

I became very close with Joe during his time with the Australian team and he still remains a dear friend. We had a fair bit in common and both considered ourselves students of the game. I even campaigned hard for him to be made the Australian coach following the departure of Frank Arok in 1985. In fact, I still believe he's the man to be the technical director of Australian football. I can't think of many better people to oversee the future of the game in Australia.

Our first international match against Scotland was played on 28 May 1967 in front of thirty-five thousand people at the Sydney Showground. Although we lost 1–0, that particular match is probably more memorable than the others in the series because the winning goal was scored by current Manchester United coach Sir Alec Ferguson. It wasn't a spectacular goal but I'm sure Sir Alec remembers it well.

The rest of the series was similarly close but we ended up losing 2–1 in Adelaide and 2–0 in Melbourne. The Adelaide match marked the arrival of Ray Baartz and Atti Abonyi on the international scene. Ray scored on debut and went on to become one of Australia's best players, while Atti also played well, demonstrating why he went on to be one of the country's best strikers and a member of the 1974 World Cup team. Ray was an incredible two-footed striker who could play in the midfield if need be, while Atti was more the skilful, penalty box expert who always kept a cool head in front of goal. It was only recently that Damian Mori eclipsed Atti's record as Australia's leading international goal scorer. I rate both players so highly that I'm sure if they had come up through today's system they would have ended up playing at the very highest level.

After the Scotland series I was lucky enough to captain the New South Wales side against the wonderful Manchester United team of the late 1960s. Their team included the likes of George Best, Bobby Charlton, Alec Stepney, Dennis Law, Brian Kidd, John Aston, Shay Brennan, Nobby Stiles, Billy Foulkes and Paddy Crerand. This was the core of the side that would later beat Portuguese giants Benfica 4–1 in extra time at Wembley in 1968 to win the European Champions Cup for the first time. They were quite obviously a spectacular side and it was an honour to play them.

We lost the first match 3–1 and the second match 3–0. In relative terms these were two very good results because our guys were still very much part-time players and were only able to train after their normal day jobs each week. It was always going to be a case of doing the best we could and making sure we were happy with our own performance. As United had some of the world's best players and were all top professionals winning the match was something we never really considered. What's more, while some big teams have been accused of treating their tours to Australia as holidays, the United players certainly treated the tour very seriously. The speed of their play was impressive but it was their teamwork, skill and professionalism that set them apart from us. In many ways, we were just like guinea pigs that were told to run around with them while everyone else made a lot of money out of their visit.

United obviously had a great following all around the world then as they do now and there were always big crowds turning out to see them on that tour. Unfortunately, there were no functions arranged for the two teams so we didn't get the chance to mix with them. However I developed a great respect for the manager, Sir Matt Busby. Just as in the case of Manchester United's tour to Australia in 1999, where young defender Simon Colosimo was seriously injured in a horrible tackle by United striker Andy Cole, there was an unsavoury incident in one of the matches in 1967. The famous Scottish international Dennis Law actually headbutted and broke the jaw of our midfielder Ronny Giles. Ronny spent many months recuperating from the injury. But I believe Busby, unlike the people leading the last United tour to Australia, handled the situation beautifully. He was not only one of the great managers of world football but he was also a fine ambassador and diplomat. He arranged for some of the United players to visit Ronny in hospital and made sure the United team had a whip-a-round to provide Ronny with some money. They probably ended up giving him the equivalent of three months worth of wages and it was a memorable gesture of goodwill. It was a far cry from the Manchester United response when

Simon Colosimo was injured. The response of the 1967 team ensured that relations didn't become strained. It was that sort of diplomatic approach that set the Manchester United team of that time apart.

It was not only playing the great Manchester United and my boyhood hero, Bobby Charlton, that defined this period of my life. It was a time when both on and off the field everything seemed to come together to allow me to immerse myself in pursuing a life in football. 1967 marked my coming of age.

6

The Birth of the Socceroos: The Vietnam War

⚽ WHEN DR VENGLOS decided to return home to Czechoslovakia, I was pleased to see Joe Vlasits, or 'Uncle' Joe as he was affectionately known, appointed as his replacement. Uncle Joe had a history of winning the most titles in the New South Wales championship and had experienced great success with Prague and my old club Canterbury, in particular. However, he had also performed well with teams like Budapest and Pan Hellenic and was perhaps even more importantly well known for giving Australian youth a chance at senior level. I knew this better than anyone as he had been one of the people responsible for giving me a start in the Canterbury team when I was only a teenager and he had been club coach, something for which I am eternally grateful.

Uncle Joe was undoubtedly one of the greatest coaches in Australian soccer because he was pivotal in developing the game in Australia by instilling the importance of and the need for specialised coaches in the minds of soccer administrators, clubs and players. Along with his good friend Denes Adrigan and former star player Bill Vrolyks he worked tirelessly to establish the Australian Coaching Federation. All three men recognised that Australia had to produce its own knowledgeable and properly trained players and coaches if we wanted to improve our standard of play. In my time in soccer I have always wholeheartedly supported young coaches for this very reason. It is why I was supportive of the appointment of Frank Farina to the national team in 1999.

When it was announced that Australia would take part in an international tournament in Vietnam, Uncle Joe stuck to his youth policy and immediately changed the composition of the Australian team. While there had been three or four young Aussies involved in the 1965 team, the rest of the boys had mainly been British ex-pats. They had been selected because they were among the best players playing in Australia at the time, but they, in a sense, had a very limited future in the national team because of their age. Now, Uncle Joe brought in a lot of young Australian boys to replace the more seasoned British ex-pats. In fact, it is worthwhile looking at a list of Uncle Joe's team just to demonstrate how young the guys were. There were goalkeepers Ron Corry (26) and Roger Romanowicz (20); defenders Stan Ackerley (24), George Keith (23), Gary Wilkins (22), John Watkiss (26), Dick van Alphen (30) and Manfred Schaefer (24); midfielders Ray Lloyd (24), Frank Micic (26), Alan Westwater (21), Ray Richards (23) and myself (24); and forwards Atti Abonyi (21), Ray Baartz (20), Ted De Lyster (20), Tom McColl (22), Nick Pantelis (22) and Billy Vojtek (23). In this sense, Uncle Joe was already looking forward towards the 1970 World Cup. It was an important decision for Australian football because another coach might well have simply picked the best eleven, even if it meant picking players that were thirty years old, in order to get the best results and save his job. But Uncle Joe consciously decided to pick young, untested Australian players in a bid to ensure the future of the game in Australia.

Unfortunately, Nick Pantelis, whose son Luke now plays for Adelaide City and recently played for the Young Socceroos, was ruled out of the tour at the last moment because he had not been in Australia long enough after arriving from Greece to be naturalised. But, of the squad, there were eight players who made a significant contribution to getting Australia to the World Cup in 1974. In this sense alone, Australian soccer owes Uncle Joe a huge debt of gratitude.

Australia's invitation to the tournament in Vietnam came in 1967, while the Vietnam War was still raging. It came via the Australian government and was essentially part of a public relations exercise to help win over the Vietnamese people to the cause of the United States-led forces. The South Vietnamese government of the time was very much a puppet regime of the United States and they were happy to stage a soccer tournament to showcase the support they enjoyed from the various nations in the region. These included New Zealand, Singapore, South Korea, Malaysia, Thailand and Hong Kong and all these nations' participation resulted in the tournament being called the Friendly Nations' Cup, or the Friendship Tournament.

Soccer was considered the perfect public relations vehicle because it was the most popular sport in Vietnam, adored by the public. There was certainly never any suggestion of staging a rugby or cricket tournament that may have better suited Australia's sporting tastes because those sports were simply unheard of in the Asian region.

Before the team left for Vietnam we enjoyed a brief training camp at the Swedish Seaman's Union in North Ryde, Sydney. The sauna baths there were fantastic and we were looked after so well that it would become the team headquarters for many years to come. But even after a week in camp it felt strange flying out of Australia to the tournament. The team was so young that most of us had little idea about the war or the situation into which we were flying. We knew that some of our mates were actually over there fighting but we had no idea what was actually going on there. If the team had been unprepared going into Cambodia in 1965 we weren't in any way prepared for what awaited us outside the football field in Vietnam in 1967.

At the time though, the trip seemed to be an adventure. Travelling far away from home seemed exciting and exotic. We were essentially a new squad that had been earmarked as the squad to prepare for the 1970 World Cup and we were all looking forward to proving ourselves. The behind-the-scenes politics of the trip were never really contemplated by our young and rather naive minds because we were all completely focused on the football. It wasn't until years later that I realised how the team had been blindly steered into helping the war effort.

The French were the colonial rulers of Vietnam up until the Second World War. During the war the Japanese invaded but Vietnamese leader Ho Chi Minh declared the country to be independent at the end of the war. Vietnamese communist insurgents famously defeated the French army, who had been fighting to resume their colonisation of Vietnam for ten years, at the battle of Dien Bien Phu in 1954. The victory resulted in an internationally sanctioned agreement to separate the country into two distinct nations—the communist North Vietnam and the democratic South Vietnam.

It was later during the Cold War that Vietnam became the setting for the ideological battle being waged between communism and the West. The United States took a particular interest in Vietnam because it was genuinely fearful that the communist north would simply take control of their southern neighbours as part of a relentless march south. Because of its geographical position, South Vietnam was very much seen as a crucial link in the popular 'domino theory' of the time—the premise being that the fall of one country to communism would lead to the domino-style fall of more countries further down towards Australia. It was an effective and fear-provoking analogy to promote among the nations of the West because it suggested that once one country fell to communism it would become increasingly difficult to stop others from following. Communism was already dominant in Russia, China and North Korea and there had been sympathetic uprisings in Malaysia, so the fear that the 'red wave' was simply washing down through the whole of southeast Asia towards Australia was quite real. South Vietnam became the crucial link in the chain.

The liberation army of the north, the Viet Cong, was already infiltrating the south and engaging in a civil war of sorts in the 1960s. The Americans responded to what they perceived as an increasing menace by sending advisers to Vietnam in 1961. The United States officially first entered Vietnam in an advisory role but the South Vietnam government was essentially set up as a puppet regime used to try and block the communist advance. By 1964 there were two hundred thousand American troops in Vietnam and by 1965 this number had grown to four hundred thousand. Not long after, both sides were engaging in full-scale war.

The United States and its allies literally bombed Vietnam to pieces. In fact, there were more bombs dropped on the country during the Vietnam War than were dropped during the entire period of the Second World War. The American forces used napalm to clear the dense forests, chemical weapons such as Agent Orange, and anything else they could think of to try and combat the guerilla tactics of the Viet Cong. But they were fighting a battle on enemy turf and they were losing.

One of the means of attempting to block the communist insurgence used by the United States and its allies was to try and win over the minds of the people of South Vietnam to the ideologies of democracy and capitalism. Staging a major sports event was a way of simultaneously signalling the strength of the allied forces and demonstrating the advantages of Western rule. As a firm ally of the United States, the Australian government was only too willing to lend their support to this cause. Suddenly, the Australian soccer team, usually of little consequence to the national interest, became a necessary part of the war effort.

I was particularly interested in what was happening in Vietnam and other foreign places to which we travelled with the national team in those days because I was studying economics at university and was fascinated by the politics behind the war. But, while I was conscious of asking questions to try and ascertain exactly what was happening, soccer generally put such considerations, at best, on the backburner. It was difficult to get involved in the politics behind our war effort when I knew I was there to play soccer. I had been appointed captain and by this stage I really considered the team as my boys. So my first responsibility had to be to the team.

The team managers for our trip were John Barclay and Jim Connell. John, in fact, remained team manager right up to and including the World Cup finals in West Germany. The team doctor was Brian Corrigan and Lou Lazzari stayed on as our masseur. We also had senior *Daily Mirror* journalist Terry Smith, who has only recently retired from News Limited, and ABC radio broadcaster Martin Royal accompany the team. Martin was the golden voice of Australian radio at that time and an avid soccer follower. He created an enormous amout of goodwill for the game with his highly regarded national coverage. They were all great soccer fans and completely devoted to the game so we were glad to have them with us. We were also happy to have Qantas sales representative Tom Patrick travelling with us because he proved to be an integral and invaluable part of the squad. The ASF also decided to take referee Tony Boskovic to help officiate the tournament so we were quite a large contingent by the time we flew out of Australia.

The trip to Vietnam was an experience I will never forget, simultaneously frightening and exhilarating. Our hotel, the

Golden Building, was absolutely terrible. I can't imagine a more inappropriate name. I remember one of the boys turning on a light switch when we first arrived and literally being thrown across the room by a mini-explosion. It was only some bad wiring but it's not the sort of incident that helps the nerves in a war-torn country. The place was also filthy. There were gecko lizards everywhere and we were immediately banned from eating any food prepared there or consuming any local drinks.

Dr Brian Corrigan, was at pains to make sure that none of us fell ill by drinking the water in Vietnam so encouraged us to drink beer (but not too much) rather than the local water. Brian was a pioneer of sports medicine in Australia so it was reassuring to have him with us in a foreign situation. He had been the Australian Olympic team doctor for many years and has been immortalised in our Olympic history by a famous photo of him helping legendary Australian distance runner Ron Clarke at the 1968 Mexico City Olympics. Clarke had collapsed and the photographer captured Brian providing him with oxygen. For us, Brian was not just an invaluable member of the squad because of his medical expertise but also a friend and a terrific tourist. Brian was a walking chemist shop with a large suitcase full of stomach tablets, vitamins, glucose and salt tablets, anti-malaria tablets and all manner of other pills, potions and bandages. With him in attendance, there wasn't any repeat of the sickness that had disrupted our preparation in Cambodia.

After we arrived in Saigon we immediately began mixing with the troops in the Australian army headquarters, called 'The Canberra'. I took every opportunity to talk with the troops and observe their routines so I could understand their experience in a war zone. We ended up eating with them most days because of the rule that the team was not allowed to touch the food at the Golden Building, so we eventually got to know some of the troops quite well. While they went off to fight, we went out to play football. It was a surreal experience.

There were guards stationed outside the mess hall and it was their job to protect the area in front of the hall by keeping it clear. Anyone who stopped outside the mess hall was considered a danger because they could easily leave a parcel or drop their bike with a bomb attached. So the guards would carefully scrutinise everyone who moved along the walkway. If anyone stopped they would blow a whistle. If the person didn't move on, they would shoot over their heads. If the person still didn't move, the guards were supposed to shoot them. I can remember some of us playing billiards in the mess hall one night when we suddenly heard the machine guns firing. The guards had started shooting over someone's head. All the players were under the table in the blink of an eye.

As no one wanted to get sick from the local food Tom Patrick decided to take action and rang Warrant Officer Bruce Glossop, a guy he had met in Singapore in the 1960s, to see if he could help us out. Bruce was more than happy to assist as he was involved with looking after the movements of any Australians, mainly troops of course, through Vietnam. He did a wonderful job in ensuring our safe passage everywhere. (Bruce now lives in Canberra and was president of the Ainslie football club there for many years.) He introduced the team to Australian Captain Tommy Moyes who was granted approval from the United States forces to allow us to eat at the American Officers' mess, called 'The Five Oceans' on many occasions. The mess had great dining facilities and was the other place, outside of 'The Canberra', where we regularly ate during our stay.

Two other Australian Army Officers, Warrant Officer Bill Smith and Lieutenant/Warrant Officer Warren Campbell, also became involved with the team and made sure our needs were met as much as possible. We considered them part of the team by the end of the tour because they took care of our security, attended our matches and made every effort to ensure that we were all right.

Our team trained at a small field that was really just the local park. At our first training session, while some of the team were involved in shooting practice (which is obviously a strange term to use when you are in a war zone) a ball disappeared into the field behind the goals. As one of the players headed off to jump the fence to retrieve it people came running from everywhere to stop him. The field was full of land-mines. It was one of the best incentives I have ever encountered to keep shots at goal down during training.

Some of these incidents, in retrospect, are quite funny but I am still amazed that the Australian national soccer team was placed in that dangerous situation at all when you consider that nowadays the Australian cricket team refused to play their group matches in Sri Lanka during the 1996 World Cup because of a terrorist bomb that had gone off in Colombo and that the Australian international rugby league team, the Kangaroos, were reluctant to play in Europe, after the events of September 11, 2001. Vietnam, and Saigon in particular, resembled something out of a Hollywood war movie. The Robin Williams movie *Good Morning Vietnam*, in particular, reminds me of the scenes that we were thrown into. There were military people everywhere—including American soldiers, South Korean troops, South Vietnamese forces (or the ARVN as they were known) and our own Australian soldiers. There were always military vehicles all around and, of course, mixed into this crowded landscape was the Viet Cong. We simply didn't know which people in the street belonged to the Viet Cong but we were warned about them and we knew they were always around. The person serving breakfast could well be working for the Viet Cong at night. It was impossible to know.

Our team manager, John Barclay, later revealed that several Viet Cong operatives had been caught during our stay only half a block from our hotel. They had been carrying explosives and later confessed that they were planning to blow up the floor of the hotel on which the Korean team was staying. The Koreans happened to be on the floor below us so I don't even like to contemplate what could have happened had those people not been apprehended.

Strangely though, the rest of the players and I were never really fearful for our lives during the tour. Because our whole trip was very basic we remained focused on soccer the entire time. There was nothing else. The team had occasional embassy functions, but mostly we trained, including regular gymnastics sessions on the roof of our shoddy hotel before breakfast. We were being paid the princely sum of fifty dollars a week while on tour, with an allowance of ten dollars a week, but there really wasn't much opportunity to spend it.

All the matches during the Friendly Nations' Cup were played at the Cong Hoa Stadium in Saigon. Needless to say, playing soccer with a war raging around us was a strange and unforgettable experience. The surrounding skyline was constantly illuminated by flares that the United States military used to help their bombers and there was a constant buzz of helicopters hovering over us. The sound of gunfire in the distance could be regularly heard and there were armed guards everywhere. Adding to our astonishment was the packed stadium; an unfamiliar sight to us back home. We were always happy to see a small group of Aussie troops in the crowd yelling their support and reminding us of Australia.

For the first match against New Zealand the field was particularly muddy and heavy. I remember the conditions because they proved to have a marked impact on the career of our centre back Frank Micic. He was a very skilful player, similar in some ways to today's Ned Zelic, but he struggled in the first half because the conditions were so poor. The heavy ground simply didn't suit his game and Uncle Joe decided to bring on Manfred Schaefer for his first international. Manfred ended up playing so well that he not only kept his position for the next match, but would hold on to it for the next eight years. Frank, however, would only play for Australia three times after that match. We won the match 5–3 and it still amazes me how such events of a single game can change a football career. Who knows how many times Frank would have subsequently played for Australia if the conditions that day had been dry and he hadn't been replaced?

Our match against South Vietnam was one of the most memorable of the tournament, not so much for the winning goal that I scored in the 1–0 victory, but because the team found out later that the country's Vice President Nguyen Cao Ky had gone into the dressing room at half-time and offered the Vietnamese team six months' salary to beat us. Their players were all army guys so I'm sure the money would have meant a great deal to them. It also shows how much was at stake for a symbolic win in the tournament. But we were playing pretty well by this stage and managed to deny South Vietnam their bonus. They must have been bitterly disappointed and the home crowd obviously felt the same way.

That game was one of those matches that just clicked for me. When you play in the midfield, some days everything just happens for you, and that was one of those games for me. I don't vividly recollect scoring the winning goal but I remember the dead silence that greeted my goal. There was a full stadium but no noise! I had to look to the referee just to check that my goal hadn't been disallowed.

After the match, we were advised to wait in the dressing rooms until the crowds, who were obviously disappointed, had dispersed. When we were finally allowed to board the team bus, an Australian soldier climbed aboard and calmly told us that while there was no need for alarm, could we all please lie on the floor of the bus with our bags over our heads! Even after a personally satisfying game like that against South

Vietnam, we always had to remain aware that the team was in a war zone.

If I was asked to write a list of the best games Australia has ever played then the final of the tournament against South Korea would be one of them. It was a truly spectacular, incident-packed football match, played amidst an unbelievable atmosphere in front of a full stadium, with President Thieu, Vice President Ky and Prime Minister Loc all in attendance.

There was drama even before the match started because we found out that the Australian troops who had been cheering us on throughout the tournament weren't being allowed entry into the stadium. We were told that the stadium was completely full and there simply weren't seats available to accommodate the Aussie troops. We were so incensed that our officials informed the organisers that if the troops weren't allowed in then there wasn't going to be a match. I think the organisers must have realised we were serious because seats right next to the sideline became available very quickly after our ultimatum. After the support the troops had given us, playing without their attendance would have been unthinkable for us.

The Cong Hoa Stadium had a huge tunnel running out from the dressing sheds onto the ground. I still remember the sensation of the hairs standing up on the back of my neck as I stood in the tunnel with the boys waiting to go out on the field. Even now, every Christmas I receive a card from my old friend Atti Abonyi with the words, 'Remember the tunnel in Vietnam 23.10.67'. When we emerged from the tunnel we were shocked because the crowd was cheering for us. The South Vietnamese disliked the Koreans and had obviously decided to put all their energy into supporting us. Needless to say, we were not used to full stadiums actually cheering for us given the relatively lacklustre support for soccer from mainstream Australia back home. It was one of those moments that I knew I was going to remember for the rest of my life.

The match itself was a thriller. We went behind 0–1 in the

first thirty seconds but came back to lead 2–1 with goals from Ray Baartz and myself. The Koreans levelled it at 2–2 before Atti Abonyi found the net to snatch the game 3–2. It was a great contest between two well-matched teams and the game was never in the bag until the final whistle. It was a fitting way for us to win Australia's first international trophy. The team had beaten New Zealand, South Vietnam, Singapore, Malaysia and South Korea on the trot and really deserved to be rewarded. I proudly stepped up to receive the trophy from President Thieu and it now has pride of place in my living room as a constant reminder of a significant milestone for both Australian soccer and for me personally.

The trophy was not actually all that was at stake that night. Before the match, team manager John Barclay announced a 'special reward' for defeating South Korea. We were told that each player would be allowed to keep his tracksuit if we won! You can imagine Frank Farina offering today's Australian team that sort of incentive before a big World Cup qualifier—he would be laughed at. Back then it was an incredible bonus.

The day after our victory the team was flown by Caribou aircraft, usually used to transport troops, one hundred and twenty-five kilometres south of Saigon to visit the troops in Vung Tau and we ended up playing a match against them. The aircraft was open at the back and we sat along the sides with a bird's-eye view of the ground thousands of metres below. Unfortunately, the team had thrown a bit of party in the hotel the night before to celebrate our victory so most of the boys were feeling a bit sore and sorry and weren't in a condition to appreciate the view properly. I can still remember the two pilots, who were both younger than me, deciding to buzz some of the troops who were out swimming at the beach before we landed in Vung Tau. They took the plane right down over the water and we could clearly, and perhaps too closely, see the looks of surprise on the faces of the troops as we passed so close overhead. Everyone aboard the plane was laughing and carrying on so it really didn't feel like we were in the middle of a war zone.

The troops at Vung Tau really seemed to enjoy our visit and our game of soccer with them. We had been in Vietnam for nearly three weeks and had come to know some of the troops quite well so it was with mixed feelings that we eventually left. We knew they didn't have the luxury of going home.

The team didn't head straight home after Vietnam. We stopped over in Malaysia and Indonesia, where we played the Indonesian national team and the touring New Zealand national team. Overall, we played ten games on that tour and won all of them. It was an amazing performance which was even noticed back in Australia. The team received an unusually warm reception from the public when we returned to Australia, particularly from our club fans who turned out in force to greet us at the airport. Suddenly, players in the team were attracting publicity in the commercial media and forging a name for themselves. Uncle Joe's gamble on young Australian players had paid off.

Beyond the impressive results of the tournament in Vietnam, I felt it was a valuable experience to travel to Vietnam during the war because it forged a resilient bond between the players and built a strong team spirit. That's why I always say that the first real Australian team was born out of the Vietnam War. A new coach, a new team and a new philosophy had all been tried and proven in the most severe environment imaginable. Promoting young Australian talent and giving players a chance had been a successful enterprise and the team was strengthened as a result. From that moment onwards, the team spirit that had developed during that tournament was always one of our strengths and Uncle Joe deserves the major credit for it. Terry Smith's words in the *Australian* after the tournament in Vietnam really prove my point:

> The Australian team's triumph is inseparable from that of the coach 'Uncle' Joe Vlasits, who so skilfully used the Spartan conditions under which the touring party existed in Saigon to develop a team spirit which brought success. This was sport on the verge of a war, gun-toting military police and soldiers ringing the stadium, bursts of mortar shells in the background. Australia's feat in completing the tour unbeaten was a classical team effort.

While there were plenty of different personalities in the team, the overall chemistry was right. I even picked up my nickname 'Skippy' on this tour (Skipper was shortened to Skippy) and it's a name reserved for the use of players of that era. The conditions of the tour had the effect of pushing us all together because no one was ever out sightseeing, shopping or on the town by themselves. We did everything together and it was never claustrophobic; there were no tensions. It probably helped that most of us were from similar working-class backgrounds and had the same passion for the game.

Most of the guys were first-generation migrants. They had come to Australia as kids with their parents and playing for Australia was a big thing for them. I believe this was a completely different attitude to the one that had existed in the 1965 team. This wasn't the fault of the players in the 1965 side because they were playing professionally in Australia and were selected because they were among the best players in the country. The new team simply had more of a connection to the nation because they had learnt their football in Australia. They were representative of an increasingly multicultural population. In this sense, the 1967 team represented a sea change for a nation which had previously imported footballers and was now just starting to establish its own line of home-grown players.

My own role was also different in 1967. I went from being a vice-captain in training in a team full of older players to being appointed captain of a young, relatively inexperienced team. I had seen what had happened in Cambodia when we had gone in blind and I wanted to ensure it didn't happen again. I tried my best to make sure things were improved both on and off the field. The players were properly educated about the risks of travelling and we ensured that everyone was match fit. We learned from the mistakes of the past.

Ironically, if it hadn't been for the Australian government wanting to use soccer as a diplomatic exercise during the Vietnam War our particular team probably would never have got together. It was only the need to compete in the Friendly Nations' tournament that called for an Australian team to be selected at that time. If the tournament hadn't been held, the next Australian team would have been chosen more than a year later and it would most likely have been made up of completely different players from those that travelled to Vietnam. I guess that's why the tournament in Vietnam is so special to the guys involved and is permanently connected with the birth of the team that later became known as the Socceroos.

I often say that the team should march in the Anzac Day parade because of the role we played in the war. Even the entertainers that toured Vietnam were in a controlled situation at the Australian bases, while we were right in the middle of the action. Here we were, a bunch of young kids, who were expected to play soccer while a major war raged around us. I don't think the team has ever received the recognition it deserved for its war efforts. Having said that, I wouldn't hesitate to do it all over again.

7

The Mighty Saints

⚽ WHEN I RETURNED to club football from the Vietnam tour with the national team it was to a St George team that was going through a golden period. Some people even say that the 1967 team was the best team St George has ever had. That's what makes it so hard to fathom what happened during the next season. How did such a brilliant team go from such dizzying heights to such dreadful lows in the space of one season?

It's all the harder to believe because we started well enough. We lost a tight Ampol Cup final to Hakoah 1–0 but our state of play still appeared to be quite healthy. But from there our form in the league deteriorated. In the end, we limped home in second-last position and it was only Manly that saved us from being relegated to the second division. While it's not too strange for a team to experience a downfall after a great year, this was something more. We had literally gone from the penthouse to the cellar. There is a delicate balance in a successful team's chemistry and, for some reason, that chemistry had been affected. In more recent times, the 2001 grand finalists Wollongong Wolves and South Melbourne, who had been the top teams for several years in Australia came undone in the following season and at the halfway mark of the championship were holding up the bottom of the table.

The first victim of our poor form, as is usually the case, was our coach Laurie Hegyes, who left mid-way through the season. It was terribly sad to see Laurie go because he was the heart and soul of the club and he had always been the man the club automatically turned to for advice when things went wrong. But this time, sadly, he was made the scapegoat of our poor performance.

I remember the supporters and officials of the club were furious about our performance in 1968. Even worse than this, they felt humiliated. The team's performance on the field was seen as a reflection of the entire club and coming second-last was simply not acceptable. Immediate action was demanded and so former Hungarian international Gyula Polgar was brought in to replace Laurie. Polgar had played in the 1938 World Cup final for Hungary and was a big name in the Hungarian community. As a result, his appointment was enough to fill the club with hope again even though the 1968 season was effectively over. In reality though there was little he could do in such a short time to redeem our reputation.

During our disappointing season at St George, I played for the national team against Japan in a series involving three matches in Sydney, Melbourne and Adelaide. Although an ankle injury I sustained in the first drawn match in Sydney ruled me out of the final two matches, the series is still particularly, and bitterly, memorable because of the behaviour of our home support. For some reason the crowd was so pro-Japan during that series that it felt like we were playing away matches. The one image that still sticks in my mind is the Japanese captain Kamamoto triumphantly being carried off the field by the Australian crowd in Adelaide after we had been beaten 3–1. I quite simply couldn't believe it. Here was the opposition captain being carried off the field by our own crowd who should have been supporting us. Unfortunately, that sort of confusing display was not a rarity. Vigorous cheering for our opponents was par for the course. It was one of the most disappointing aspects of suiting up for the national team at home. Everyone in the team was out there doing his absolute best and we hoped the entire nation would get behind us. I guess the situation was partly a by-product of Australia's ethnically diverse population where supporters would often barrack for their country of origin. Also, the Australian public's response to our national team was still very parochial at a state level. If we played in Adelaide and there were no players from South Australia in the team, the crowd would most likely support the visiting team. If there were no players from Victoria and the match was played in Melbourne, a similar situation would arise. It was always disconcerting for the boys who understandably thought they would have the entire crowd behind them. However, Sydney was the one place where the team was usually guaranteed strong home support, primarily because most of the players in the team at that time either came from New South Wales or were currently playing in the New South Wales competition. Nevertheless, times when the crowd started barracking for our opponents really hurt everyone involved with the team.

The three-game series against the Japanese was very competitive because they were a particularly strong side at that time. They had come to Australia as part of their preparation for the Mexico City Olympic Games tournament, where they would eventually win the bronze medal, and they were probably the best side Japan has ever produced. The series was ultimately tied at one victory apiece with one draw which, although slightly disappointing, was not a disastrous result for us. Our victory in Vietnam had left the team with high expectations though and I think we had all wanted to do better.

Back on the local scene, one positive to be taken from the disastrous 1968 season was that it led to the arrival of Frank Arok at St George for the 1969 season. Frank had been working as a journalist at the 1966 World Cup in England when he had a chance meeting with Australian soccer writer Andrew Dettre. Frank expressed an interest in Australian soccer and the possibility of coaching out here so when Andrew returned to Australia he mentioned Frank to president of St George, Les Bordacs. Negotiations continued over the next two years until Andrew's then colleague at *Soccer World* Lou Gautier travelled to the 1968 Olympics in Mexico where Frank was working at the Games and passed on the St George contract. The next thing the players knew, we had a new foreign coach, of whom we knew nothing, arriving to take charge of us.

The historical importance of Frank's arrival at St George was that he became the first real manager in Australian club history. He represented the first step in developing a professional Australian club competition and he also represented the first step in Alex Pongrass's dream to have St George operating under one figurehead. Alex wanted someone to run the whole show at St George. I was still playing and was too young to take on such a responsibility. The calamitous season of 1968 forced Alex's hand somewhat and he decided to take a bit of a gamble on Frank by appointing him full time and giving him complete control of the management and administration of the team. It was an unprecedented step in Australian soccer.

I can still remember driving to Frank's house to pick him up for the first day of training. I had never met him and was naturally curious as to what he would be like, having heard several stories and rumours. On that particular day I had already been to work and university, so I turned up at his house ten minutes late. Frank's first acerbic words to me were, 'You're not very punctual are you?' I immediately realised that our relationship was going to be an interesting one.

Frank's arrival at St George heralded a revolution at the club, a revolution that continued throughout the entire Australian soccer establishment for years to come. From the first day he walked in, Frank took control. Although he was only in his mid-thirties, he had a real intensity about him that made people sit up and take notice. Frank took his role as a professional coach extremely seriously and immediately made it clear to the team that maintaining discipline was paramount to success. The players were informed that training would be increased to four nights a week and lateness would not be tolerated. In fact, Frank began fining people for being late, something unheard of in those days. He even banned us from going to the club at any time other than official social functions. It was a new regime and was a complete culture shock for me and the entire team. Frank's rationale was that players should develop good habits from the game. It worked because even today I am very punctual.

Frank was a visionary in terms of Australian soccer. He introduced new and innovative training sessions, which simultaneously challenged and improved us. For the first time in my soccer experience there was a ball for everyone at training. It was a simple improvement but it made an amazing difference. Where in the past we would endure the hard slog of ten-kilometre road runs to increase our fitness, Frank concentrated on interval training to build up our endurance. It was much easier on the body and was much more effective in terms of match fitness. Even the system we played was changed when Frank introduced a sweeper, or libero, system. This system freed one of our defenders from any man-marking duties and placed him behind the main defensive line. He was an insurance policy, if you like, effectively protecting the goals by 'sweeping' up any ball or player that got through the defence. However, the system also allowed the sweeper to push forward into the midfield and beyond to create an extra man in attack, much in the way the legendary Franz Beckenbauer made famous. Quite amazingly, no team in Australia had ever played with a sweeper up until then.

Even the team talks given by Frank were a revelation to us all. He would put down his watch and say, 'I will talk for five minutes,' and off he would go. He would simply tell the players directly what he thought of them and what he expected: bang, bang, bang, out it all came. It was a shock at first but it was certainly effective. After five minutes to the very second Frank would stop. It was such an amazing style of delivery.

Frank literally cleaned the club out from the start of the 1969 season. As soon as he arrived he began rewriting player contracts because he believed the existing system was bad for the club in that the players were guaranteed money regardless of performance. So, whenever a player's contract came up for renewal, if Frank wanted to keep him, he would change the contract to an incentive system.

The new system changed our attitudes completely. We had to adopt a new professional approach to the game because if we wanted more money we had to perform. Before Arok's arrival, we had played to win but there wasn't a financial incentive involved in the result. We would be paid regardless. Now we were penalised for losing. It was a critical difference and an important transition to a more professional attitude.

Because I was working at the club I used to speak to Frank all the time about football. He turned out to be the most influential person, along with FIFA coach Dettmar Cramer on my football life. The professional way he approached the game really impressed me and showed me how dedicated you have to be to succeed. The disciplined way he motivated a team, organised training sessions and planned matches was all entirely new to me and I look at his arrival as a blessing, both for Australian soccer and for me. Even today, every time he opens his mouth I learn something.

All of Frank's methods produced immediate results. In his first year in charge we finished second in the premiership to South Coast by a solitary point. Finishing so close to first place was hard to take but we did make it through to the grand final against Apia and were desperately hoping for revenge. The game was played at the Sydney Sports Ground and ended in a 1–1 draw, meaning we would have to turn out for a replay. Unfortunately the national squad was flying out to Seoul in South Korea to start our World Cup campaign only two days after the replay was to be played and the ASF decided that any national squad member involved in the grand final couldn't play in case we were injured. This meant Manfred Schaefer, Atti Abonyi and I would miss out for St George, while Stan Ackerey, George Keith and Billy Rorke would miss out for Apia. It was disappointing for all of us but there was nothing we could do about it.

It's strange watching any match from the sidelines, let alone a grand final, when you know you're fit and could be playing, but I was quite content when the team was leading 2–0 with about ten minutes to go. That contentment turned to despair in a flash when Ernie Campbell, a future Socceroo himself, scored three goals to snatch the match for Apia. I could scarcely believe it and was devastated that I hadn't been out there trying to make a difference. Losing against Apia made the result even harder to swallow.

The 1969 season was also memorable because a player called Tommy Anderson joined the club; a former Scottish youth international who had gone on to play professionally with many British clubs before coming out to Australia. While he played with several other clubs in Australia he spent two seasons with St George while I was there. Tommy was in the twilight of his career when he came to St George but the way he always gave a hundred per cent on the field was an inspiration to me. He was a very hard-working, team-oriented player who was usually used to mark the opponent's key striker. It certainly wasn't the most glamorous role but a player needed to be mentally tough to do it successfully. He became a critical member of our St George line-up. After he finished playing, Tommy went on to become a soccer writer for the *Daily Mirror* in Sydney and did a lot of great promotional work for the Socceroos. Personally though, Tommy's toughness and determination were a great lesson to me of how important those qualities were if I wanted to go on playing football at a high level for any period of time.

In 1969 the national team played another friendly three-match home series, this time against Greece. I had well and truly recovered from my ankle injury by this time and took part in all three matches in Sydney, Brisbane and Melbourne. The matches were considered very important because they were viewed as the start of our preparation for the 1970 World Cup qualification series. Greek football had been steadily improving; their top club sides Olympiakos and Panathinaikos were doing very well in Europe, and everyone in Australia with a Greek background had been warning us how good the national team was. As a result we were prepared to be really tested.

It was a noteworthy series because it marked the international debut of Adrian 'Noddy' Alston—one of Australian soccer's greatest strikers. He came out from England as an eighteen year old to join Jim Kelly's South Coast United side and made an immediate impact. A very tall guy, he got his nickname 'Noddy' because he scored so many goals with his head, always nodding them in. Even when Adrian wasn't playing he was an invaluable part of the Australian team because he was always the life of the party, telling jokes and acting as a circuit breaker when the pressure was really on.

Noddy was also a terrific player. He was the national team's top scorer in the qualifiers for the 1974 World Cup and even after the World Cup in Germany, he was the only player to go on to play in Europe. Most of the rest of us were probably too old anyway but Noddy must have really impressed the talent scouts because he got an offer from German side Hertha Berlin and eventually ended up going to English first division side Luton Town. He later moved to Cardiff before heading over to the United States to play for many years in the North American Soccer League with the Tampa Bay Rowdies. I am still great friends with him and always recall that Greek series as the start of Noddy's long international career. (Noddy has coached Port Kembla for the last twelve seasons in the Illawarra league, winning the championship nearly every season. He is the classic example of Australian soccer not utilising past players who have something to contribute.)

The team for the first match of the series at the Sydney Cricket Ground was made up of Ron Corry in goal, Manfred Schaefer, John Watkiss, Alan Marnoch, Stan Ackerley in defence, Danny Walsh, myself and Ray Baartz in the midfield, and Billy Vojtek, Atti Abonyi and Adrian Alston up front. I remember the first game very fondly, mainly because it was the first time I had played at the SCG. It was a huge occasion for everyone because while most of us had played many matches at the Sydney Sports Ground and the Sydney Showground, none of us had played on the same turf on which the great cricketers and rugby league players had performed so heroically in the past.

The match was the day after Neil Armstrong walked on the moon and there was a palpable sense of excitement around the place because of the moon landing. A crowd of thirty-one thousand people turned up, and although half were probably supporting Greece, there was an electric atmosphere. The match was personally memorable for me because it was one of my better games for the green and gold. Andrew Dettre's match report from the game in *Soccer Weekly* reads in part:

> Warren was the best man on the field, a bundle of atomic energy, incredible determination, astonishing speed and polished skill. This indeed was his finest hour and a half... Warren took the

entire midfield in his two bare hands and began his most unforgettable 45 minutes of soccer. He seemed yards faster than any other player on the field, he covered some 90 yards in length on one run, only to be thwarted by the Greek goalkeeper. He covered the whole width of the field tackling, intercepting, prompting and occasionally letting fly with some piledrivers. A couple of times he burst through in the middle in the best Beckenbauer style—at least one of his sorties deserved a grand goal.

Everyone on the team played well that day. Our eventual 1–0 victory through a penalty from Atti Abonyi could have been, and should have been, greater. We had had chance after chance but just could not find the back of the net. Anyone who has played the game will know, however, that sometimes, no matter how many chances you have, the ball just doesn't want to go into the net.

I believe the team always played better when we were not expected to win. We always loved proving people wrong because no one in Australia ever expected us to win in those days. Unfortunately we didn't play as well in the next two matches and the Greeks, as expected, responded to their first match disaster and lifted their play. The second match in Brisbane ended in a 2–2 draw and we were beaten 2–0 in the third game in Melbourne. Overall it was an important series for us to play because the Greeks were strong opposition and they provided excellent preparation for the World Cup qualifiers that awaited us.

In Frank Arok's second year in charge at St George we again fell short of the championship by one point. Hakoah proved slightly too good for us in the league and our frustration grew, even though we remained confident of knocking them over in the finals. In 1970 the format of the finals had changed to a round robin series from which the two top teams would play off in the grand final. The last game of the round robin saw us drawn against Yugal. We had already managed to upset Hakoah but because of other results we knew that if we beat Yugal by more than four goals we would play Hakoah in the grand final. On the other hand, if we won by four goals or less, we would be facing Yugal again. Everyone was unanimous that we would rather face Yugal in the final than Hakoah.

After half-time we were leading Yugal 3–0, which led to the comical situation of our players running towards goal in the second half and having to turn back the other way so we wouldn't score more than four goals. In the end we just tried to keep the ball. Of course there were Hakoah fans at the match and they went berserk once they realised what was going on. We weren't concerned at the time though and when the match eventually finished 4–0, we had knocked Hakoah out.

The ironic thing about that whole incident was that after all the controversy we went on to lose to Yugal in the grand final. It had rained cats and dogs leading up to the game and the pitch was completely waterlogged. But for some reason, Tony Boskovic, Australia's first FIFA accredited referee, decided to play the match when we all thought there was simply no way it should have gone ahead. We were very much a passing team and knew we would suffer in the conditions because it was nearly impossible to knock even a five-metre pass. Even though Yugal had five or six players out suspended or injured they still walloped us 4–0. They were inspired by Joe Alagich, who I knew from my school days as a Combined High Schools soccer representative, and who became well known in Australian sporting circles because he was a very good rugby player who also represented New South Wales at soccer and even became beach sprint champion. Joe was a very fast, attacking forward who always caused defenders trouble because of his pace. In that final, he not only scored a hat-trick but he also set up the other goal with a great cross from out wide.

The game really was a bit of a farce though and was not only disappointing but also financially costly. Under Frank's performance-based incentive system each player would have been up for fifteen hundred dollars in bonuses if the team had beaten Yugal. That was a huge amount of money in those days and everyone probably mentally had the money spent before the match was even played. The upset meant that we all earned a lot less money that year under Frank's incentive scheme than we had the year before. That was the nature of the system though and it only strengthened our resolve for the forthcoming season.

It was during this period in my life with the mighty Saints that I decided to approach the *Sun* newspaper about writing a regular column on soccer. Englishman David Jack, the son of legendary Arsenal and England international David Jack—the player who scored the first goal at Wembley, was the main soccer writer for the *Sun* and it was through him that I got my foot in the door in 1969. I had been writing a column called 'Saintly Soccer' in the *St George Leader* newspaper for the past two years but I wanted to access the wider New South Wales community. There needed to be some avenue through which I could inform people about how marvellous the game was and how important it was for Australia to develop its playing ranks. I was actually angry at the way the game was being ignored by the mainstream media and when I went in to meet with the *Sun*'s sports editor Jack Tier, we ended up having a huge argument about soccer, because Jack almost immediately told me that no one in Australia was interested in the game. Those words were like a red rag to a bull and by the time we were finished arguing Jack said I could have my column. He seemed to like my passion for the game and even though he had a gruff exterior, he was a terrific person once I got to know him. He told me I would get paid fifty dollars a week for my column and I could write on just about anything to do with the game I loved. It was the start of my long involvement with the media in Australia.

Because the *Sun* was part of the Fairfax media empire, I was also offered a spot on the 'Today Show' that appeared on Channel Seven. It was a great coup for soccer because I ended up having a regular segment on Friday mornings where I would discuss the game with the hosts Bruce Webster and Patty Lovell. Sometimes I would demonstrate the skills of the game, other times I would promote upcoming international matches and we would always be running competitions for the kids to enter. I still have scrapbooks full of drawings that young children sent in to Channel Seven as part of my 'Today Show' segment. I always got a big kick out of receiving paintings and drawings of soccer players from young kids because I believed I was having an impact on the future generation of Australian sportsmen and women. The segment was my first proper introduction to television appearances and I immediately felt comfortable in front of the camera. In fact, the segment was usually my favourite part of the week. I think the segment only ever had one complaint from a viewer. A lady wrote in to complain that her dog kept going crazy every time a soccer ball was bounced on the show!

My involvement with the 'Today Show' led me to regular appearances on Rex Mossop's 'Sportsworld' program on Channel Seven. 'Sportsworld' appeared on a Sunday morning every week and covered all the sporting action from around Australia and the world so it was another big breakthrough for soccer to have someone on the program to talk about the game. At this stage the *Sun* was also using me as the figurehead for school holiday soccer coaching clinics. The clinics were more about promoting the newspaper than actually training the kids but they did wonders for the game in New South Wales. We held the clinics all around Sydney and usually had more than a thousand kids show up to each clinic. I roped in some other players and coaches to help out and the kids would be given soccer photos and posters, prizes of soccer balls, drinks free ice-creams and hats to take home with them. The clinics were such a success that I can remember some of the players

I brought along with me being forced to sign autographs for hours at the end of the day. Famous Australian rugby league coach Phil Gould even told me recently that he had attended one of the clinics when he was growing up. I guess we mustn't have done a good enough job convincing Phil about the wonders of the round ball.

I wrote my column for the *Sun* up until 1975 and began writing for the *Daily Telegraph* and the *Sunday Telegraph* from 1979. Eventually I moved back to writing a regular column for the *Sun Herald*.

For over twenty-five years I've also been involved with 2UE's evening sports programs and with most of their programs during big Australian games. Over that period I have also worked, at some stage or another, for 4BC, 5AA, 2SSS-FM, 5RPH, 5DN (the Dom Rinaldo soccer show) and 6PR. I enjoy radio—it's instant, I find the radio people more laidback than those in other media, and I never have to worry about my appearance! One of the highlights of my radio career has been working for 6PR over the past three years covering the Perth Glory away games. Peter Vlahos, a former colleague from the time we covered Italia '90 in Italy for SBS is the head of sport at 6PR and he approached me to be part of their soccer commentary team. Peter has been the driving force for doing for soccer on radio what SBS did for the game on television. He has ensured that there is extended coverage and live broadcasts of not only Glory games but also a wide range of other Australian soccer games. Only last year we covered the three big games; against France in Melbourne and the two games against Uruguay. 6PR sent a team to Montevideo that not only covered the match but also held its daily two-hour sports show from the Uruguayan capital. Apart from a weekly spot on the 6PR sports show, I work with one of the great characters of Australian sport—commentator George Grljusich. George is a man of immense experience in covering all sports from Olympic to Commonwealth Games to AFL and now soccer. It has been a delight and honour to be involved with him and 6PR.

My involvement with the media, that commenced during my days with the mighty Saints, has always been ambassadorial, enjoyable and educational. It has been pioneering work for football in Australia.

8

The Curse on Australian Football

⚽ On 1 October 1969 the team flew out for Seoul for the first elimination round of the 1970 World Cup qualifications games. We had been drawn in a round robin series against Olympic bronze medallists Japan and the Asian champions host nation South Korea. So much for a neutral venue! The African nation of Rhodesia (now Zimbabwe) was also supposed to be in the round robin series but South Korea had refused to allow their team into the country for political reasons. It was a situation we didn't think much of at the time but the decision to exclude Rhodesia would come back to haunt us down the track. (In those days there were only sixteen nations that played in the World Cup—fifteen that qualified and then the host nation which automatically qualified. Asia/Africa and Oceania were only allowed one representative so, in other words, over one hundred and twenty nations in these regions were limited to one World Cup spot between them.) As it was, we would play four matches, two each against Japan and South Korea, to see who would progress through to the next round. It was already a daunting prospect, and we knew winning wouldn't necessarily even guarantee us a spot at Mexico. This was only the start.

I remember the final match of that tournament vividly. We only needed a point against South Korea to win the round robin and progress through to the next stage of qualifying. We had been playing well and had two wins and a draw in earlier games. There was a full house of around forty thousand people at the match, all supporting the South Koreans, but our confidence was high after our earlier results.

I scored probably the best goal I have ever scored in that game only to have it ridiculously disallowed by the referee. I must have dribbled through about six players before somehow managing to slot the ball past the goalkeeper and into the net, only to hear the referee blow his whistle for offside. It was an unbelievable decision, one that the boys still marvel at today, and I think even the South Koreans were astounded. The referee didn't stop there though and also awarded the South Koreans a penalty which quite simply should have never been given. It was another disgraceful decision and the boys were starting to get upset. Some great reflexes from goalkeeper Ron Corry saved the day though and we somehow held on to draw the match 1–1. The draw provided the point we needed and we were through to the next round. Although it was only the first stage of qualification it was a major achievement. We had played four games against the best sides in Asia on their home turf. We not only won qualification to the next round but were unbeaten in four games on foreign soil.

The team was then informed that we would have to play off against Israel in Mexico to qualify. The winner of the match would simply stay on in Mexico for the World Cup. This seemed like a fair scenario and we were genuinely excited to be so close to making the finals. To think that we could be playing against the likes of Pelé and all the other great players of world football was simply unbelievable. Although they were just names to us—we had never even seen them play— we had heard all about them and were awestruck by stories of the magic they could weave on the football field. We knew the World Cup was our only chance to not only match our image of them with the reality but also to compete on the same stage.

As it turned out though, the match against Israel in Mexico never eventuated. The world of international politics and the international politics of football itself conspired to ensure that Rhodesia became our next opponent. For reasons relating primarily to the apartheid practices in South Africa and Rhodesia, most of the African nations decided not to enter the qualification campaign in protest against Rhodesia's participation. In the end, Rhodesia was the only African nation wanting to qualify for the World Cup. They would obviously have to play someone else from another qualifying zone because they could not just walk into the tournament but they were refusing to compete against Israel, also for political reasons.

As has often been the case in Australia's dealings with soccer's international governing body, the national squad was given the short straw. We were informed that we would have to play Rhodesia in the Portuguese territory of Mozambique. (Portugal was the only country that would accept Rhodesia to play on its territory. If this was the case I wonder why we couldn't play in the Portuguese colony of East Timor.) While it was supposed to be a neutral venue, it was basically a corner kick from Rhodesia and on the other side of the world from us. If we could beat Rhodesia then we would qualify for a two-leg home-and-away series against Israel. Although it seemed that our path to Mexico had taken a giant leap forward, it was now clear that we had actually been moved two steps back.

The trip to Rhodesia and Israel was one of the most physically and mentally draining times I have ever experienced. The squad spent an incredible number of hours in aeroplanes, airports and hotels during our campaign and I'm sure it eventually took its toll on us. Because of the break between winning in South Korea and FIFA's decision to schedule the series against Rhodesia, we had had four weeks off before we flew out of Australia. All the players had thought our next match would be against Israel in Mexico before the World Cup, and because the local league was not in season, we were not ideally prepared for competition. We were out of season.

We were expected to easily beat Rhodesia but the series against them didn't turn out quite as we hoped. The Rhodesian goalkeeper Robin Jordan was simply outstanding in goal during the first two matches and we were left needing a third match to resolve the series after only managing two draws. (I missed the second game due to food poisoning. Many believed I had been nobbled.) It was soon after the second drawn match that our team doctor Brian Corrigan and the team's Qantas travel consultant Tommy Patrick, who handled all our travel arrangements and had become an integral part of the team, were sitting in a bar with a local journalist discussing the team's inability to score and the amazing performance of the Rhodesian goalkeeper. They weren't sure we would ever progress through to our next match against Israel if the Rhodesian keeper kept performing such heroics.

Brian and Tommy's lamentations prompted the journalist to suggest that they contact a local witch doctor, hinting that maybe some black magic could help the team out. Tommy and Brian obviously thought they might as well give it a go and proceeded to hold a somewhat bizarre meeting with the local witch doctor at his offices at the back of a nearby bordello. He was immaculately dressed in the finest of clothes and spoke Oxbridge English. The witch doctor promised to help our cause by placing a spell on the Rhodesian goalkeeper before the third match and told Brian and Tommy to meet him at the football ground at dawn the next day. The idea was that the witch doctor would bury some bones under the goal at the stadium, pointing towards the Rhodesian goalkeeper, and this would render him useless during the third match.

Unearthly forces seemed to help us because by the third match I had recovered from my food poisoning and I was back leading the team. Amazingly, the Rhodesian goalkeeper who had been our stumbling block in the last two games started throwing them in his own goal. I even managed to score a goal in our comfortable 3–1 victory. One report has it that I scored the goal from the halfway line but I'm sure I would have remembered it if I had. As it turned out, the Rhodesian keeper had little effect on the match and was ultimately carried off the field after colliding with Ray Baartz. The curse had apparently worked. Certainly the witch doctor thought so because he turned up at the hotel before we departed for Israel demanding a thousand pounds in cash as payment for his efforts.

When he was told that there was no way he was getting a thousand pounds, the witch doctor was extremely upset. He felt he had been doublecrossed and cheated out of a payment that was rightly his. He followed the team around demanding money right up until we left and declared that if the money wasn't paid he would seek revenge by putting a curse on the team and Australian soccer. There was no way anyone would have had access to a thousand pounds even if we had wanted to pay him and so in the end, the witch doctor carried through his threat and put a curse on us. It must have worked because things went progressively downhill for the team from that moment on.

After the protracted three-match series against Rhodesia our travel plans were cast into total disarray. The extra match had meant that we were already three days late for the next leg of the tour to play in Israel. The qualification marathon was entering its final stages and we were now only two games away from Mexico but things seemed to be getting unnecessarily tough for us. We technically had a couple of days before our first match against Israel in Tel Aviv but most of this time was spent in transit. First we caught two small twelve-seater planes from Mozambique to Johannesburg in South Africa and from there we flew to Luanda in Angola. Unfortunately a civil war had broken out and the situation was considered so dangerous that we were not even allowed off the plane for several hours until we flew out again, this time to Lisbon in Portugal.

Planes were not allowed to fly directly over Arab territory at that time so we were forced to virtually circumnavigate Africa to get to Portugal. When we finally arrived in Lisbon we had an eight-hour stopover before flying on to Rome and enduring another six-hour stopover. Then we boarded another plane to Athens, had a four-hour stopover there before finally touching down in Tel Aviv in Israel. The trip had taken an unbearable thirty-six hours and anyone who has travelled internationally can imagine how we were feeling by the time we arrived in Tel Aviv. What's more, it was less than twenty-four hours until we were scheduled to play Israel. In terms of preparation, I don't think there could be much worse. Two of our best players, Ray Baartz and Alan Marnoch were so travel sick they could not play. This was one of the biggest games of our lives and we were exhausted before it had even begun.

The atmosphere in the Ramat Gan stadium in Tel Aviv for the match was extremely intimidating. The sixty thousand-strong crowd of Israeli supporters gave the home side a tremendous advantage and they were fiercely supportive of their team. We didn't help our cause much by conceding a disastrous own goal in the early stages of the match after Israel was awarded an indirect free kick back outside our eighteen-yard box. It was a dangerous position to concede a free kick and as it turned out we paid a high price for it. The free kick hit the shoulder of one of our players in the defensive wall and deflected into the corner of the goal. The deflection obviously could have gone anywhere but luck was against us. Then again, maybe the witch doctor's curse was already working!

After the first goal we knew we had to show some fighting qualities or we would be in trouble. The crowd sensed blood and were ecstatic when Israel was awarded a penalty. Goalkeeper Ron Corry came to the rescue though by saving the penalty. He was a real specialist at saving penalties in big matches and this time he really kept us in the match. Although we couldn't sneak an equaliser, the 1–0 loss seemed a good result with the home leg to come, especially considering we had conceded so early.

It was our first loss of the entire qualifying campaign but we boarded the plane back to Australia still confident we could do enough at home to make the World Cup. We were playing at home and knew exactly what we had to do. It would be attack, attack and more attack. Unfortunately our preparation for the match was ridiculously poor.

Instead of remaining together when we returned to Sydney on Tuesday, the team dispersed for a few days. Everyone was told to go home while the ASF decided whether they could afford to put us into camp. While they realised it would be beneficial for us to go into camp, the financial cost involved was making them think twice. In the end, they only called the players back together on the Friday before the match on Sunday. It still seems incredible to me now and the logic behind the decision escapes me. Even when the squad actually did reassemble, our training suffered because everyone had lost the stamina and fitness during the break which touring always provides. Israel, on the other hand, had flown to Australia with us and were straight into training on the Tuesday. They were training while we were at home. The preparation of the two teams couldn't have been more different and, as usual, it was us that had it all wrong.

Having said all that, I don't want to make too many excuses because we could well have won the second-leg match at the Sydney Sports Ground. In the end we were probably too keyed up and spent all our energy too early. We came out at a million miles an hour, which was great, but we didn't get the crucial goal we needed and Israel eventually started to get more of the ball and create some chances. As each second of the match ticked by without us scoring, we became more desperate and the thirty-two thousand-strong crowd became increasingly frustrated.

We attacked and attacked but just didn't take the chances that were provided to us or that we created. We had a contentious penalty appeal for handball turned down by the referee and then, as always seems to happen in soccer, the Israelis scored against the run of play late in the second half. The goal was the result of a missed half-volley clearance by George Keith, one of our most reliable players, one which he would normally have cleared in his sleep and the ball ran through to the Israeli captain Mordechai Shpigler who thumped it into the net. Even though we managed a late equaliser through John Watkiss, the Israelis had done enough. The match finished 1–1 but we had lost the series 2–1. After nine games we had finally been knocked out of the tournament and our dreams of reaching Mexico were dashed.

The players were devastated. We had given four months of our lives attempting to reach the World Cup and by the end of it we were physically and emotionally exhausted. Players lost jobs, loved ones and their health because of their devotion to the cause and to come so close to qualifying for the World Cup only sharpened the pain. Then to really rub salt into our wounds, each player subsequently received a cheque from the ASF for the grand total of $13.27 for nine games. It was our reward for the sacrifice and effort we had put in. The team had played in front of hundreds of thousands of people during our qualification odyssey and it had been deemed we deserved less than fifteen dollars in return. It was a disgrace and we would rather have been paid nothing.

I took the payment insult worse than anyone else in the team because I felt responsible for the rest of the players. I was the captain and the one who had negotiated the so-called 'deal' with the ASF that the profits from the series would be split amongst the boys. But when it came to the crunch the ASF let everyone down with how they distrubuted the money.

I had committed them to a deal and when it had fallen through there was nothing I could do about it.

I always thought the 1969 team was the team that was most likely to qualify for the World Cup. The team really deserved more for its efforts because it played nine games during qualification, eight of these away from home, and only lost one match. Even today, I doubt if the Socceroos would qualify playing South Korea and Japan away in four games, Zimbabwe away three times and Israel home and away. Still, in the end this effort counted for little and I guess that's why people don't remember this team's greatness.

Every time I look back on 1970 I can't help thinking about the series against Rhodesia, the witch doctor and his curse. As the disasters and freak occurrences that have befallen Australian teams since 1970 pile up, my belief in the curse has only strengthened. Our series against Israel in 1969 with the cruelly deflected goal in Tel Aviv and George Keith missing the half-volley in Sydney. Losing to New Zealand at home in the 1982 World Cup qualifying campaign and drawing with Scotland at home when we were by far the better team in the 1986 campaign. The series against Israel for Italy 1990 when captain Charlie Yankos was dispossessed, which was totally out of character and even the accidently but costly deflected own goal of Alex Tobin against Argentina in the 1994 qualifying series. Let alone the disaster against Iran at the MCG in 1997 and our loss against Uruguay in the 2002 World Cup qualifiers. The list is as long as it is painful.

Even the last under-17s World Cup in New Zealand where the Joeys lost on a penalty shoot-out against Brazil in the final springs to mind as another event that could be explained by the curse. One of the Brazilian penalties hit the post, went across the goal line and into the opposite side of the goal, while one of ours hit the post and stayed out. The recent

Olympic Games in Sydney also saw individual defensive errors cost us matches against Italy and Nigeria. The errors came from players that you would normally put your house on in terms of reliability and just left me amazed at how often such misfortune has occurred. The bad luck always seems to come in big matches.

So every time some new disaster befalls our national teams I think back to Mozambique. I can't help wondering if there's something extraordinary to blame. I think Soccer Australia should send someone to Mozambique with a thousand pounds to track down the witch doctor and get him to lift the curse. It could be worth a try anyway.

9

Our Revenge

For those involved in the '69 campaign and its marathon effort we were all totally devastated in its aftermath—it was all so close, so far, so unfair. We all felt cheated and bitter about the experience and we felt done in by events beyond our control. Many of the boys involved in the campaign formed the basis for the 1974 World Cup attempt and, to a man, vowed that the experience that we'd just had would never be repeated. We couldn't wait to exorcise our anger and avenge our unfair loss.

Shortly after the series I, somewhat controversially, said we had been 'crucified' in Israel. But I don't back away from that statement because the ASF hadn't looked after us at all. The travel arrangements had been terrible, we hadn't gone into camp early enough, the organisation of the matches worked against us, we had played only one match at home and we weren't paid what we deserved. Everything had conspired to make it difficult for us. Even today, when I catch up with my 1969 teammates like Atti Abonyi, Adrian Alston, Ray Baartz, John Watkiss, Ron Corry, Jim Fraser, Billy Vojtek and Manfred Schaefer, we all talk about how much harder 1970 was compared to 1974.

However, we found some consolation in another tour to South Vietnam after our failure to qualify for the World Cup in Mexico. We were invited to play in a three-nation tournament involving South Vietnam, Hong Kong and ourselves. The team was invited by the South Vietnamese government because of the success of the Friendly Nations' tournament in 1967 and our visit was again supported and fully funded by the Australian government. The South Vietnamese were very grateful that we agreed to play and both countries saw it as a good opportunity to further strengthen relations.

We easily defeated Hong Kong 6–2 and then overcame South Vietnam 1–0 to win the tournament. The tour was significant because it saw the introduction of new players like Jack Reilly, Jim Mackay, Peter Wilson, Mike Denton and Gary Manuel. These players would go on to play a major role in our campaign to reach the 1974 World Cup and were another example of Uncle Joe's youth policy at work. The rest of the team for the trip consisted of Ron Corry, Dennis Yaager, Manfred Schaefer, Sandy Irvine, Johnny Perin, Danny McKinnon, Jim Armstrong, Adrian Alston, Billy Vojtek and Gary Quested.

The team was given a lecture by Australian embassy officials when we arrived in Saigon and although it was only to be a short visit we were allocated sixteen permanent soldiers to look after us while we were there. The embassy officials instructed us not to touch the drink or the food, not to go out of the hotel at all, to keep away from windows, to stay clear of unattended bicycles (which in a city that has thousands upon thousands of bicycles was a big ask) in case there was a bomb attached, and to be vigilant of packages that appeared to be unattended. It was still obviously a very dangerous place to be. The South Vietnamese actually tried to calm our nerves by explaining that the rockets going off all night were only going out of Saigon, not coming in. I'm not sure if this actually reassured us but the trip went off without a hitch.

After the team returned from winning the three-nation tournament in South Vietnam in the early part of 1970, the ASF announced that Uncle Joe was being replaced. I was immediately angry because I felt Joe had been made the scapegoat for our failure to qualify for the 1970 World Cup. He certainly didn't deserve to be blamed considering we had played eight of our nine matches away from home and still almost made it. But I guess the ASF felt someone needed to be held accountable and they decided it would be Joe. My own personal regard for Joe probably made their decision even tougher for me to deal with but I knew there was little I could do about it. At least winning the tournament in South Vietnam had given him a better send-off and meant he didn't depart on a sour note.

The ASF, to its credit, didn't waste time and moved very quickly in planning our assault on the next World Cup by appointing Rale Rasic as the new coach. Rale, as a thirty-five year old, was fairly young to be a national coach but he was very ambitious and already well respected for what he had done as coach of Melbourne club side JUST and the Victorian state team. Unfortunately, in those days there wasn't the interplay between states that we have in today's soccer so I didn't really know that much about him.

As always happens when a new coach takes over, the team changed. Although the core of the national squad didn't change a great deal, Rale brought in several new players. So while players like Ron Corry, Adrian Alston, Atti Abonyi, Manfred Schaefer, Ray Richards, Ray Baartz, Billy Vojtek and myself were selected again, players such as Col Curran, Harry Williams, Jimmy Rooney, Doug Utjesenovic, Branko Buljevic and Max Tolson were chosen as additions to the national set-up.

Alongside the players who had joined the team in South Vietnam, this squad of players picked by Rale, full of old and new faces, would form the nucleus of the team which would get Australia to the World Cup for the first time.

I quickly got the impression that Rale was the sort of coach who wanted to play his best team in every match. He didn't rotate his run-on team unless he was forced into it by injury, suspension or an extended run of bad form. This meant some players were selected to play in every match while others always sat on the sidelines. In a way it was understandable because he was a new coach and I believe he wanted to prove that he was up to the job by getting immediate results. When you consider that the national squad played fifteen matches in ten different countries over a period of just thirty-six days after leaving on a world tour in October 1970, you can appreciate just how tough Rale's policy could be on the players who were selected to play every game.

The world tour started on 25 October 1970 when we beat New Caledonia in Noumea 1–0. We then thrashed Macau 9–0 in front of their home crowd, with Mike Denton scoring a hat-trick. I even managed two goals myself in what was a clear mismatch. The national team of the tiny Portuguese colony was clearly a few rungs below us on the international soccer ladder. We used the matches against teams like New Caledonia and Macau as warm-up matches and while they weren't much of a challenge on the field, they were interesting places to visit. Macau was a major gambling destination and I can remember our match there was actually played on a field inside a greyhound track. I even met some Australian greyhound trainers who were plying their trade over there because it was such a major sport in Macau. Luckily, I didn't know much about the dogs so I was never tempted to have a wager.

After Macau the team travelled to Iran where we pulled off an exhilarating 2–1 victory in Tehran in front of a crowd of twenty-two thousand. The match against Iran was a considerable step up in class from our previous warm-up matches but our preparation had been good and we competed extremely well in front of a hostile crowd. We also played two matches against an Iran 'A' side, drawing both games and maintaining our unbeaten record. The three matches in Iran were all played within a five-day period so we were extremely happy with our performance, even if we were starting to feel slightly tired. What the team didn't realise at the time was that our experience in Iran—becoming accustomed to the hostile crowd and the conditions—would prove invaluable down the track when we returned with much bigger rewards at stake.

The next match was probably the most satisfying on the tour because we were able to exact some revenge on Israel. Beating them 1–0 in Tel Aviv in front of a twenty-five thousand-strong crowd at the Ramat Gan Stadium was particularly satisfying for those of us who'd been members of Uncle Joe's team because we were still hurting from Israel knocking us out of the World Cup. Even the new members of the team seemed to appreciate how much that win meant to the senior players. Beating Israel certainly didn't make up for not going to the 1970 World Cup, but it went some way to easing the pain.

But while exacting some revenge on Israel was gratifying, our victory over Greece in the next match was more significant in terms of the international game. The Greek side of that era was probably the best international team that country has ever produced and most of the side was part of the tremendous Panathinaikos squad which later played in the European Cup final at Wembley against Ajax in 1971. Beating them 3–1 in Athens was quite an amazing feat for a group of part-time players like ourselves. The Greeks had not lost for five years at home and the Australian team was probably the last team they would have thought could end their run of victories. It was the biggest defeat the Greek national team had ever experienced in Athens and they weren't happy about it. The media even reported that the Greek players were fined three thousand drachma for losing to us, a reasonable amount of money back then and more than a week's work for us! To hold the Greeks to a 1–1 draw two days later was probably just as significant a result considering how keen they were, after the first match, to beat us. It was a spiteful match that was marred by some nasty incidents but again we held out.

After the success in Greece we were unbeaten after eight games on the tour and we were slowly forging a formidable reputation. The team was obviously in good spirits but, at the same time, the heavy schedule was starting to take its toll on all of us. By the time we got to Britain for the next leg of the tour everyone was beginning to tire. The first team we played in Britain was top English second division team Luton Town. I can remember they had famous striker Malcolm Macdonald, or 'Super Mac' as he was known, playing for them. The night we played them was particularly cold and the pitch was wet and muddy—classic English conditions. That's probably why our 2–1 victory was more impressive than it sounds. Two St George boys, Mike Denton and Adrian Alston, scored the goals. Adrian's winner cost his dad (who was in the crowd) his prized cap which he had thrown on the field in delight when Adrian had scored. The cap was subsequently trampled in the mire.

While we were an international side, Luton Town were the professionals. Even if they were only a second division team, they were full-time players while we were merely part-time players. And, of course, English football was really seen as a benchmark in Australia in those days. Beating any English club in any fixture was a big win for an Australian side. What's more, the icy conditions were foreign to us and we were feeling the pinch of a long tour.

Our next English opponent was first division side Manchester City. Unfortunately the match at Maine Road signalled the start of our slide. The rigorous playing schedule just caught up with all of us in the end.

Playing an English first division side in the mud on a cold English night wasn't top on my list of things I wanted to do at a time when I felt like I should be rugged up in bed with some chicken soup. But I knew all the boys were doing it tough and I didn't want to let anyone down. In the end, we lost 2–0 although I think our performance was good, all things considered. Manchester City players were top-notch professionals and we were playing in their backyard. Who knows what would have happened if we weren't so exhausted? But as it was, we were almost spent when we stepped onto the field to play Manchester City. We then also lost to the Republic of Ireland in Dublin.

By the time we got to Mexico for the last match of the tour we were physically and mentally exhausted. Our 3–0 loss to Mexico at the wonderful Azteca Stadium on 1 December was hardly surprising given how everyone was feeling. While we gave our all, the Mexicans' skill on the ball made it tough for us. They were a quality side, having just reached the quarter-finals of the 1970 World Cup, and were obviously experienced in playing at a higher altitude than we were used to. Having Ray Richards sent off during the match didn't help matters because he was a key player in our side. He was a hard-working, midfield ball-winner and losing him meant everyone else had to work that extra bit harder. I can remember Ray, or 'Ricky' as he was known, getting absolutely pelted with fruit and seat cushions from the crowd as he left the field. He eventually must have had enough because he picked up an orange and hurled it back at them.

One of the clearest memories I have of the Azteca Stadium is the oxygen tanks they had outside the change rooms. The air was so thin at that altitude (2240 metres) that it was more difficult than usual to breathe and even the Mexican players were inhaling oxygen from the tanks at half-time. Unfortunately, we didn't have any oxygen, so we had to soldier on without it. The other factor about playing at altitude was the movement of the ball. The thin air made the ball dip and swerve in the air and it also meant the ball travelled a great deal further through the air. One of the great memories I have from football is hitting a shot from a long way outside the box at the Azteca Stadium during our match against Mexico and watching it fly towards the Mexican goal before crashing against the bar. It was one of the best shots I have ever hit and I knew the goalkeeper had no chance. It was one of those shots that you think is in the back of the net from the moment that it leaves your boot. I'm sure the high altitude had something to do with it. Lou Gautier's match report of the game in Mexico for *Soccer World* describes the strike:

> In his latest international appearance against Mexico at the fabled Azteca Stadium on December 1, 1970 [Johnny Warren] came within centimetres of scoring a memorable goal. Bursting through in the best Beckenbauer-style, he shook off two Mexican defenders and from 45 metres let fly with a sizzling right-foot drive which crashed on the bar, the Mexican goalkeeper Castrejon too petrified to move.

I doubt if the keeper was petrified but I really couldn't have hit that shot any better. It was disappointing that it didn't go in because scoring at the Azteca would really have been something to remember. I think the Azteca Stadium is one of the best in the world. It was built for the 1968 Olympics and it is quite simply an awesome place to play football. The stands seem to rise straight up into the air and, as a player, you feel like the crowd is almost right on top of you. Because the crowd is so close, it becomes very difficult to hear your teammates and you can really feel the pressure building in the air as the Mexican supporters start to get excited. It was so special for us to play there because, having missed out on the 1970 World Cup finals which were hosted by Mexico, we at least got a taste of what it would have been like. Just thinking that we were playing on the same ground where Pelé and all the other great players of world football had competed was inspiring. After the match I was lucky enough to swap shirts with the Mexican captain, Pena. He was a national hero in Mexico and I thought it was a great honour to get his shirt. I still have it and pulling it out of the cupboard brings back wonderful memories.

Even though the last couple of games were a letdown, the tour had still been a great success for the national squad. It had been tough and we certainly weren't well rewarded (we weren't receiving match payments or bonuses for wins and even had to pay for any personal laundry we needed done) but looking back, the tour represented the start of a new era. It allowed us to put the disappointments of 1970 behind us and begin concentrating on qualifying for the 1974 World Cup. In a way it also toughened us up for the dramas of the qualifying campaign to come.

After the 1970 season, Frank Arok decided to accept the job of technical director of the Yugoslav Football Federation. Before he left St George he appointed Rale Rasic as his successor. As Rale had recently been appointed Australian coach I had, of course, had a chance to get to know him before he came to St George.

Before the start of the 1971 New South Wales season, St George was invited to compete in a four-team tournament in Japan. The tournament was organised by journalist Andrew Dettre—a big fan of the club enthusiastic about expanding Australia's relations with Asia—and by Japanese Football Association President Shun-ichiro Okano. Okano had been the coach of Japan when I captained Australia against them and I had come to know him quite well. So the tour was not only considered to be a good way to introduce new coach Rale Rasic to the St George team and prepare the side for the season ahead, it was also thought to be a valuable opportunity to strengthen ties between Australian and Japanese football.

The other three teams in the tournament were the national team Japan and the reigning Olympic bronze medallists, a Japan B side and Danish leading first division team Frem. This was obviously strong competition and we knew if we looked at the trip as a holiday we would probably get thrashed and have to return to Australia with our tails between our legs. All the players at St George were keen to impress Rale in any case.

The first match against Frem probably demonstrated how focused we were because we recorded a comprehensive 4–1 victory in which we not only shook off the pre-season cobwebs but also played some quality football. The next match against Japan B saw an even more impressive 6–2 victory and the final 0–0 draw with the Japanese A side was good enough for us to finish on top of the table and win the tournament.

Our victory was a milestone for Australian soccer because it was the first time an Australian club side had won an international tournament. It was even more impressive because we were playing against high-quality opposition, serious about winning the tournament, on their home turf. What's more, we also won the two other matches we played on tour, including one against our sister club Toyo Kogyo. They were based in Hiroshima and were financed by the wealthy auto manufacturer Mazda, so beating them wasn't too bad an achievement either. Our other victory against Hitachi FC left us unbeaten after six games on tour. Things could hardly have gone any better for us.

St George was really very strong for a club side in those days. Having a number of players in the national team and being coached by the national coach meant we weren't your average club side. We actually had ten players participating in Australia's qualification campaign for the 1974 World Cup so we were an unofficial national team in a sense. Even now when people talk about Australia qualifying for the World Cup in West Germany, I sometimes joke that it was actually St George that really qualified.

I was playing some of the best football of my career and was honoured by being voted player of the tournament. When I received the award I decided to present it to our young fullback George Harris. He had just been included in the team and I felt he was the future of the game in Australia. I decided that presenting him with the award might encourage him to push on even further with his career. I could understand how hard it was to make a career out of soccer in Australia and I wanted to make it a bit easier for him. George went on to represent Australia and became a top-class player so I think I had the right idea.

The St George team was a very tight-knit bunch off the field and we really enjoyed our time in Japan. In fact, the guys still remember it as the best tour they have been on. Even though many of our players played in the national team, there was much more camaraderie at St George. Club teams are usually able to develop tighter bonds than representative sides simply because of the circumstances of selection. The national team didn't play regularly, there were usually new faces and the competition for spots was intense. At St George we spent most of the year together, all pulling in the same direction.

When I look back at our success in Japan I can't help but shake my head in wonder at the subsequent opportunities Australia has wasted in terms of embracing Asian football. The fact that there is still such limited contact between Australia and Asia in terms of football is a real failing of the people who have been running the game. Even now, the sport's administration and the media talk about Australian teams playing in Asia as if it's something new. They obviously don't realise that we were there thirty years ago playing our hearts out. What's more, we showed how much of a success embracing Asian football can be.

Botany Methodists under-12s team, 1950. I'm seated in front row, first from right, aged seven, two years after my older brothers guided my hand across the registration pages to sign up for the team because I was too young to write. Directly behind me are my brother Geoff (second from right) and cousin Keith (first from right). My dad, Victor, at the back was the team's manager, coach, gear steward, bus driver and true friend to all the players.

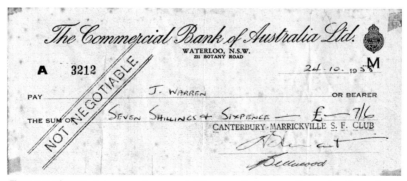

First pay cheque. A bonus of seven shillings and sixpence from the Canterbury Marrickville Soccer Club was my first payment as a soccer player. I never banked the money but kept the cheque as a treasured memento.

State champions. I was selected for the Canterbury district representative team in 1958 and we became the NSW State Junior Champions in the under-16 grade. Back row (l-r): me, M. Teague, D. Wilson, W. Collins, I. O'Reilly; Middle (l-r): B.W. Brackenberry (Sec.-Treas.), W. Webster, S. Lanyon, G. Stevens, R. Abercrombie, L. Kirkaldy, C. Barlow (Pres.); Front (l-r): S. O'Reilly (Co-Manager), D. Buchanan, K. Warren, B. Hamilton, G. Thyrde, C. Payne (Manager).

Soccer: a family affair, 1959. My brothers and I each played for different first-grade teams—me (at left) for Canterbury Marrickville, Geoff (middle) for Auburn and Ross (right) for Concord. Dad's car ran hot driving all over Sydney during the season to watch all our games. If we played each other, Mum and Dad would usually end up barracking for the son on the losing side.

Lesson from a schoolboy. One of two goals I scored for Canterbury against Apia, in the 1960 Federation final. We won 3–2 in extra time which secured us a place in the grand final against Prague. A newspaper report of this match read: 'John Warren, Canterbury's 17-year-old star, gives a lesson on how to score a goal to Apia's veteran centre Joe Marston...' Playing against my lifetime hero Joe Marston was a dream come true and this picture was displayed on posters all around Sydney to promote soccer—the world's greatest game.

On the TV. I first appeared on TV on a Channel Seven sports show hosted by Ray Connolly in 1960. I've always considered my media career a pioneering role for soccer in Australia.

No mateship here. After both playing for the Canterbury team, my childhood friend John Watkiss joined Apia and I later transferred to St George Budapest. In this match, we were pitted against each other. Later, we went on to play for the Australian national team—not a bad effort from two boys from Edward Street, Botany. The street also produced rugby league international Brian Hambly.

Opening Ceremony, Friendship Tournament, Saigon, 1967. I'm still amazed the Australian national soccer team was sent to Saigon in the midst of the Vietnam War for the 'Friendship Tournament'. During our time training and playing there, the sky was constantly lit with flares that the United States military used to help their bombers, there was a constant stream of helicopters buzzing overhead and the sound of gunfire could be heard in the distance.

Australia's first ever international soccer trophy. The proud Australian national team in the dressing room in Saigon after winning the Friendship Tournament by beating New Zealand, South Vietnam, Singapore, Malaysia and South Korea—our first international trophy. President Thieu of South Vietnam had just presented me with the Cup and medals. I'm in the bottom row, second from left.

Australia vs Greece, 1969. As preparation for the 1970 World Cup qualification series the Australian national team played a three-match home series against Greece. Here, I am leading the team out onto the field at the SCG, followed by Atti Abonyi, John Watkiss and Ray Baartz. It was the day after Neil Armstrong walked on the moon so the atmosphere of the 31,000-strong crowd was electric. Australia won 1–0.

Australian national team in Tel Aviv 1969. We had just arrived in Tel Aviv after a gruelling thirty-six hours of travel from Mozambique to play the most crucial match of our lives, twenty hours later—our World Cup qualifier against Israel. Back (l-r): Bordacs (manager), Uncle Joe (coach), Lazzari (physiotherapist), Perin, Baartz, Zeman, Alston, Abonyi, Fraser, Corry, Schaefer, Sandell, Barclay (manager). Front (l-r): McColl, Rutherford, Watkiss, me, Walsh, Marnoch, Vojtek, Keith, Ackerley.

Tehran, 1970. Australia line up for our match against Iran—part of our national team's world tour organised by new national coach of the time, Rale Rasic. Australia won, 2–1. (l-r): me, Reilly, Wilson, Doyle, Alston, Yaager, Richards, Schaefer, Denton, Vojtek, Roche.

Celebrating in Greece, 1970. In Athens on our world tour we beat Greece 3–1. The Greeks had not lost for five years at home and we—a group of part-time players—were probably the last team they would have imagined could end their dream run. (l-r): Blues, Richards, me, Roche, Denton, Curran, Schaefer.

St George win international tournament.
My club side, St George Budapest, competed in a four-team competition in Japan in 1971. We won the international tournament and arrived home to a warm reception by St George fans. Players, in suit and tie, back (l-r): Ainslie, Alston, Schaefer, Donovan, Sandell, Abonyi and me. Front (l-r): Taylor and Campbell.

Knee injury. Seconds after this photo was taken of St George Budapest playing against Prague at Wentworth Park in 1971, my right knee collapsed, resulting in the first knee reconstruction operation in Australia, six weeks later. With me is former Olyroo and Assistant National Youth Coach Raul Blanco—he was incorrectly blamed afterwards for causing the injury but he didn't even touch me.

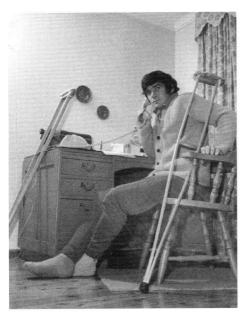

Dark days. After my knee reconstruction, performed on my twenty-eighth birthday, I spent ten weeks on crutches with a full-length plaster on my leg. Lifting the phone was about the only thing I could do. I had been successfully playing the sport I loved, captaining my club and captaining my country as the Socceroos prepared to qualify for the World Cup and now my career seemed finished.

10

The Dark Days

⚽ I WAS ON a high when I returned to Australia after St George's tour to Japan. I was twenty-seven and I felt I was at my football peak.

Things couldn't have been going any better on the field for me. I was enjoying playing, I was captain of my country and captain of my club. I had just come back from a great tour to Japan, the Australian team was already building up for the next World Cup qualifiers and I was scoring my fair share of goals. I even felt like I had really improved and matured as a footballer. Off the field, I was enjoying working full-time in football in public relations for St George. It was simply one of those golden periods in life when everything seems to fall into place.

The incident that shattered my period of prosperity seemed fairly innocuous at the time. St George was playing against local club side Prague at Wentworth Park during the 1971 season and when I went to turn, my right knee simply gave way. Raul Blanco, the former Australian Olympic coach and a very good player in his own right, was actually blamed for causing my injury but he didn't even touch me. There was no dramatic incident or vicious two-footed challenge. My knee simply collapsed under me. As I limped off the field, I didn't really have any idea what was wrong and yet somehow I knew it was a serious injury.

Once the doctor had examined my knee, he decided it needed to be aspirated to reduce the swelling. I knew this procedure would be fairly unpleasant, having experienced it when I hurt my knee playing for Canterbury as a sixteen-year-old schoolboy. To make matters worse though, the doctor wasn't sure what was wrong. In the end he simply told me to rest and see what happened.

I remember being stung at the time by some people's suggestion that the injury was all in my head. I suppose people were sceptical because I could still make certain movements before my knee would suddenly give way on me. The criticism and the uncertainty about the injury probably contributed to my decision to make a comeback only four weeks later. The knee didn't feel one hundred per cent but I wanted to get back on the field.

My return match was against Western Suburbs at Hurstville Oval and it was a particularly wet, unpleasant day, certainly not the sort of day to be returning from a bad knee injury.

It didn't take long before I was hit in a tackle from behind. My knee just buckled completely and I was immediately in agony, the pain so unbearable that I had to come straight off the field. I asked my mate John Economos to drive me home but quite amazingly, in hindsight, I didn't go to hospital or get any medical attention for the injury whatsoever until the next day. For the rest of the day I just sat on the floor at home and feared the worst.

When I saw the doctor he thought it was likely that I had damaged some of the cartilage in my knee so he immediately booked me in for an operation to fix the problem. The date for the operation just happened to be 17 May 1971, my twenty-eighth birthday. Ironically, twenty-eight is the optimum age for a footballer, say the experts—you're experienced and you're at the height of your physical condition. Unfortunately, the birthday present I discovered when I came out of the anaesthetic at the Waverley War Memorial Hospital in Sydney wasn't quite what I had been hoping for. My entire right leg was in plaster from the upper thigh down to my foot. My leg was bent at a slight angle and was completely immobilised. When my surgeon, former Australian rugby union captain Dick Tooth, visited me, he told me that he had needed to perform a revolutionary operation on my knee—I had in fact undergone the first knee reconstruction in Australia. I had ruptured the anterior cruciate ligament in my knee and so literally had to have a new one screwed into place. My first question was whether I would be able to play again. The doctor was direct enough to say he didn't really know for sure but that it was extremely unlikely. It was the one thing in my life that I didn't want to hear and I was completely devastated.

The following period of my life was absolute hell. I was in plaster for ten weeks and unable to walk. I obviously couldn't drive either and work was definitely out of the question. The only thing I was able to do was lie on the floor and attempt to do some leg exercises. Not surprisingly I became very depressed. It's a cliché, but in that sort of situation you really find out who your friends are. When the severity of my injury became public some people in the soccer media, and even some people that I thought were my friends, suddenly disappeared. They obviously thought I was finished and decided they didn't want anything more to do with me. It came as a shock to me and soon even some people that I considered I was very close to drifted away as well. They were all people that I had become friends with through soccer and as soon as my soccer career looked in doubt, they disappeared.

It would eventually turn out to be a valuable lesson for me but at the time it was difficult to come to terms with.

For an athlete there is nothing worse than being forced to sit out and watch other people play. I had been playing sport all my life, since I could walk, and now I simply couldn't do a thing. During my time in hospital, the Socceroos were scheduled to play a side representing the English Football Association and I knew it would be a great series to participate in, considering the interest in English football in Australia. Knowing I was missing it made me feel even worse and even though I was slightly cheered up by a visit from England's captain Mike Keen at the hospital, the improvement in my mood didn't last long.

Having to watch someone else lead out the team when Australia played was worse than I had ever imagined. As captain, I felt it had been my team and now someone else had taken my place. My confidence plummeted as I realised I might never return to international level. My whole sense of self was centred on my achievements in soccer and now I believed I wasn't someone special any more. When you are a successful athlete, even as a soccer player in those days, people want to talk you and want to know how you are going and how you are feeling. I guess I had grown accustomed to the attention and the limelight and when it was suddenly taken away, I felt unsure of myself. It sounds melodramatic but I really felt like my life was over.

When the plaster was finally removed, my leg was so skinny that it looked like my arm. It had literally wasted away to nothing. I was still in shock and as I tentatively started doing some rehabilitation work, I simply didn't know what to do with my life. I had never considered life without football before and it was a daunting prospect when it was eventually forced upon me. I was still able to do some office work at the club and I desperately tried to keep myself busy there but I obviously wasn't able to perform my duties in the same way I had prior to my injury. I couldn't go out to schools and take training courses because I could barely walk. So I spent most of my time feeling sorry for myself and cursing my situation.

The incident that first turned my life around occurred during a visit to the pool at the Prince Henry Hospital in Sydney. I was having regular hydrotherapy sessions as part of my rehabilitation. At the time I was probably the most miserable person in the world. I can remember feeling particularly sorry for myself one day as I watched several young kids laughing and carrying on in the pool because their overt happiness seemed to make my own situation even worse in my mind. But as I lowered myself into the pool I saw a large pulley being swung over and into the water near where the kids were playing. I realised that the pulley was needed to help them out of the pool because they were disabled. How stupid and self-pitying I was being hit me like a sledgehammer. Here were these kids who would never have the chance to walk or to play sport, and yet they were making the most out of life.

Not long after being given this valuable lesson in perspective at the pool I had the good fortune to cross paths with the legendary German coach Dettmar Cramer. It would prove to be another crucial moment in my recovery. Dettmar was in Australia holding coaching courses and because I already knew him from a previous meeting during my playing days, I got talking with him when he gave a lecture at the St George club. He was very sympathetic to my situation and urged me to come to a FIFA coaching course in Malaysia that started in January 1972, the next year. He told me the course would consist of four months of intensive physical preparation and study of the game; six days a week, twelve hours a day. It seemed to offer me some much needed direction and I was immediately interested.

At this stage my leg was slowly getting better but there was still a huge question mark over whether I would even play again, let alone return to the highest level. Dettmar's suggestion really made sense because if I didn't make a comeback as a player the course would allow me to become a young coach. At the same time the course would be an excellent test of whether my leg would recover away from the pressures of the club scene. It appeared to be the best possible course of action for me to take.

The combination of these two chance incidents changed my attitude completely. As quickly as I had become depressed, I just as quickly decided not to feel sorry for myself any more. My entire mindset changed and I was suddenly determined to come back and prove people wrong. I realised I hadn't properly appreciated how important playing football was to me. It was only after my injury that I realised I had taken playing football for granted. While I enjoyed playing, I had never appreciated how important it was to my existence. I decided then and there that I would give everything I had to try and make a comeback and I decided my first step would be to throw all my efforts into the coaching course.

My knee injury proved to be a blessing in disguise because my time at the coaching course in Kuala Lumpur was unforgettable. But before I could reap the benefits of the course I had to attend to the small matter of actually getting there. At the time I was writing a column for the *Sun* newspaper and I decided to go to sports editor Jack Tier, my old sparring partner, to ask his advice on how to fund my studies. Jack was a real old-time newspaper guy, as rough as guts but with a heart of gold, and he liked the idea of me going to Malaysia. We were eventually able to reach a deal where the newspaper would sponsor my trip and I would write articles for them while I was away.

The course in Kuala Lumpur was run by a man named Peter Velappan, who is now General Secretary of the Asian Football Confederation and one of the most powerful people in world football, but Dettmar was actually in charge of most of the activities. There were fifty-six other coaches from countries all over Asia, including Korea, Iran, Japan, Thailand, Malaysia, Singapore, Indonesia and India, enrolled in the course and we all stayed on campus at the University of Kuala Lumpur. It was an appropriate setting because the course itself was very much like a university degree. We studied every aspect of football imaginable, from technique, tactics, physical preparation, physiotherapy, physiology and anatomy, right through to the laws of the game, the use of other sports, first aid and the art of teaching the game to others. At the end of the course we were tested with thirty-six hours worth of stringent physical, technical and written examinations.

Although the course was held at a university and was like a university degree, there was none of the parties and revelry usually associated with university life. Breakfast was served between 6.30 am and 6.50 am and from there it was constant work right up until dinner was served at 7.30 pm. Everyone on the course had separate rooms, with a bed and a desk, and at night I would usually return to my room to study before going to bed. The course was very demanding and I was trying to secure some sort of future for myself, so I wasn't interested in going out anyway.

I also had the responsibility of writing my columns for the *Sun*. The newspaper had helped me get to Kuala Lumpur so I always made sure I filed my column on time. I would usually concentrate on some aspect of my time at the course, such as the training techniques I was learning or Dettmar's coaching philosophy, and then phone through the copy to the *Sun*. It was a good arrangement and the *Sun* was happy with the way it turned out. I can remember writing one column on a game called Sepak Takraw. Popular in Malaysia, it was regularly played in streets and parks across the country. It is a three-a-side game played on a small court with a cane ball and is like volleyball in a sense because it is played over a net with much the same objective. Each side is only allowed a certain number of touches and has to try and keep the ball in the air so it does not land in their own court. The players are not allowed to use their hands and so there is some spectacular action, such as amazing overhead scissor kicks and flying volleys. The game develops a whole new set of soccer-related skills, so studying it and its relationship with soccer became an integral part of the course.

Dettmar was particularly meticulous in demonstrating the finer points of soccer. Things like passing and heading a ball correctly were constantly demonstrated and practised. Even though I was twenty-eight years old and had been captain of Australia I really only learned how to properly head a ball during my time in Malaysia, as amazing as that sounds. I was brought up like every other young kid of my generation, with a heavy ball that was a nightmare to head, especially if you caught the big laces that ran around its middle. That was why most Australians generally weren't good headers of the ball in those days. They would have the ball thrown at them in junior football and it would petrify them. The first thing they would do would be to close their eyes. As a result they would not learn the basics. I was lucky that, albeit towards the end of my career, I was properly instructed with the correct technique.

The underlying theory behind the course was that coaches had to be able to demonstrate what they wanted from their players. Talking about the game was pointless unless you could do it or demonstrate it yourself. It was a logical theory but meant, in practice, that we were expected to master almost every element of the game during the course.

Sometimes we would be taken to matches to analyse them. We would then be expected to present our ideas about the game and to highlight any important tactical aspects. It brought my awareness of the sport to a new level of understanding. Dettmar believed that each game could show you what and how a team needed to train. He was a visionary in terms of football and all his coaching principles still apply today. Dettmar was so meticulous in his approach that it eventually rubbed off on me.

One quite painful extension of his coaching philosophy was a tremendous focus on fitness. Guys who were overweight when they arrived left the course in far better condition—as practically new men—because Dettmar worked all of us incredibly hard. He was in superb condition himself and he would push me to do extra because he knew about my knee. He would have me training in the pool and doing the infamous Cooper twelve-minute run every second or third day. We started doing ten sit-ups and push-ups at the end of each session and by the end of the course we were doing two hundred! After four months of steadily increasing my physical condition, my knee gradually strengthened and improved.

Being able to test out my knee in competitive matches also helped my rehabilitation. The FIFA coaching team would play the various state teams of Malaysia—Penang, Johore, Selangor—with all gate monies donated to charity. I can remember after one game when I must have played particularly well Dettmar took me aside and said: 'Johnny, today you can play anywhere in Europe, let alone in Australia.' It was a wonderful thing to hear from such a respected figure and after the bad times I had been through it did wonders for my confidence.

When the course finished I was named dux of the school and awarded the course medal. I had worked very hard for it and was extremely proud of my achievement considering there were fifty-six coaches at the course, including one who is now technical director for Asian football. In the end it wasn't that difficult for me because I enjoyed the course so much and made a lot of good mates. I had been studying economics at university in Australia and now here I was studying football. The two simply didn't compare because in Malaysia I was doing something I loved.

Even after finishing the course, I was still not thinking about becoming a coach when I returned to Australia. The course had, if anything, only strengthened my resolve to return to the playing field and prove wrong all those people who had written me off. My knee was feeling good and before I went back to Australia I even started doing extra training. That was something I had never done before in my life and I guess it demonstrated how determined and fixated I was on returning to the game.

By the time I returned to Sydney from the coaching course in Malaysia, Rale Rasic had left St George to go to Italian community club, Marconi. It was actually an important coaching change for me because the club called back Frank Arok to take charge again and he proved crucial in helping me complete the final stages of my recovery. He was immediately very keen to get me back into the St George team and had me training with the team after I had only been back in the country a week. His attitude was that I was someone special at St George and that every effort needed to be made to return me to playing. If I needed special privileges then so be it. He was going to make space for me because the team needed me back. His faith and confidence in me was a real boost to my morale.

My first game back was at Lambert Park against our old archenemy Apia. I was quite nervous before kick-off and I can remember being surprised when the ground announcer made a point of welcoming me back. I was even more surprised when the crowd gave me a round of applause! It was a generous gesture considering we were in 'enemy territory' and it was certainly not what I had been expecting.

When I say I was nervous I was probably more anxious about how I would play than concerned about my knee holding up. Returning from a major injury is primarily a psychological matter of getting your confidence back. I had worked so hard on my recovery and been through hell to return to the game so I knew I couldn't have done any more. If my knee went, it went, but I was confident it would hold up. I was more worried about whether I would be the same player. I knew I had been out of the game for fifteen months and I knew people would be watching closely to see if I struggled.

As it turned out I didn't have a particularly good game against Apia and I never really got into the rhythm of the play. Things even started particularly badly when I gave a penalty away in the first couple of minutes. Our keeper Jimmy Fraser saved it and has never let me forget it even though we went on to win the match 4–2! I was lucky that the boys encouraged me throughout the match. Right towards the end I managed to give the pass for our last goal and it was a major source of relief. I walked off the field reasonably satisfied.

My form eventually picked up from that game, although it took probably seven or eight games before I felt like I was back to my old self. There were some people who were sceptical that I would ever return to my previous form. People still argue over whether I was a better player before or after my injury. But the vast majority of my teammates, friends and associates from soccer were so supportive of me that I was always confident of coming back to at least the same level at which I played before. At the time I was simply happy to have proved all my critics wrong and be back on the field. There's no doubt though that aspects of my game changed when I returned in 1972. I was certainly a smarter player, in the sense that I didn't dive into situations on the field where I was only ever going to come out second best. It wasn't a case of trying to protect myself or shield my knee, it was simply that I thought more deeply about my role on the field and put my energy into where it would be best utilised. My overall game didn't change. I still loved to get forward and I still won tackles and competed for the ball. I was simply wiser about the game and started to use my experience from the coaching clinic to play a smarter game.

In my view, the 1972 team was the best St George ever produced. We won the Ampol Cup, the league championship and, while we lost the grand final to Marconi, we made up for it by beating them in the Cup final a week later. It was a brilliant squad, full of internationals and top-class players, many of whom later contributed to getting Australia to the World Cup in West Germany in 1974—players like Manfred Schaefer, Jim Fraser, George Harris, Doug Utjesenovic, Bobby Hogg, Adrian Alston, Atti Abonyi, Harry Williams and Mike Denton. We also had two young players, in Brendan Grosse and Neville Morgan, who went on to play for Australia. In the last game of the season against Hakoah, I scored three goals in a 4–2 victory, and Frank Arok turned to me and said: 'I didn't know you could score so many goals.' I replied, 'Well, you've always got me back doing all the donkey work!' I have always said I should have been a striker.

The matches against Marconi in 1972 had some extra excitement for us because, in those days, it was never imagined that coaches would leave St George for another local club; it simply wasn't done because St George was one of the biggest names in Australian soccer boasting up to half of the national squad. So Rale's decision to leave for Marconi had sent shockwaves through the club. The players were more surprised than anything because we had enjoyed such a successful season and many players on the team were part of Rale's Australian squad. The immediate result of Rale's departure was to create a new rivalry between St George and Marconi. The rivalry was of course heightened when St George managed to convince Frank Arok to come back to replace Rale. By the start of the 1972 season, the St George officials, coaching staff and players all had a reason to want to beat Marconi.

The games against Marconi that season were always tough and unforgiving affairs. Marconi had several Australian internationals in Peter Wilson, Alan Maher, Ray Richards and Max Tolson and was our main competition that year. The Cup final against Marconi was our most memorable encounter that season because I was involved in a huge argument with Frank in the lead-up to the match. The week before the Cup final we had been beaten by Marconi 1–0 in the league grand final and I had written a newspaper column congratulating our opponents on their victory. I didn't really think much of it at the time because I thought it was the only gracious thing to do. However, Frank was furious with me because he thought I had used the newspaper article in an attempt to butter up Rale who was, of course, coaching Australia at that stage. He also accused me of playing within myself in the grand final so that I wouldn't get hurt before the upcoming Australian tour to Asia. Frank actually had a go at all the Australian representatives in the team, telling the team that there were too many players trying to protect their legs. It was probably the worst insult you can give a player and I was extremely upset with Frank for even suggesting it.

The Cup final was played in very wet, slippery conditions and the match became a real 'take no prisoners' encounter. I was still fuming at Frank and I played the match with a real anger and intensity. At one stage, I simply yelled at Frank, using some fairly colourful language, to try and make him bring on Adrian Alston. When Frank eventually brought Adrian on, he scored almost immediately and levelled the match up at 2–2. The match was a thriller and I was lucky enough to score the winner in extra time to clinch the match 3–2. But, rightly or wrongly I was still so angry with Frank that I didn't attend the club's presentation night—my Mum accepting the club's Player of the Year award on my behalf. As it turned out, I soon left with the Australian tour to Asia and Frank decided to go back to Yugoslavia again, so I didn't speak to Frank after that Cup final for about nine years. However, we eventually patched things up and remain good friends today.

Funnily enough, Frank finally discovered that the way to get me to really perform was to stir me up and make me angry—a winning formula. Despite these tempestuous encounters there was a feeling that things were coming back together for me—confidence, some goals, club success and now the World Cup qualifiers around the corner. My next goal was to establish myself in the national team.

11

Australia Makes It: The 1974 World Cup

⚽ It had not been until 1971 that the *Daily Mirror*'s chief soccer writer Tony Horstead, writing under the name 'Hotspur', first coined the term 'The Socceroos' for the Australian national soccer team. I'm not sure whether Tony wanted the nickname to become the national team's permanent unofficial title, but that is exactly what happened. The Australian rugby league team was known as the Kangaroos and Tony wanted to create something similar for the soccer team, to recognise the link it had established with the nation. So when the Australian team assembled in October 1972 for a tour of Asia as part of our 1974 World Cup qualification preparations, we left as the Socceroos.

We played matches against Indonesia, New Zealand, South Vietnam, South Korea and the Philippines on the tour but our stay in South Vietnam was easily the most unforgettable part of the tour. Our first match against South Vietnam was at the Cong Hoa Stadium in Saigon, the same stadium we had played at in 1967. The stadium was located in Cholon, the Chinese quarter of the city, which was a big gambling district, and a lot of money had obviously been wagered on the result of our match because after our 1–0 victory, which was a bit of an upset, there was a huge riot. The packed crowd literally went crazy and our entire team, including the coaches and officials, was trapped on the field. It was an unbelievable experience because there were hundreds of machine-gun-toting troops surrounding us and thousands of people pelting rubbish, stones and anything else they could find from the stands at us. As we stood dazed on the field, a bag full of kerosene, used by the take-away food merchants to fuel their stoves in the stadium, came sailing through the air and exploded onto our Qantas travel representative Tommy Patrick's eyes and face. He immediately started screaming, obviously terrified that he was going to lose his eyesight. There was little any of us could do for him at the time because we were standing in the middle of the pitch surrounded by an angry, violent mob! Some of our team officials looked after Tommy as best they could until more troops arrived and managed to shepherd us back into the dressing room.

The dressing room was a mess, with all the windows smashed and glass lying everywhere. We were all in shock. Tommy was still screaming as our doctor poured water over his eyes to clean out the kerosene. At the same time we could hear the crowd screaming as the riot continued outside. Eventually we were herded onto the bus, which also had its windows smashed in, and commanded to get down on the floor while we drove out of the stadium. It was a frightening situation and when we eventually arrived back at the hotel everyone knew we were lucky to have got out of the stadium at all. The thing was, we all knew we were scheduled to play another match against the same team the next day.

The players called a meeting straight away. We were still all very shaken up and it was unanimous that we didn't want to put ourselves back into that situation again the next day. Tommy hadn't sustained any lasting damage to his eyes but everyone realised that the situation had been out of control and his injuries could have been worse. Standing out in the middle of the pitch we were really at the mercy of the fans and what they decided to hurl at us. The Vietnamese officials sent security officers to the hotel to guarantee us that there would be increased security for the next match and the Australian ambassador also arrived to try to settle our nerves and convince us to play the next game. However, we were really shaken up and remained adamant that we just wanted to leave South Vietnam—NOW!

The team meeting had probably been going for a couple of hours when team physiotherapist Peter Van Rjn stood up and delivered one of the greatest speeches of my time with the national team. Peter was from a Dutch background and was the Hakoah physiotherapist back in Australia. He had been with the national team since 1970 and had become a valued member of the squad. He was a real character and was usually at the centre of any practical jokes carried out on our tours, on the receiving end of just as many as he masterminded himself. When Peter stood up he was visibly shaken with the emotion of it all. I obviously can't do the speech justice but Peter told everyone on the team that we were like his sons. He had lived with us, travelled the world with us, and seen all the hard work we had put in and admired us greatly for it. 'I'm not born in Australia,' he said, 'but I know you guys are doing the wrong thing. You are letting your country down.' It was an amazingly heartfelt address which underlined how important the team and the players were to him. Everyone looked up to Peter and his words had an immediate effect on the whole team because the entire mood in the room changed and we decided to reconsider our decision not to play the next day and agreed we would play if better security arrangements were put in place. I think everyone still thought we were taking a huge risk but Peter's speech had inspired us to think beyond our own personal fears for the time being. When we ran out onto the field the next day we took the orange and red South Vietnamese flag out with us and ran around the field holding it aloft for a few minutes. It was a sort of peace gesture and it immediately got the crowd back on side. There were no incidents during or after the match but after we won we made sure we got off the field and out of the stadium as soon as possible. Everyone was happy to leave because we were all a bit frayed around the edges. If it wasn't for Peter I still don't think the second match would have gone ahead.

When people speak to me about my experiences with the Socceroo team that qualified for the 1974 World Cup in Germany, they often assume I was captain of the side. I guess it's a widespread assumption because I was, and have been since, strongly associated with the national team of that era. But the fact is that I was only the vice-captain. Even now I feel I should have been captain so it's something that I look back on with a great deal disappointment and regret.

My feelings about the World Cup and the captaincy really go right back to 1967. Ever since I had captained the Australian team in the Friendly Nations' tournament in South Vietnam I had considered the national squad to be my team. It was a young team and I felt like my role was somehow more than just being an on-field leader. I really thought of the team as my boys. The core of the team had grown so close during our tour to Vietnam and our subsequent attempt to qualify for the World Cup in 1970 that I really enjoyed my leadership role and it became the focus of my life.

Maybe I didn't realise just how important my role as captain had become to me until I hurt my knee. Watching the team play and watching someone else lead the Socceroos out onto the field was like a knife in my side. I couldn't play for fifteen months and I was virtually out of the national team for two years but throughout the recovery process I focused on the goal of making a comeback and captaining Australia again. I really thought it was just a case of getting back to full fitness and being given back the role of captain which I considered was mine. It was a goal that saw me through some tough times.

My path back to football at club level had been made relatively easy because everyone at St George wanted me back and gave me tremendous support. Even though I had been out of the game for such a long time, all the players and coach Frank Arok adopted a 'we'll help you' attitude during my rehabilitation. I was put straight back in the team even when I was still a bit unsteady on the knee and I was given every opportunity to recover my form. It was great for my confidence and I expected that I would get the same treatment from the national team.

Of course, I knew that the national team wouldn't come to a standstill waiting for me to return but I somehow expected to be treated with a little special consideration because of my record. As it turned out though, the entire Socceroo set-up had changed during my time out and my own status within the national team had diminished. Upon my return I discovered the Socceroos clearly wasn't my team any more and had very much become the domain of new coach Rale Rasic. He had become the team's new figurehead. While I expected to come straight back into the captaincy, Rale had other ideas.

Rale had made defender Peter Wilson captain in my absence and he stayed in that position right up to and during the World Cup. I had nothing against Peter of course, it really wouldn't have mattered who was in the position, but I truly thought I deserved to wear the armband. While in retrospect I can understand Rale's decision, at the time I was extremely disappointed. I thought Rale should have placed more weight on my previous efforts and position in the national team. I had been vice-captain of the team in Australia's first World Cup qualifying attempt, I had led the team to its first international tournament victory in the most inhospitable and testing environments and I had captained the team through the most arduous qualification campaign imaginable for the

1970 World Cup where we missed out by a whisker. Throughout it all, I had given my best for the team and the nation and felt I had been a real ambassador for the entire sport in Australia. It's not a case of being big-headed; I simply considered the Socceroos were *my* team in those days and the centre of my existence.

I still believe that in any other country I would have been reinstated as captain. If West German great Franz Beckenbauer had been hurt and spent a year on the touchline, he would have come straight back into the national team as captain when he recovered. That's just the way I believe it would happen, no matter what had occurred in between. Now I realise I'm no Beckenbauer and, at the same time, the Socceroos were not the German national team. Suddenly, though, I discovered I had become just another player. I felt I wasn't being given the appropriate recognition for my accomplishments as previous captain and it was hard for me to deal with not being given the chance to captain the Socceroos once again.

Not surprisingly, Rale and I had our fair share of blues after I returned to the national team. It wasn't that we didn't get along—Rale was actually very close to my parents—but when it came down to business we had a difference of opinion on certain things. One of them was obviously the captaincy and in the end it became a bit of a problem between us.

All the players in the national team were extremely supportive of my comeback and I was happy to be back playing with them. But at the same time they were also competing for a spot with me. It wasn't like at St George where it was accepted that I would be back in the team if I was fit. In my absence the set-up for the national team had changed and other players had moved in. So there was a situation where the guys were, on the one hand, supportive towards me but on the other hand worried about their own positions. And of course that was fair enough. I certainly didn't expect them to step aside for me. I really don't want people to think I wasn't happy just to be back in the team, because I certainly was. It was just that I thought I should be back in the captain's position that I had left.

My comeback to the national team occurred with the tour to Asia in 1972. During my time out with injury I had missed out on playing against the Football Association XI from England and a three-match series against Israel. I also missed out on playing against the famous Brazilian club side Santos when they toured here. The Australian team had drawn 2–2 with Santos in front of a full house at the Sydney Sports Ground and it was a big occasion. Missing any game for Australia was bad enough but as I would have really loved to have played on the same field as Pelé, sitting on the sidelines had been even more painful.

Pulling on the Australian jersey against Indonesia was a great feeling because of all the hard work I had put into making my international comeback. People had told me I would never play the game again, let alone play for the national team, so it was a vindication of my belief in myself. I came on as a sub for Jimmy Mackay and although my first game produced nothing outstanding, it was exciting to be back playing at that level again. By this stage Rale had almost settled on the team he wanted to play in the upcoming World Cup qualifiers, so I knew I had my work cut out to get back in the run-on team.

The team played six matches on the tour against Indonesia, New Zealand, South Vietnam, South Korea and the Philippines. We returned home unbeaten after winning five matches and drawing one. It was a successful tour. It wasn't until our 2–0 victory over South Korea in Seoul, however, that I really began to feel that I was back to playing my best again.

While I managed to get back in the starting line-up by the time the World Cup qualifiers finally arrived in 1973, I had not been able to win back the central playing role I really wanted. I was being played out on the right, and although I would have played anywhere, I was probably still a bit frustrated when the team began our official campaign.

At the back of everyone's mind throughout 1972 and the early part of 1973 were the World Cup qualifiers. The desire to reach the World Cup was always paramount among the players, the coaches and the administration. The ASF and Sir Arthur George still deserve much recognition and congratulations for the job they did in organising the qualifying campaign in 1973. Obviously they had learnt from the mistakes made in 1969 because our path to the World Cup in Germany was far easier than it had been to Mexico.

The ASF made the bold decision to host the initial round robin qualifying tournament between Iraq, Indonesia, New Zealand and the Socceroos in Sydney. We would have to play New Zealand away, but the remaining five games would be at home. It was a good decision because the home support helped us through what turned out to be a difficult round robin series. We drew twice against our archenemy New Zealand, had a draw and a win against Iraq and recorded two solid victories against Indonesia. In the final match against Indonesia we had needed to win to ensure our qualification through to the next round and the emphatic 6–0 victory was a great way for us to end the series and thank the fans for coming out and supporting us so strongly. We finished a point ahead of Iraq on the final ladder so we had done enough to qualify for the next round.

Our next opponent was Iran. While we had played them on the world tour in 1970, we still didn't know much about them these three years later. There was no television coverage in those days to keep track of international games so we had no idea what they had been doing. This had led Rale to go on a scouting mission over there before the series. I can still remember him bringing back photographs of the Iranian players and sticking them up on the wall in the training shed.

He told us to memorise the face of the player we would be marking or playing against.

Maybe the photographs worked because our team put on a great display in the first leg match in Sydney. There was a big crowd of thirty-one thousand people at the Sydney Sports Ground and the boys played so well that the eventual 3–0 victory was probably slightly disappointing. It's hard not to be happy with a 3–0 win but it really should have been a lot more. Of course, at the time we didn't realise how handy a couple more goals would have been to take into the return leg in Iran. No one had any idea of what was awaiting us in Tehran.

The return leg was a week after the first match so both teams ended up flying out of Australia on the same plane. I can still remember trying to talk to some of the Iranians about the match while on the flight. It was a strange situation, not just because we were in a confined space with a team with whom we were about to lock horns in one of the most important games of our careers, but also because of the scoreline. We were pretty confident because we were 3–0 up, but at the same time we knew the qualifier was not yet over. It was hard to know how to feel. The Iranians were probably thinking it was over for them but not wanting to give up without a fight either. That's what makes two-legged series so interesting because the mental side of the preparation becomes so important.

The first thing that greeted us when we stepped off the plane in Tehran was the sight of thousands of angry soccer fans. The funny thing was that they weren't there to heckle us—they had all turned out to demonstrate against the Iranian team because of their performance in Australia. The crowd was pelting everything they could lay their hands on at the Iranian team and, in the end, the police had to escort both teams out a back exit of the airport. Everyone was taken aback by the reaction of the home crowd because we realised the Iranian players would be keen to make sure the demonstrations didn't get any worse. We were all wondering what would happen if they were beaten at home.

Still, even though the Iranian team was in disgrace, it didn't stop the Iranian public from letting us know where their true allegiance lay. Everywhere we went in Tehran people would hold up four fingers for us to see. It didn't take us too long to figure out that they were letting us know that we were going to get beaten by four goals. None of us even wanted to contemplate that happening.

The culture shock on arriving in Iran wasn't too destabilising because the team had been there before in 1970. We had brought our own food and knew what to expect in terms of accommodation and training facilities. Unfortunately there was one major element that had changed since 1970 and that was a new massive stadium. The Azadi Stadium had been built on the outskirts of the city and had an amazing capacity of one hundred and thirty thousand. I was amazed by the sheer size of the place when the team went for a training run there prior to the match. It was daunting even with no fans in there, so my mind was immediately flashing forward to what it would be like full to the brim with fanatical Iranian fans screaming their support for the home side.

In the end nothing could have prepared us for the atmosphere in the stadium on game day. The noise from the crowd, was simply incredible. The sound was distinctly shrill, and piercing and I still don't know whether the crowd was making it intentionally or not. All I knew was that it was a sound like nothing I had ever heard before.

Players these days are used to huge stadiums and intimidating atmospheres, although I think even the current team would admit playing in Tehran is something else. We had not come from a background of playing in major overseas leagues every week. This was something completely new for us. The intensity, crowd and intimidation were all fifty times greater than we were used to. And there's no doubt it had an effect on us. In a sense it was frightening because we just couldn't communicate with each other. Suddenly our 3–0 lead didn't seem quite so large. To make matters worse the Iranian team came out like men inspired. They hit us with everything they had from the first minute and were all over us. Before we knew it, thirty-one minutes had elapsed and Iran was 2–0 up. We were completely rattled because it certainly hadn't been in our game plan to concede two goals within half an hour! Iran was right back in the contest. The one hundred and thirty thousand-strong crowd was going mad and their team was growing in confidence every second. We knew we were in big trouble.

In the end, it was probably only our team spirit, goalkeeper Jimmy Fraser and a bit of luck that saved us. Jimmy was brilliant and made some tremendous saves to keep us in the match. But the whole team battled to ensure that we didn't concede a third goal. It certainly wasn't pretty and we had our backs to the wall for most of the game, but we survived. It was one of the great strengths of our team that we would never give up and would always show grit and determination. Our tenacity saved us on many occasions.

We knew we should have won the first leg by more, so in a way it was a classical home and away series. People always wonder how a team can be so much on top at home and then go away and get absolutely thrashed. Well that's what happened to us and I'm still not sure why. At the end of the day you just have to hope the home advantage balances out. For us, our determination and spirit saved the day.

The team was excited about beating Iran but it was muted excitement because we knew there was one more hurdle to cross. The final qualification series pitched us up against one of our oldest foes, South Korea. While people always think of New Zealand as Australia's greatest rival, in reality there is probably a stronger rivalry with South Korea because we have played them so many times in crucial matches. In fact, the Socceroos were probably South Korea's bogey side for a long time because we always used to beat them. Our record against them was amazingly good and, although that has changed in more recent times, in 1973 we were confident about beating them. Unfortunately other circumstances intervened before the match even kicked off that would harm our chances.

Throughout the World Cup qualifying campaign, the more experienced members of the team, those who had been around for the previous World Cup attempt, had become increasingly concerned about what the financial arrangements would be if we qualified. Some of the players had made some tentative enquiries to the ASF about the matter because we didn't want to be left with a cheque for $13.27 like we had been after the last World Cup qualifiers. After all of our effort and sacrifice to get where we were, we understandably wanted to make sure we weren't going to be deprived of our appropriate remuneration. Even the newer members of the team were concerned, having heard the story of our payment for the 1969 qualification series.

Unfortunately the ASF kept postponing discussions until after the qualification campaign. They just wouldn't talk. So, in the week before the first match against South Korea in Sydney on 28 October we decided we would have to force the issue. A delegation of senior players, made up of Ray Richards, Manfred Schaefer, Peter Wilson, Ray Baartz, John Watkiss and myself demanded to see ASF president Sir Arthur George on the Thursday before the weekend match. The timing probably wasn't ideal but the official team list for the match had been given to FIFA by this stage and it couldn't be changed, so we knew we had some bargaining power.

I can still remember Sir Arthur and ASF general secretary Brian Le Fevre driving into our training camp at the Wahroonga Travel Lodge in a Rolls Royce. Brian is only a small bloke and it was a funny sight watching him steer the big car into the camp. However, it was the only laugh to be had for the rest of the day.

After sitting down with Sir Arthur and explaining our position, he told us that the federation was not in a position to make any financial commitments to the players. He did however give his word that the players would be looked after. It was the same old story we had all heard before. Sir Arthur had been appointed as ASF president quite late in the previous World Cup qualifying campaign and most of the troubles we experienced were already beyond his control by that stage, so we didn't hold him totally responsible for the poor treatment we felt we received in 1969. He was a successful businessman outside his role with the ASF and he also had a great public speaking voice and demeanour that always impressed me. In fact, I got on with him quite well. We believed he was being genuine in his promise to look after us, so we told him that we would have to take his assurances back to the players. I can remember him telling us to hurry because he had to be at a meeting in the next hour or so. It wasn't a great surprise to find him in a dark mood when we returned about two hours later.

Predictably, Sir Arthur's mood only darkened further when we told him that we couldn't accept his promise to 'look after us'. He was furious. Before he drove off with Brian in the Rolls, he told us to pack our bags and leave the camp. The match against South Korea was looking extremely doubtful.

The promise to 'look after us' might well have been enough for us at one stage but you have to remember how badly some of the players had been treated in the past. The delegation had taken Sir Arthur's promise to the boys and although the young players weren't that concerned about it, the older guys knew what could happen if we didn't get concrete financial arrangements in place. We really thought it was time to make a point. It wasn't simply about money, it was also about being treated properly for the effort and loyalty we had given to the game and its administration over a long period of time.

Some of us had actually started packing our bags to leave camp when Brian returned and summoned the delegation to meet with Sir Arthur again. It's still hard to believe that all this was happening two days before one of the biggest matches of our lives. He was now much more willing to deal with us. He explained that the ASF didn't know how much money they were going to receive if the team qualified but he promised to put the players on a percentage of the television rights and any other revenue. The team eventually decided to accept his offer.

In the end, I think we all realised that we had made our point. The thought of letting down both the public and ourselves by not playing was something none of us actually wanted to contemplate and it appeared that our message had been heard by the ASF. So we accepted their deal and the game was suddenly back on again. I actually have a great deal of respect for Sir Arthur and the job he did in organising the entire 1974 World Cup campaign and in subsequently promoting the sport in Australia. In some ways I wish I had got to know him better. Unfortunately, circumstances regularly put us on opposite sides of the fence.

The postscript to all the drama of that Thursday was that each player ended up getting paid probably the equivalent of a year's club salary for playing in the World Cup. While it still wasn't a huge amount of money, we were happy with it because it was recognition of the personal sacrifices we had made to get Australia there. It's important to realise that the World Cup was only just becoming the massive, worldwide media event that it is today so there simply wasn't as much money involved as there is now. The ASF has never been in a strong position financially either so the end result of our payment terms was a good one for both parties.

Making our point had, however, not helped our preparation for the match. Rale had already been worried that we weren't adequately prepared because the local competition wasn't in season and the team's last match against Iran had been more than a month before. The end result was that we had missed training and our focus on the match had been displaced. People's minds were elsewhere and I'm not sure if they returned in time for the opening match in Sydney.

South Korea had already eliminated Israel and Japan to get to the final qualification stage so we knew they were a team in good form. They were going to be a handful in any circumstances but given our lead-up to the match, they were only going to be tougher. The eventual 0–0 scoreline probably flattered us but was also not really unexpected given our disjointed preparation. Our team lacked its usual aggression and fire. The crowd of thirty-two thousand at the Sydney Sports Ground was no doubt as disappointed as we were and it was a classic case of the Australian team not being able to perform at home in big matches.

The Koreans had decided to man-to-man mark me in that match and I barely touched the ball. My opponent was only a little guy but he didn't leave me for the entire match. I thought he was even going to follow me into the change rooms at half-time! I absolutely hated being marked that tightly because it always made playing difficult. As a player, it meant you were never in any space and there was always added pressure on your first touch. I took being man-marked as a sign of respect but I never enjoyed it. My own performance and the result meant it wasn't a match I remember with any fondness but I'm sure the pay dispute had a lot to do with our average performance. It meant that we would have our work cut out for us in Seoul if we wanted to see the fruits of our labour in our qualification quest up until now.

Just how much work we had in front of us became strikingly apparent when we were 2–0 down during the first half of the second leg in Seoul. I was confident the team had regained its focus during the week between the two matches but the South Koreans absolutely massacred us in the opening stages. The home crowd was going berserk and the Korean players were feeding off the excitement. They were probably already planning their World Cup finals campaign after scoring the second goal. Luckily for us Branko Buljevic scored a goal for us almost immediately after South Korea scored their second goal. Needless to say, our goal changed the entire complexion of the match. It suddenly gave us some confidence and took a bit of the heat out of the home crowd.

It was a brilliant feeling when Ray Baartz scored the equaliser in the second half. We had come back from the dead and I don't think the crowd could quite believe it when we held on to secure a 2–2 draw. Unfortunately, in those days, away goals did not count as double, like they do today. Otherwise, Australia would have qualified on the away-goals rule, which means if scores are level after both games, away goals count as double.

The draw in Seoul meant another match needed to be played at a neutral venue and so the decider was played in Hong Kong. Although it didn't have the drama of the second-leg rollercoaster ride the team really played well. Our 1–0 victory was secured by a wonderful goal from little midfield dynamo Jimmy Mackay. It was an absolute cracker that flew straight into the top corner of the goal and I'm sure it probably even disturbed a few spiders that had been living there quite peacefully. The goal probably should be more recognised in Australian soccer because it was the one that put the nation into its first and only World Cup.

Amid the jubilation there was a sense of disbelief among the team after the match. After all our struggles it was hard to believe that we had actually made the finals. For me it meant that the ghosts of 1970 had finally been laid to rest and my own personal struggle to recover from my knee injury had not been in vain. We were going to West Germany!

The thrill of reaching the World Cup was made even sweeter on 1 January 1974 when I received a telegram informing me that I had been awarded an MBE for my services to Australian soccer. The news came out of the blue and was a dramatic boost to my spirits. It was the first time anyone had received such an award for soccer and it was special because I felt it was not just acknowledgment of my own efforts but also recognition of the game in Australia. It remains a highlight of my career and topped off what had been a satisfying phase of my football life.

Nowadays the World Cup is an international football extravaganza with blanket media coverage but back in 1974 things were markedly different. The World Cup was only starting to build up into the event it is today. Of course, we had some idea of how big it was, but in reality we really had no idea what to expect. We had never even seen the World Cup on television.

Everything about international soccer was pretty new for us in those days because the players simply didn't have that much knowledge about the world outside Australia. We certainly didn't know anything about the teams as there was no video footage of the teams that we could analyse and study like there is today. The East German players were a mystery, we didn't know anything about the Chilean team and we only knew some of the West German players by name.

Rale had more of an idea of what was awaiting us. He seemed to make a conscious decision that the team needed to be as fit as possible to compensate for some of our shortcomings in terms of skill and technique so he ensured that our preparation for the finals was extremely physically demanding and very well organised. In fact, the entire organisation of our World Cup campaign was very professional thanks to the efforts of Rale and the ASF.

On 21 May 1974 we kicked off our preparations by defeating Indonesia 2-1 in Jakarta. It was soon after that match that I was elected the team's vice-captain. It was a nice moment when the boys immediately chose me although I won't lie and say it erased the disappointment of not being captain.

After our brief trip to Asia we travelled to Israel and went into a training camp. We were situated right near the beach and every day Rale would have us running kilometre after kilometre across the sand. They were always long-distance runs because the first thing Rale wanted to do was build up our endurance. He had travelled over to see the East Germans play and had immediately been concerned that they would be too physically strong for us, so he devised a plan that he believed would make us as fit, if not fitter, than any team at the tournament. The plan started with the long beach runs in Israel. In fact, I don't think we saw the ball too much during our camp in Israel. We did play an international against Israel during our stay, however, losing 2–1 in Tel Aviv. That match was almost a reversal of what had happened in 1970 because on this occasion we were going to the World Cup and they had to be content with a morale boosting win. Obviously it wasn't the result we wanted but we weren't too worried. Everyone's mind was already on the big World Cup games ahead.

The team then spent ten days in Switzerland in a huge house in Zug, just outside Zurich. It was a wonderful place for us to prepare because it was always quiet and peaceful, with no distractions. I still remember that the people in the village made the most amazing chocolate and it was always a temptation after a long training session. The weather was also perfect, with Switzerland just entering spring. Switzerland was not one of the big European football nations but it still offered professional football set-ups, which meant we had good training pitches, goals, nets and dressing sheds; basically everything we needed. During our time there we played three matches against Swiss first division sides. We beat St Gallen 4–1 in Zurich, with Adrian Alston scoring a hat-trick, defeated Young Boys of Bern 2–0 and drew 0–0 with Neuchâtel Xamax.

Everyone felt fit and inspired during our lead-up games in Switzerland. We were given our first opportuntiy to train like professionals and were actually being treated like professionals for the first time in our lives, not in Australia, but on the other side of the world where football is the religion. We weren't 'sheilas', 'wogs' and 'poofters'—we were accorded the same respect as the greats of football. We would get up in the morning and all we would have to do was train or play football. That was it. There was no going to work or university and then desperately trying to make training on time. All our attention was focused on improving our skills, our fitness and our overall performance. The difference to our confidence and our performance was enormous. In fact, the lead-up games in Switzerland were easy to play because we quickly realised that the opposition was nothing special. Our players had grown up with the attitude that overseas football and players were superior to our own standard. In many ways they were because Australian players simply couldn't match the technique, fitness, tactical skill and experience that resulted from playing professional football. But we now realised it wasn't a question of talent or application; it was simply the difference between playing football for a living and playing it on a part-time basis and in Australia, we'd never had the opportunity to play football full time.

Having realised that we could compete at the top level, it was amazing how our confidence levels skyrocketed and we really began to enjoy the competition. When I look back on those three matches against the first division sides in Switzerland I think they were probably the three easiest games I have ever played, simply because I was feeling so sharp and on top of my game.

It obviously helped that I was fitter than I had ever been. In fact, I really don't think any of us could have been in better physical condition. By the time we arrived in West Germany we had been through about a month of preparation and Rale's fitness plan had worked wonders. He had built up our endurance and stamina in Israel and then put us through several matches in Switzerland to build up our match fitness. In between, we were constantly training and working to hone our skills. We didn't do any weights or gymnasium work like a lot of teams do these days, but we were extremely prepared for playing ninety minutes of football. I can remember Branko Buljevic coming out with one of the great lines from the many team meetings we had during the training camp in Switzerland. He said to Rale, 'Can you organise that we play the World Cup without the ball, because if we do we're going to win it!' He was probably right too. Either way, we certainly weren't going to lose because of inferior fitness, that was for sure.

The team spirit was also in excellent condition. The ASF was fantastic in agreeing to bring one of our former teammates Ray Baartz on the trip as a team manager. Ray had been viciously fouled during one of our warm-up matches against Uruguay only months before the World Cup. He was literally karate-chopped behind the play in our 2–0 victory at the SCG and nearly lost his life. After spending two days in hospital he was told that if he played again and got a knock he could die. It wasn't really much of a decision and Ray was forced to retire at only twenty-eight. He had already been thinking of retirement but to miss the World Cup was a huge blow. All the players in the team felt for him because he had been through all of the hard slog to get to the World Cup, going right back to Vietnam in 1967. Rale believed Ray was the best player that he had ever coached and there is no doubt that he was certainly one of the best players of my era. He had even gone over to trial with Manchester United in 1965. The ASF's decision to bring him to West Germany was a stroke of genius in terms of team morale.

There were similar feelings in the team for Bobby Hogg. He would have certainly been in the squad at the World Cup but he broke his leg in a club game two years earlier after going into a tackle with his national squad roommate Ernie

Campbell. It was an injury from which Bobby never really recovered. So much effort and hard work go into playing top level sport that injuries like that always seem such a cruel twist of fate. I knew better than anyone about that. But while we would have loved to have Bobby in West Germany as well, it wasn't possible to bring everyone along. The same applied to Terry Butler who had been the baby of the team for the past three years. Terry was Australian-born and played for Apia, and along with George Harris, I felt he should have been in the squad. The squad for West Germany was made up of three goalkeepers in Allan Maher, Jimmy Milisavljevic and Jack Reilly. It was a particular disappointment that one of the real heroes of the qualifying campaign, goalkeeper Jimmy Fraser, decided to pull out of the squad. Rale had promised Jack Reilly the number one goalkeeping spot in the side at the World Cup even though Jack had been unable to play in any of the qualifying matches. Jimmy was understandably upset and decided to stay at home and concentrate on his security business. He had probably done more than anyone to get us to West Germany so it was a real letdown that he didn't come with us. It was also disappointing that Ronny Corry, the inaugural Socceroos goalkeeper, wasn't selected for the team.

The defenders in the side were Col Curran, Ivo Rudic and my old friend Manfred Schaefer. What the boys in the team didn't realise then was that Manfred was going to attract star attention when we arrived West Germany because of his German heritage. He was literally mobbed by people wanting his autograph and was in constant demand from the German media. He really was the local boy returning home to a hero's welcome. The other defenders in the squad were Doug Utjesenovic, John Watkiss, Peter Wilson and Harry Williams. Harry was the only Aborigine in the team and had actually been first picked for Australia after only playing six club games for St George. He was a tremendous talent and a terrific bloke to have on tour. He played as an attacking left-sided winger and was one of those players who loved to entertain the crowd with fancy tricks and dazzling skills. All the boys used to call him 'Fancy Nancy' because he was always trying something out of the ordinary.

I was personally disappointed that my St George teammate George Harris wasn't selected for the trip. He had been in the team for a long period of time before we reached West Germany and I thought he was particularly unlucky not to make the final selection. George was the brother-in-law of Doug Utjesenovic and it was Doug who won the battle for the right back position in the World Cup squad ahead of George. But Doug was a skilful player, probably more at home as a libero where he could read the game and inject himself into attack. He was a fabulous passer and crosser of the ball with the outside of his feet. I believe it's worthwhile paying tribute to players who missed out, like George, because they put in just as much effort and hard work as everyone else but didn't get to enjoy the brief taste of football paradise that we did.

The midfielders in the squad were Dave Harding, Jim Mackay, Ray Richards Jimmy Rooney and myself. Jimmy was a real workhorse in the middle of the park. It seemed like he could run all day. I always thought he was a robot because he never seemed to stop. Jimmy was also good with the ball and he very rarely gave up possession. The other Jim in the midfield—Jim Mackay—was our qualification hero. He was one player who you could guarantee would lift in standard when he pulled on the green and gold for Australia.

Adrian 'Noddy' Alston, Atti Abonyi, Branko Buljevic, Ernie Campbell, Gary Manuel, Peter Ollerton and Max Tolson provided the team's attacking force. Scoring goals is always going to be tough in a World Cup but I thought we had enough good strikers, particularly in Adrian, Branko and Atti, to cause our opponents some problems.

It wasn't a huge squad but Rale was never a coach to use a big squad anyway. With Rale everyone had a fair idea of who was going to be in the team long before any match. There was never any 'down to the wire' decisions on who he would pick. So while there was pressure on some players for their place in the team, no one was under illusions as to what the initial line-up was likely to be. Despite the fierce competition for places everyone stuck together and even those players on the fringes did their bit for the team.

One of the most memorable things about arriving in West Germany for the World Cup was the security. As soon as we stepped off the plane there were armed guards and security officials everywhere. The terrorist killings at the Munich Olympics in 1972 had prompted the West German authorities to take every possible precaution to ensure something similar didn't happen at this event. Armed guards became our constant companions, never leaving our sides. I kept waiting to see if they would come onto the pitch when we played!

We never entered anywhere through public entrances and were always escorted through secured areas. We could have been rock stars the way we were kept away from the public. The team was even designated a couple of security officials who dressed in our team uniforms and followed us around wherever we went. They would carry big kit bags that actually had nothing in them except their machine guns. Luckily their bags never got swapped with any of ours.

Our base camp was at the Hamburg Football Club and our stay there was a revealing insight into the life of a top European soccer professional. The club was quite famous so we were all inspired by being there. The training centre was a real eye-opener and for part-time players, like we were, it was paradise because the facilities were amazing and everything we could want was laid on. The complex had accommodation residences, physiotherapy facilities, treatment rooms, huge baths, restaurants, lecture rooms, staff quarters and even a games room, with pinball machines and table tennis, where the team could relax. We were lucky even to have our own change rooms back in Australia, let alone all of these unbelievable facilities.

There were a staggering eighteen fields available for us to train on and they were all in perfect condition. We would use one field to train on one day and then the next day we would be shown to another pristine playing surface. It was beyond all our expectations. There were hundreds of balls given to us to train with and we even had our own 'Australia' bus that took us everywhere. Our time at the Hamburg Football Club was like getting to live in the penthouse for a couple of weeks after spending our whole life in the basement. I remember some representatives from Adidas taking us to their factory one day and handing out football gear to everyone. This was a big deal after coming from a country where a pair of boots needed to last you a year. I couldn't believe it, here they were just handing them out like chocolates. A seasoned professional probably wouldn't blink at these sorts of things, but for us they were so foreign. We even had special chefs cooking our meals. I felt that if someone were to pinch me I would suddenly be back kicking around the ball on a bumpy field in Sydney.

Unfortunately, the guard dogs and guys carrying machine guns surrounding our training camp ruined the scene somewhat. No one was ever allowed out of the camp alone and nobody was allowed in to see us. Most of the team had family or friends over to watch the finals and whenever they came to the training camp to visit we had to meet them in a special room out the front. My brother Geoff had come over to West Germany for the tournament and I can remember thinking it was as if I was in prison when he came to visit me. A club official would come to tell us that there was a visitor and then we would have to go out into the special visitors' room. In the end though the team didn't have any security problems and it was reassuring to know we were being looked after so well.

Most of the team was quite accustomed to playing amidst that sort of security-conscious atmosphere anyway. Our matches in Vietnam during the war prepared us for anything and even those guys who had not been to that extreme were used to doing it tough and playing in intimidating atmospheres such as Tehran. There was never any glamour when the national team travelled and we were never out hitting the town partying. When the Socceroos went into camp, we really went into camp. Our daily routine was training, more training and then bed by 10 pm. It wasn't glamorous but the guys were feeling so elated about being at the World Cup and enjoying the great facilities that the tedium of the same routine every day never really affected us. I don't think anyone really expected to be partying every night anyway and we all knew that having a good time could wait.

By the time the first match was scheduled everyone was itching to play. We had trained so hard that it seemed to take forever for the actual event to come around. We had been drawn in the same group as West Germany, East Germany and Chile. There was obviously never going to be any easy draw in a World Cup with only sixteen teams. Rale thought we had a chance of achieving a draw out of our first game against East Germany but he knew the second game against West Germany was going to be tough. He felt it was possible to win the last game against Chile.

The opening match against East Germany was played in Hamburg on 14 June 1974. Rale sent us out with the instructions of not opening up in the early stages and keeping things very tight at the back. The tactics worked and it was an encouraging 0–0 at half-time. I think everyone in the stadium was a bit shocked that we weren't three or four goals down. In fact, as the game progressed we became more confident about our chances of sneaking a result. Somewhat ironically, it was only when we started to open up and attack the East Germans that they scored. The East German goal was, in a cruel twist of fate, reported as an own goal scored by our defender Col Curran but the ball was clearly already over the goal line when he tried to clear it. The second goal was also scored on the counter-attack, going from their end of the field to our end in about three seconds. Just bang, bang, bang and the ball was in the net. I can remember the ball came in square from the right-hand side and the East German player, whose name just happened to be Streich (as in strike), just hit it. It was a difficult angle but the ball flew straight into the top corner. It's an old soccer saying that you're most vulnerable defensively when you are on the other team's eighteen-yard box. Well, that's exactly what happened to us. But there isn't much you can do about such shots, even at the best of times.

In the end we were happy with a 2–0 loss even though we probably felt we could have achieved at least a draw out of the match. The important thing was that we had proved we could match it with a top side in a big match. In that sense, I think the result immediately earned us respect from the public, the media and the other teams. People had been expecting us to get absolutely thumped and we had proved that we weren't imposters—we were a team worthy of respect.

Unfortunately I was feeling too sorry for myself after the match to give Australia's elevated reputation too much thought. During the second half of the match against East Germany one of their players had hit me in an over-the-ball tackle. It was the sort of tackle that regularly happened in those days but in this instance my foot was absolutely crunched. Players wore particularly long studs back then and as the East German's boot came over the top of the ball I kicked into it from underneath. The studs just went right through my boot into the top of my foot. I knew I was in trouble immediately. The pain was excruciating. To his credit though Rale let me remain on the field, as I wished, even though I was limping badly.

While I was warm I managed to limp around without too much trouble and I ended up playing out the entire game and was quite satisfied with my performance. It was only when we got back into the dressing rooms that the extent of my injury really hit me. I realised that I might not actually get back on the field for the remaining two matches and it was one of the worst moments of my entire career. After all I had done to get back in the team and to make it to the World Cup the thought of missing the next two games was just beyond my comprehension.

I treated the foot with ice and reduced the swelling as quickly as I could, but kicking the ball still felt like someone hitting me on the foot with a sledgehammer. There had been so much drama and emotion to get to this point in my career that I simply couldn't believe that this was how my World Cup would end. There was nothing I could do though, the injury was too painful and I had to tell Rale I couldn't play. It was one of the hardest things I have ever had to do and it was almost as big a disappointment as injuring my knee in 1971. In a way it was worse because of all the hard work I had put in to make the World Cup. I had resurrected my career after being told I would never play again and I was at the pinnacle of the sport. Now, suddenly, I was consigned to the sidelines again. It was a nightmare finish to my World Cup dream and it wasn't the way I wanted my Australian career to end.

The West German team was one of the favourites to win the World Cup but they were extremely disappointing in their performance in the opening match against Chile. Scraping together a 1–0 victory in front of their home crowd had not been what the adoring home fans were expecting. The West

Germans were crucified by the media for their performance. This was probably the worst case scenario for us because it meant that we had to play them when they were extremely fired up. Playing the West Germans, who would go on to win the World Cup, would have been difficult at the best of times but playing them when their pride was wounded and the whole nation was demanding a good performance from them was a particularly daunting task. We would have rather gone into the match with them having beaten Chile by four or five goals. At least that way there was a chance they might be slightly complacent.

Even though I thought Holland was the best team at the tournament, the West Germans were undeniably outstanding. They had a world-class team—right from goalkeeper Sepp Maier, defender Berti Vogts and midfielder Wolfgang Overath, through to the great Franz Beckenbauer and prodigious striker Gerd Muller. While everyone was intent on doing their best, I don't think we really expected to win the game. As it turned out the West Germans scored only twelve minutes after our match kicked off at the Volksparkstadion in Hamburg. A long-range strike from Wolfgang Overath beat Jack Reilly and the crowd of around fifty-five thousand people started getting behind the West Germans. There was always a chance that the crowd might have started to become frustrated with the West Germans if we could have held out for the first half, but the early goal put us well and truly on the back foot. The West Germans scored again through Bernd Cullman in the thirty-seventh minute and the match was effectively over. The famous goal poacher Gerd Muller scored the final goal and although we finished the game strongly, the scoreline remained at 3–0. It certainly wasn't a result to write home about but the West Germans had been expecting to beat us by six or seven goals, so our team was still proud of its efforts.

Some people have since criticised Rale for the Socceroos playing too defensively during the World Cup but I don't think they are being fair. It was Australia's first time on the world stage and we simply hadn't played at a high enough level or gathered enough experience to go out and take on East Germany or West Germany really aggressively. These were some of the best teams in the world and we were just learning what it was like to be professional. Realistically, trying to establish a defensive platform was the only sensible option we had. It would have been disastrous for the game in Australia if we had come out, all guns blazing, and been beaten by a huge margin.

The final match against Chile wasn't a memorable match in terms of football. It was played in torrential rain at the Olympic stadium in Berlin and was marred by a terrible tackle on our overlapping fullback Col Curran. Col was carried off the field on a stretcher with knee problems and then Ray Richards was sent off in the eighty-third minute in an incident of bizarre refereeing. Everyone thought Manfred Schaefer was being red-carded after he fouled one of the Chilean strikers, but the Iranian referee was actually pointing towards Ray. The referee had yellow-carded Ray earlier in the match but I don't think anyone was sure why he was sent off. The referee just seemed to lose control of the match. The situation probably wasn't helped by a demonstration by a group of students protesting against the governing regime in Chile. The demonstration stopped the match for several minutes and, unfortunately, didn't help our concentration. Playing with ten men for most of the game meant we were forced to play extremely defensive football. The game was never pretty as a result and we were happy with a 0–0 draw. It was Australia's first ever point in World Cup football and it was more than most people thought we would achieve.

The non-soccer public in Australia had predicted that we would get slaughtered. They were saying we would get beaten by fifteen goals once we got to the tournament and played against so-called 'real' teams. I guess I had become used to such criticisms by that stage but the comments were still deflating, considering some of the results the team had pulled off in recent years.

The criticism wasn't just confined to Australia either. I can even remember an article appearing in one of the German newspapers, *Bild Zeitung*, asking: 'Why have we got these Kangaroos at the World Cup... How have we ended up with this bunch of no-hopers at the world's greatest tournament?' If they had known what we had been through to qualify maybe they wouldn't have been so scathing but that sort of commentary was reflective of Australia's position in world soccer at the time. We were literally nobodies and had been regarded as such for as long as I had played the game. I think all the players realised that this might be our only chance to change people's minds.

On the final ranking table after the World Cup, we finished ahead of Haiti, Zaire and Uruguay. It was a reasonable result by anyone's standards but by Australia's it was amazing. In a way the team had performed above expectations just by making it to the World Cup. As part-time players we knew we were entering the tournament on an uneven playing field. Even when I returned to Tehran in 1997 to watch the Socceroos play Iran I wondered how we ever came out on top under those circumstances back when I was playing. I think the same thing about our away victories against South Korea, Greece and Israel. The stadiums, the conditions, the crowds and even the way our opponents played were foreign to us. In retrospect the team did a great deal better than it ever should have done considering the circumstances under which we played.

Yet, by the same token, the entire experience opened our eyes to what could be achieved under the right circumstances. It was the first time we were treated as professionals in every aspect and, even more than that, it was the first time we were treated as someone important. It felt great not feeling like we were somehow inferior to the athletes who were viewed as Australia's sporting heroes—the rugby league players, the cricketers, the tennis players, the Australian Rules stars. People at the World Cup respected us as athletes and sportsmen and this was something we had certainly never experienced back among the general community in Australia. It gave the entire team an injection of confidence we'd never received before.

My good friend Manfred Schaefer was the real hero for us at the World Cup. He had migrated to Australia as a young East German boy of eight years of age and here he was, twenty-two years later, playing against East and West Germany and receiving accolades such as one in a German press article begging Australia to allow him to play in front of Franz Beckenbauer instead of German central stopper Schwarzenbeck.

The Germans quickly changed their attitude towards us during our stay. They soon became fans of the way we played, the team spirit we showed and the enthusiasm we displayed in every circumstance. Even our behaviour and attitude off the pitch left them impressed. So much so that the same newspaper which had criticised our inclusion in the competition printed an apology after we were knocked out. Part of that apology read:

> When Australia was drawn on January 5 to play in the same group as our national team, everyone laughed. What could these greenhorns be dreaming of playing East and West Germany. They will get thrashed... We would like to apologise for the statements we made. We were wrong... The Australians have been a wonderful squad. Thank you very much and goodbye and good luck, Aussies.

It was a great moment for us and a real vindication of all the effort the boys had put in. I felt like we had done our bit for the game back in Australia because the tournament was a giant step towards Australia being recognised as a football country. The team's performance generated an enormous amount of goodwill and interest, not just in Australia, but also around the world. I was told one of our matches attracted four hundred million viewers across the world. While that figure is probably dwarfed by some of the audiences watching sport today, back then it was enormous. That was why Rale and the team took our role as ambassadors for the country so seriously.

The match against East Germany was to be my last international for Australia. I was aware that my time in the green and gold was running out but I had thought I had at least three games at the World Cup left in me. To finish like I did was not how anyone wants their international career to end and I'm still disappointed about it. But after the tournament there was also a sense of relief. All the team was given a couple days off in Berlin after the Chile game and I realised how long it had been since I had enjoyed some time just to relax. The team didn't hold any special group celebrations after we were knocked out because we had been together for so long that everyone felt the need to split up and go their own separate ways for a while. We had spent more than a month in close proximity to each other and by that stage we all needed some time apart. I simply decided to go out to dinner in Berlin with Manfred and we visited a few clubs later that night and had a few drinks. We didn't indulge in any wild celebrations and I was content to sit back and relax. The next day I wandered around Berlin and explored the city with Manfred, Ray Richards, Ernie Campbell and Dr Corrigan. The simple pleasure of the beautiful sights of Berlin and having a day free from football made the day particularly wonderful. The World Cup had been such a long campaign and taken so much out me, both physically and emotionally, that I finally had time to reflect on whether I wanted to keep playing.

For some us in the team the end of the 1974 World Cup campaign was the culmination of eight years of struggle, often with little reward. And, of course, in those days when a player reached thirty they were almost expected to retire anyway. You certainly knew you weren't going to be around until you were in your mid-thirties. The players today have every incentive to stay involved because of the financial rewards offered but it was a different situation for us because jobs or careers simply took precedence around the age of thirty. So, for a lot of the players, including me, Germany was the end of a long journey.

My decision to retire was also made easier because I knew the team had done as well as it could. I think everyone realised that we couldn't have done any more than we did. It just would have been too much to ask for us to knock off one of the big football countries. It would have been one of the greatest sporting upsets of all time. The players had done everything they could to prepare, had committed themselves totally to the cause and had met all their responsibilities, not only to the game but also to the nation. So, while some players from the World Cup team played on, several like John Watkiss, Jim Mackay, Manfred Schaefer, Ray Richards, Jack Reilly and myself decided that it was time for a new generation of players to take up the green and gold. We had done our bit.

12

Goal of a Lifetime: A Dream Finish

⚽ WHEN FRANK AROK left St George to return to Yugoslavia at the end of the 1972 season, he appointed Mike Johnson as the new manager. Mike came from a good playing background having been a part of Jim Kelly's famous 'Kelly gang' team at South Coast United. He had played for the South Coast in one of the great grand finals of the New South Wales competition when they upset Apia 4–0 in front of thirty-three thousand people at the Sydney Sports Ground in 1963, a real red-letter day for football in Australia.

However, Mike was more of an intellectual coach than many other coaches were and he didn't seem to hit it off with the boys. Whereas some coaches are basically just trainers, in the sense that they simply physically prepare players for matches, Mike wanted the players to think about every aspect of the game—all of its tactics, psychology and subtleties. Unfortunately he arrived at St George at a time when the team was full of experienced players who were perhaps less open to Mike's coaching techniques than younger, less experienced players might have been. In fact, I think Mike would have been great with a bunch of younger guys. But, as it was, the team never really responded to his style. Also in Mike's defence, 1973 was a very disruptive year because of Australia's World Cup preparations. St George had such a big contingent involved in the World Cup that team selection was always a problem for him. Even though Mike did the best he could as coach, many of the players' minds were too busy thinking forward to West Germany. The team didn't perform too badly by finishing third in the league, but a better performance was expected of us considering the quality of the players we had.

It was much the same in 1974 when the World Cup became a reality. Mike was still coach but it wasn't an easy period for the club because there were so many players concentrating on making the Socceroos squad that it was easy to lose focus on the local competition. I know I certainly did. I had a feeling that there would be changes at some stage that season because St George never took too long to react to a sustained run of poor results. Still, I wasn't expecting the offer that greeted me when I returned from the World Cup in West Germany.

Although I had done a FIFA coaching course during my enforced injury lay-off I had never really considered coaching as a serious option once I returned to playing again. There just didn't seem to be the opportunity in Australia. The game simply didn't enjoy enough support and the clubs didn't have enough money to employ full-time coaches. It really wasn't a viable career path. Frank had been the first full-time manager in the Australian game but his appointment did not have a dramatic impact on changing the coaching scene in Australia. For most clubs full-time coaches simply weren't viable. It wasn't simply a case of there being no money to hire full-time coaches but more that coaching was just not a profession in Australia; it was not yet regarded as a worthy full-time occupation or pursuit. So when Alex Pongrass called me into his office and told me that the coaching job at St George was mine, I was genuinely taken aback. He sat me down and explained that things couldn't be allowed to continue the way they were going on the field and told me, in no uncertain terms, that I had to take the job for the sake of the club. Alex's skills as a negotiator surfaced again because he knew I was always going to agree to anything for the sake of the club. How could I refuse a club that had given me so much?

Still, even when I decided to take the job I was not looking at the position with a long-term view. It was already midway through the 1974 season when I took over and I had fourteen weeks to try and turn the team around. That was as far as I was thinking and in the end I accepted the job as a challenge rather than as a career change. I would still play and I knew I had a good relationship with all the boys. I had always been a talkative captain on the field anyway so I thought my role as coach really would not represent that big a change for me. I had been captain of the teams I had played in from youth grade right through to the senior national team and it was a role I always relished. It was something that seemed to come naturally to me and I was never hesitant, even as a young man among much older, experienced players, to take on the captaincy. In fact, I think being captain helped my performance on the field because I enjoyed the responsibility so much. I never had a problem with any of the players in the various teams that I captained; never any dramas or fallouts with the way I led the team and I was always conscious of making sure the boys were all pulling in the same direction.

My childhood friend John Chegwyn bumped into former South Vietnamese national team coach Karl Heinz Weigang in Vietnam some years ago. Karl had been coaching all over the world, including South Vietnam when I had led the Socceroos against them during our tour of Asia. When John mentioned my name to Karl, he replied, 'I remember Johnny well, he was a captain who had complete control of his team on the field.' It brought a smile of pride to my face when John told me the story because it had come from someone not involved with the team. It also brought back to me just how much I enjoyed and revelled in leading the various teams I captained.

Of course, my favourite aspect of captaincy was the opportunity it provided me with to serve as a voice for soccer in Australia. Leading St George and Australia gave me a platform from which I could publicise the game and discuss ways of improving it. It meant I had a profile from which I could try and help the game move forward.

I have often argued that being a player–coach is easier than being a coach because you are able to influence the match every moment in a direct way. A non-playing coach is limited in a sense because he can really only yell out comments from the sideline and gather the team together at half-time. A playing coach, however, is on the field all the time, talking and communicating with his players and he has a real advantage. That was certainly my experience anyway. The only problem with the player–coach role is the strain it places on you both physically and mentally. I soon realised that coaching is extremely tough and dealing with everything going on in the team was simply exhausting. By the end of the season I was totally spent. The dual role had really caught up with me.

The club president, Les Bordacs, was overseas when I was appointed coach of the club and so my day-to-day dealings with the administration in 1974 were with the vice-president Imre Nagy. As acting president in Les's absence, Imre proved to be a blessing for me in that first year in charge. He was always available and always helpful when I approached him with a problem and he gave me one hundred percent support from the moment I was appointed. I wasn't surprised because Imre was just a tremendous supporter of the club, even employing players at his printing factory. I will always be grateful for the particular support he showed me during that time.

My exhaustion was also eased somewhat by the results we achieved. The team made and won the grand final after a terrific run that saw us win twelve from fourteen games.

Unfortunately one of the games we lost was the Cup final against South Sydney Croatia but the run of success boosted us from mid-table in the league to near the top of the ladder. It was an incredible turnaround in form and something of which I am still proud today. Having said that, we always had a good team and I think it was primarily a matter of ensuring everyone was mentally prepared and on the same wavelength.

In the grand final against Hakoah I scored the last goal in our 4–2 victory. It was a wonderful game, full of excitement and drama, and it had finished 2–2 in regulation time. In the second minute of extra time though we scored to go to a 3–2 lead. A match report written by Andrew Dettre in *Soccer World* describes what followed:

> Five minutes later we saw the goal of the season. John Warren stole the ball inside his own half and, with nobody running off the ball, burst through on his own, passing two defenders in the process. When he got to about 20 metres out, and being pushed towards the left, he sliced the ball with his right, curving it, just like a croissant, just inside the post; something a Rivelino or Tostao can imitate at their best.

It was one of my most memorable goals and I decided to substitute myself straight after I scored it. I can remember heading into the dressing rooms and collapsing from exhaustion. I was so tired and yet so happy with what I had achieved. It had been an amazing match, we had done incredibly well just to get there, and I had scored one of the best goals of my life to seal victory.

I didn't even bother to watch the end of the match. I just stayed in the dressing room and it was during those last few minutes of the game that I decided my playing days were over. I'm not sure what it was but something at that moment told me it was the right time to retire. I was only thirty-one years old, young by today's standards, but sitting in the dressing sheds by myself I felt I had achieved all I wanted to do. I had been to the World Cup so there wasn't the desire of international football to keep me going any more and I had won everything there was to win in the New South Wales competition.

I can remember newspaper reporter David Jack coming into the rooms after the match and I said matter-of-factly to him, 'That's it, I'm finished.' We had won the grand final and I had scored a great goal to clinch the match with my last touch. What better way could there be to go out?

The next day the headlines of the *Sydney Morning Herald* match report read 'Saints Fairytale Finish' followed by the report of my retirement:

> The fairytale rise of a reluctant coach Johnny Warren ended in a dream as St George carried off the 1974 soccer championship. Fittingly it was a superbly executed goal by Warren which settled the issue beyond doubt. Speeding past flagging Hakoah defenders, Warren curled the ball round the advancing Hakoah goalkeeper, Martin Coe. As it looped into the net Warren collapsed to the ground, emotionally and physically spent, as his exultant teammates crushed him into the turf. Rising shakily and widening the eyes, Warren headed straight into the dressing room. It was an electric moment and as Warren walked from the field the crowd stood as one to applaud a fine sportsman.

Also, in the *Sydney Morning Herald* leading sports writer and columnist Rod Humphries gave me a humbling endorsement when he described the end of my career, in his article 'Epitome of a Sportsman':

> It is one of the great sporting success stories of our time that Warren came back from the operating table to play in the World Cup finals and to lead St George-Budapest to the 1974 Soccer championship... John Warren, the All-Australian boy... the son every mother hopes for... the man every sportsman should live up to...

(Little did I realise at the time that I would become great friends with Rod down the track. His main sporting interest was tennis in which he played on the fringe of the top level during the Newk and Roche era. His playing partner in those days was Roger Waugh, father of Steve and Mark. Rod, as a writer and journalist, covered boxing, rugby league and soccer. His boxing time coincided with the rise and fall of Lionel Rose, whose biography he wrote. The next time I bumped into Rod was after my appearance on 'This is Your Life' in 1978 for which, unbeknown to me, Rod was the writer. Just before Rod left Australia to marry a Texan woman, Lynne, and take up a position as media and public relations director of Lamar Hunt's World Championship Tennis based in Dallas, his last words to me were 'Call and see us' which I have done almost annually ever since. Rod and Lynne have introduced me to American professional and college football, basketball, US soccer, baseball and to every conceivable corner of Texas. In fact, their eighteen-year-old son Justin was signed by the Houston Astros as a professional baseballer in 2000.)

David Jack's article, 'A Goal of a Lifetime, then Johnny Warren Quits!' also appeared in the *Sun* on the same day, part of which read:

> Yesterday Johnny Warren scored one of the most spectacular goals ever seen at the Sydney Sports Ground ... ran straight off the field to be replaced by a substitute ... and decided he would never kick another Soccer ball ... Warren will have serious talks with the Saints committee today ... He will tell them he wants to quit as a player to concentrate on the job he really wants ... full-time manager of the team.

Needless to say, the club wasn't too happy with me for announcing my retirement to the press without talking to them first but, in my defence, it was an on-the-spot decision. A week later my great teammate Manfred Schaefer decided to do the same thing.

Probably lurking in the back of my mind was the fact that

I had seen so many players become bitter as they got older. I had seen good players coming back through second grade or third grade and simply losing their enjoyment of the game as their performances failed to match up to their expectations. I can even remember being unhappy at the way Australian cricket captain Bill Lawry was treated when he was dumped. The one thing I knew was that I wanted to finish my playing career when I chose, not when someone decided my time was up. Although I still miss playing the game, I have never regretted the timing of my retirement. It really was a dream way to finish my career. I went out right at the pinnacle.

When I made the decision to retire I was already thinking about ideas for my next year as a manager. I was in charge of the entire coaching program, including decisions about players, contracts and tactics. While most things were done in consultation with the various staff, I was the person who had the ultimate responsibility. I soon convinced Manfred to coach the team and I brought my old friend Vic Fernandez back from New Zealand to look after our youth set-up. My brother Ross was coaching the third-grade team and I was feeling very comfortable with the way the entire coaching system was working. I think everyone at the club was also fairly content with where St George was at that stage. Andrew Dettre had given me a major boost after the grand final when he wrote in *Soccer World*:

> Warren should take most of the credit for the incredible revitalisation of the side after he took over. This was their tenth win in eleven games. The Saints do not have to search for Arok's successor anymore. The Warren/Schaefer duo should be able to manage and coach the team for many years to come.

Before the start of the 1975 season I took the boys up to Jindabyne for pre-season training to prepare them at altitude.

The team was so fit and strong when we returned that we dominated all the other teams in the pre-season Ampol Cup. The team, you guessed it, finished second in the league behind Apia but went on to beat them in the grand final. It was sweet revenge for me and meant that in one-and-a-half seasons as manager coach I had seen my team take home two grand finals. I was extremely proud of the team and I was happy with my own part in the club's success.

Beyond the results on the field though, I was more excited with St George's off-field football set-up. We were so far ahead of every other club in terms of producing our own players, implementing a professional management structure and entrenching ourselves in the district. There were so many things going for the club that the future seemed overwhelmingly bright.

It was at the height of the club's success that St George and I had a falling out. The club was progressing so well in 1975 that I wanted to move the structure of the football operations to another level. I was considering giving up coaching the senior team and creating a new general manager role for myself, which would have involved looking after the marketing of the club, building up the supporter base and primarily ensuring that the club would grow and prosper in the future. It was something I was particularly enthusiastic about because I loved the club and wanted it to lead the way for a new and brighter era of soccer in Australia. I thought I could establish a structure that all the other clubs in Australia would be keen to imitate. Unfortunately, a friend broke my confidence and informed the club committee about my plans before I was ready to tell them. It wasn't a case of me trying to keep the plans secret but I wanted to have everything worked out before I went to the committee and made a proposal. My falling out with the club was a messy and regrettable period of my life and I realise now that my inexperience and ambition probably fuelled the explosive situation. I tried to change the club too quickly because I had my own ideas of where the club should be heading and I didn't stop to consider how the old guard at the club might view my actions. Still, I believe that the club perceived my actions in the wrong way and people reacted without hearing my side of the story. Looking back I realise there was blame on both sides.

It was a particularly sad period of my life because St George really was *my* club. We were one and the same for such a long period of time. Even though Canterbury gave me my first chance at playing senior football, I spent thirteen years at St George and it was a huge part of my football education. I played my best football there and enjoyed some of my best experiences on the football field wearing the St George colours. I also recognised that the club had done so much good for the game in Australia during my time there. They were the first club to develop playing links with Asia. They were one of the first clubs to begin producing their own players from junior ranks while other clubs continued to bring in players from overseas. They played a major role in the establishment of the national soccer competition and they willingly gave up their Hungarian ethnicity that meant so much to them to try to establish themselves in the broader community. They built a social club, a stadium and established junior soccer development programs in the St George region. I had played for the club, captained the club, coached the club and even worked for the club, so St George was my entire life. I simply wouldn't have believed it could happen if someone told me back in 1975 that one day St George would not be a focal point of Australian soccer. St George, though it still exists and competes in the New South Wales state league, bears no resemblance to the old St George club as I knew it.

13

Football: The First Sport to Go National

⚽ ONE OF THE great things about the Socceroos making the 1974 World Cup was that we helped put soccer on the map in Australia. The numbers of kids playing the game increased markedly after 1974 because of the exposure our participation in the tournament had given the sport. The team had now been prominent back page sports news in Australia for a couple of weeks and even made the front page of the newspapers on occasion. Most of the players became household names back in Australia, giving young soccer players someone to admire and emulate. I think people also began to realise just how internationally popular soccer was and what Australia had been missing out on.

Still, among all the positives, there was one worrying thought that stuck with me after the World Cup. I couldn't help wondering how Australia was going to get better and begin competing with the rest of the world on the same terms. I knew that everything that had gone towards making the 1974 team successful had still not been enough to compete on equal footing at the highest level. At the same time, I knew we had played to our utmost capability and I didn't think our preparation could have been any better. So the nagging question I was left with was where did that leave Australia as a soccer nation? How should we go about creating an environment where our soccer players are able to not only match it with the best in the world but also to defeat them?

I have no doubt that the players in the 1974 World Cup team would all have made it overseas as professionals if they were given the same opportunity that our young kids enjoy today. They were simply the best players of that particular era and, as it was, they were good enough to give a good showing against the best in the world. But the system they had grown up in and the competitions that they played in didn't give them the opportunity to reach their potential. The World Cup brought home how important it was for Australian soccer to be given a complete makeover.

Even today, after our failure to qualify for the 2002 World Cup, there is still a great misconception that the national club competition will suddenly take off in Australia when the national team finally qualifies for another World Cup. Many people believe that all the problems at club level will be solved once the public sees the national team competing against the best in the world and is exposed to the thrills of the international game. There was a similar thought process in place when Australia qualified for the World Cup in West Germany in 1974. However, while the World Cup certainly increases the general level of interest in the game, it is not the magic answer to all of soccer's problems in Australia. People slowly realised this after 1974.

There was no immediate effect on the state league competitions when I arrived back in Australia from the World Cup in 1974. The competitions had become increasingly predictable and it was usually easy to pick which teams would finish in the top four because there were several big clubs who were continually dominant. Attendances, rather than growing after the World Cup, were actually dropping in 1975 because longstanding supporters were quite literally dying out and not being replaced by a new era of fans. There were twelve teams in each state competition and the standard of play was simply too diluted because all of Australia's top players were spread far and wide geographically and only played for their local teams. The World Cup might have given the sport publicity but it did not send people rushing out to catch a glimpse of the domestic competitions. The competition at the state level was in desperate need of an overhaul.

It was visionaries such as Alex Pongrass at St George and Frank Lowy at Hakoah who soon realised that the World Cup by itself had not been enough to increase soccer's popularity in Australia. They began to appreciate that something extra needed to be done to take the sport to another level and cash in on the impetus provided by West Germany. The current system of separate state based leagues simply wasn't going to attract the public's attention and support, particularly after the glamour and excitement of the World Cup. People had appreciated the World Cup because it was the best teams playing the best. That was part of the reason why the public became so interested in Australia's participation in the tournament. Unfortunately, the existing state league system in Australia was not producing enough quality football to match up to the pulbic's expectations of a high standard of play. It became obvious that soccer needed a competition where the best were playing the best week in and week out.

The answer was the creation of a national competition. The national league would create a new elite level of football competition in Australia, in which only the best players in the country competed, and it would bring together players from interstate to compete on a regular basis. The separate state based leagues would no longer be the highest level of soccer in Australia. The national competition would also cater to interstate rivalry by pitching city against city and state against state and would give soccer some prestige from which to sell itself to the mainstream Australian public. It would also serve as a way to create a better career path for young footballers by giving them a level of competition to strive towards and therefore an incentive to keep playing the game.

Of course these are the underlying principles of all the national competitions, like the National Rugby League and the Australian Football League, that exist today. But at that stage there was no other national sporting league for club sides operating in Australia for soccer to model itself on. There was a national competition for cricket, the Sheffield Shield, but it pitted state against state rather than being a national competition between the club sides of different communitities and regions. In considering a national league, soccer was literally breaking new ground and again proving to be the leading innovator on the Australian sporting scene. All the national competitions that now exist followed soccer's lead.

Unfortunately, being the pioneer in terms of forming a national sporting competition meant the process wasn't easy or particularly smooth, and initially there was a lot of resistance from various clubs to the proposals put forward. I experienced such resistance first-hand because I, as manager/coach of St George was one of the people making phone calls to the various clubs in an attempt to get things moving in 1975 with our president Alex Pongrass and Hakoah president Frank Lowy as the initiators of the quest.

The very first meeting about the proposed national competition was held at the St George club on 5 April 1975. Representatives from West Adelaide Hellas and Adelaide City, Lions (Brisbane), Brisbane City, Adamstown (Newcastle), Marconi, Hakoah, Western Suburbs, Apia and St George were there. However, there was not one single representative from Melbourne. The meeting was convened by Alex and Frank and continued for four hours before the delegates signed a resolution of intent in relation to the formation of a national competition. But even though things were well and truly underway it was agreed that it wouldn't be possible to have everything in place for the 1976 season. It was a sensible decision because there was a great deal of politics and administrative matters to be sorted out, first of which was convincing the Victorian clubs to join. They were unsure about the competition, primarily because of its origins in New South Wales, and needed convincing that they were going to have a significant stake in the league. Creating a national competition from the ground up necessarily meant that some clubs and some people, who thought they should be involved, wanted more of a say or missed out completely. There was a great deal of politics involved in deciding who would be in charge, which teams would be involved and which states they would come from. Getting the administration right was a major task and the final product was far superior as a result of waiting until 1977 to start the league.

By 1977 the National Soccer League, Australia's first national sporting competition for club level sport, was ready to kick off. The league was made up of West Adelaide Hellas, Adelaide City Juventus, Mooroolbark, South Melbourne, Footscray JUST, Heidelberg, Canberra City, Sydney Olympic, Hakoah, St George, Marconi, Brisbane City, Brisbane Lions and Apia. Socceroo skipper John Kosmina would score the league's first goal playing for West Adelaide against Canberra City at Manuka Oval.

The league proved a great success in its early years and serves as a tribute to the vision of those clubs who were involved in its formation but sadly my own involvement ended at the end of 1975 when I fell out with St George. While the clubs set about organising the details of the new competition I was travelling around Australia and busying myself elsewhere as a freelance coach. As fate would have it, I would eventually return to take part in the opening match of the new NSL but it was a strange and twisting path that led me there.

After severing my ties with St George in 1975, I had to make some decisions about my future in the game. I soon decided to go out on my own and so I started running coaching clinics around Australia. I was able to negotiate arrangements with dozens of local soccer associations to provide a soccer course for the kids, parents and coaches involved in the game in each particular area. The course wasn't simply a coaching clinic where I would show the kids how to kick a ball. Instead, I tried to provide a total package which would improve everyone's knowledge and appreciation of the game. I would usually speak about my time in the game and my philosophy on playing soccer and then, as well as holding a coaching clinic for the kids, I'd also hold a separate clinic for the local coaches. I always thought that actually coaching the coaches was more important than having one session of ball-kicking with the kids because it is the coaches who impart their knowledge and skill to the kids, day after day, long after I've been there. I would also hold an information seminar with parents, explaining the game to them and convincing them of its benefits to young children. Any other time I had would be used appearing at promotional events and publicising the game to the town or community I was in at the time.

I travelled extensively throughout Australia, places as far as Alice Springs in the Northern Territory and Broken Hill in western New South Wales. I visited Cairns, Port Macquarie and Wauchope and dozens of other communities along the way. I also coached more locally in the Sydney area. It was an eye-opening time for me because I began to truly appreciate how much love for the game there was around the country. Everywhere I went, the kids seemed to genuinely love playing soccer and kicking the round ball. I can distinctly remember going up to visit an Aboriginal community outside Alice Springs and being amazed at the joy the young kids got from just kicking the ball around. So while I wasn't making a great deal of money from my freelance coaching, it was keeping me afloat and still providing me with a sense of giving something back to the game.

It was in the early part of 1976 that I received a phone call from two Fijian soccer players who were in Australia after winning a competition run by the *Fiji Sun* newspaper. They had been sent to train with two Australian clubs but didn't feel like they were being looked after properly here and had been given my number in Sydney when they had contacted the *Fiji Sun* about their problems. The connection between myself and the *Fiji Sun* went back to the year before when I had visited Fiji to help out my brother Ross with some of his business interests there. During my brief stay I had met some of the people in the local soccer community and had done an interview for the newspaper. I had enjoyed my stay in Fiji but I never thought it would lead to me being asked to look after two young guys back in Australia. I didn't have the heart to say no when they rang me.

The two boys, Anand and Jimmy, ended up living with me for the remainder of their stay. I trained them every day, took them to various matches, showed them videos and basically gave them a brief soccer education. I actually enjoyed it because they were very enthusiastic and keen to learn about the game. They obviously had some kind words to say about me when they returned to Fiji because I was asked to come over to Fiji and conduct some coaching clinics, first by the Nadi district football association and later by the Fiji Football Association. As it turned out, I spent some of my most unforgettable times as a coach in Fiji.

I must have spent more than six months coaching there on an irregular basis in 1976; irregular in the sense that I would coach for a couple of weeks in one part of Fiji and then return to Australia. The Fijian soccer authorities would then call me up and ask me to return for another couple of weeks. The arrangement suited me and I coached at every school in the entire country during that year. It seemed like every member of each school would come out to watch the clinics I ran, even the teachers. There would be kids hanging from trees to get a better view of the skills I was demonstrating. It was all quite basic, such as teaching the correct passing technique, but the locals loved every minute of it. The clinics were so well received that I was soon asked to coach district teams and, at one stage, was even drafted to take charge of the national team.

Taking charge of the Fijian national team was a brief but extremely rewarding time for me because Fiji had somehow arranged to play a match against English first division side Tottenham Hotspur. Spurs was one of the better sides in England in those days with players such as Ralph Coates, Steve Perryman and Martin Chivers in their line-up, and they would have been formidable opposition for most teams around the world, let alone a small island in the Pacific like Fiji.

I was in the Nadi district coaching when the match was confirmed and the Fiji association immediately came to me and asked if I could help with the team's preparation. They were understandably very nervous about playing the famous English club, thinking they were going to get beaten by twenty goals. I didn't hesitate to agree to help out because I realised that you don't get to coach against a top English team too often in your life.

I already knew a lot of the players in the Fijian national team from coaching the various district teams anyway, so it was not a huge leap into the unknown for me and I certainly wasn't complaining when I arrived at the national team training camp on Mana Island. It was a beautiful resort island and I began to appreciate why Tottenham were coming such a long way to visit. I spent a week there with the team before the match and it was one of the most beautiful places I have ever been. Things were never more idyllic for me than coaching soccer on a picturesque resort island.

I knew I had a job to do though. My aim was to make sure that the team was competitive because I obviously wasn't going to be able to turn the guys into world beaters in a week. I decided to concentrate on building up everyone's confidence and immediately ridding them of any fear they had about playing Tottenham. Some of the Fijian players were petrified about playing against an English team and I knew it would ultimately affect their performance. Of course, it wasn't surprising because even in Australia at that time playing against an overseas team was a bit intimidating. For the Fijians, who had even less access to the world of international football than we did, it was like playing against someone from another world. I made sure I kept on reminding the players: 'They only have two legs, they are not going to be used to the heat and we are going to train to be prepared for what they are going to give us.' I wasn't lying to them either because that was exactly how I saw it.

I knew Tottenham was very much a crossing team in the sense that their game plan was to get the ball to the flanks and whip it into the penalty box for their strikers. So I made sure the team practised dealing with cross after cross after cross. We worked on tactics as well, always totally focused on preparing for the opposition. This was very much the philosophy I had been taught when I did the coaching course in Malaysia and it seemed the only sensible approach to take in preparation for a one-off match. It wasn't difficult for me to train the team because I became very good friends with them. It was clear that we wanted to do well for each other. That sort of team spirit is always important and made my job so much easier and pleasurable.

The match against Spurs really couldn't have gone any better. Fiji played as well as could be expected and only lost 3–0. The team was so prepared for a barrage of crosses that Spurs posed little threat from out wide. Fiji's marking was spot on and they managed to nullify Tottenham's main route of attack. Of course the heat was a leveller too. The English players seemed to almost pass out in the hot, sticky conditions. Even Australian teams struggle when they play in Fiji so you can imagine how the Spurs guys were feeling after coming over from England. I thought it was a tremendous effort from my team, and everyone involved was elated. It is probably one of the few times when losing 3–0 feels like winning the World Cup.

I actually became involved with the Fijian national team again as part of their preparation to play Australia in Suva in early 1977 but unfortunately didn't get to see the match because of other commitments. It turned out to be a huge upset with the Fijians knocking off the Socceroos 1–0 and, while I wasn't in charge of the team, I like to think I played some part in the victory. Not that I wanted the Socceroos to lose of course, but the Fijian team had a special place in my heart and I was still really happy for them.

I had no great plans to get back into coaching at a senior level during my time freelance coaching around Australia and in Fiji. I was quite content working at a grassroots level and trying to influence the young generation of players. Things changed however when I received a phone call from Steve Doszpot while I was coaching in Alice Springs. Although I didn't know Steve, his dad had been a big supporter of St George and I was familiar with the Doszpot name. He didn't beat around the bush and told me straight away that the national league was definitely starting next year and that a team from Canberra had been admitted. Would I be interested in the coaching job? Here I was, up in northern Australia coaching juniors, and I was suddenly being asked to coach a senior team thousands of kilometres away in the nation's capital! It was an out-of-the-blue proposition and I wasn't really sure whether I was interested or not. I knew I had little to lose though so I agreed to fly down and see for myself what the set-up in Canberra was like.

During my coaching stint at St George there had always been tremendous pressure on the team to win. Obviously that pressure always ultimately rests on the shoulders of the coach.

As long as the team won, played well and brought home the title the club was happy with you. That all went with the job description. But while it was a simple enough equation to grasp it was obviously extremely difficult to actually achieve. It meant there was constant pressure in every game the team played. Of course with the great players, wonderful support and excellent set-up I had had at St George there was a certain balance to it all, but it was a tough environment nonetheless.

When I arrived in Canberra I immediately discovered that I was walking into a completely different situation. This was a club simply trying to establish itself and winning matches wasn't nearly as important as making sure the club itself laid some deep foundations in both the local soccer community and the national competition. All the people involved with the club, blokes like Steve Doszpot, Theo Moulis, David Dillon, Hal Leslie, Pat Stanley, Peter Vidovic, John Ward and Peter Windsor, were also extremely enthusiastic and keen to make sure the club was a success. They were real soccer people who just wanted Canberra to be part of the big time. It was a refreshing change and I think their enthusiasm rubbed off on me.

When I met with the club officials they decided to take me to lunch. I can remember going to lock the car and being told that there was no need. I'm not sure if I locked the car or not but I quickly realised I wasn't in Sydney any more and began to appreciate that Canberra had a few attractions that I hadn't really considered before. After lunch (the car was still there when we came back) we decided to take a drive around Canberra and passed by the site where the Australian Institute of Sport is now located, in the suburb of Bruce. Back then there was simply nothing there and it was quite literally just a sheep paddock. When I was told that there would be a major stadium there within the next twelve months I just smiled and nodded to myself, disbelievingly. I had heard it all before.

The first day I was in Canberra I also ran into a guy called Billy Smith. He was an Englishman from Newcastle and he later ended up being the Canberra team's physiotherapist and team manager. He was a terrific bloke and he was so excited because he had heard I might be coming to coach. I went with him to have a pizza and I can still remember him singing 'We're gonna win the league, we're gonna win the league!' This was before I had even made up my mind to take the job, let alone put a winning team together. But that was the thing that struck me about Canberra. Everywhere I went people were excited about getting into the national competition and making a real go of it. There was no other national competition for Canberra teams to compete in so this would be the city's first shot at the big time. There was a real buzz about the place.

But while everyone was so positive in Canberra there was one big problem. It was the same problem I have always encountered with soccer in Australia. There was simply no money. The bottom line was that taking the position wouldn't simply entail coaching a national league side. I would also have to serve as director of coaching for the entire Australian Capital Territory. This would entail taking charge of the entire coaching program in the region, effectively meaning that I would have responsibility for ensuring the development of the game, particularly at the junior level. It was a big responsibility and no NSL coach would dream of doing it these days. However, I wasn't totally dissuaded. I've always felt it was my duty to ensure that the future of the sport was being looked after. The real problem was that I wasn't sure I would be able to build and coach a national league side simultaneously.

I was genuinely impressed with what I had seen in Canberra and the feeling remained with me just as strongly when I returned to my home base in Sydney. I knew the position would be a huge challenge for me and markedly different from what I had done before, but I was still excited about it. It wasn't something I was ever one hundred per cent sure about doing but in the end I decided to accept the job and see what happened. From a stable existence at St George I had gone to

Fiji, to Alice Springs, to Broken Hill and somehow ended up in Canberra.

I remember turning up to one of the first training sessions as coach of Canberra City and someone asking if there were any balls around. Everyone immediately looked at each other and, of course, no one had actually brought any balls to train with. It certainly wasn't something I had thought I would have to worry about and I guess everyone else thought the same. Unfortunately that was just how things were at the start. There was plenty of enthusiasm and people were always willing to help, but the club itself simply wasn't ready. It was a completely new organisation that had decided to build a team from scratch and while it had a name, a group of administrators and a sponsor, it had none of the hands-on elements that are necessary for sending a good soccer team out onto the park each week. The club quite literally had nothing, including, I might add, players.

I had met the team's major sponsor, local car dealer Brian Pollock, when I had first arrived in Canberra and the club officials had told me that the sponsorship was thirty thousand dollars a year for three years. This was the figure I was using to try and pull a team together and I was quite happy with the sum. I would have liked more but I was confident of creating a reasonable squad. I already had a couple of St George players that I wanted to recruit and they had expressed some interest in coming to Canberra City. I wanted them to form the heart of the team so that I could then attempt to build the rest of the squad around them. But about a month into the job, when the players from St George were nearly ready to sign, the club told me they had made a mistake. The sponsorship was actually thirty thousand dollars *over* three years. This was a massive difference to the original sum I believed we had in sponsorship and the alarm bells in my head immediately started to ring.

I arrived in Canberra around November in 1976 and the league started in March the next year. With the Christmas period in between, there wasn't a great deal of time to build a club from scratch. My new budget had forced me to drastically change my plans and I started looking more closely at the local competition. Attracting players when you have a limited budget is never easy and this was certainly the case in Canberra. Even the local clubs wouldn't let us buy the players we wanted. Players like Baz Giampaolo and Walter Valeri were simply priced out of our league. It wasn't a case of us not being willing to pay the money; the money just simply wasn't there.

I have always been a supporter of giving young players a chance though and I knew there was a lot of talent in the region, so my next step was to trawl through the youth competitions and identify some talented youngsters. It didn't take long before I recognised the talent in three guys, Danny Moulis, Mike Milanovic and Steve Hogg. They were only young at the time but they became an integral part of the team in the first year of the NSL and later went on to play for the first Young Socceroos team in the qualification for the first World Youth Cup in Paraguay in 1979. As fate would have it, Danny went on to run the Canberra Cosmos and Mike went on to coach the Cosmos for a brief period.

But I obviously needed more than a couple of good young players if I wanted to be competitive. You can't build a team around youth alone and I knew I needed a few senior players with some experience. Before I arrived, the club had signed Ron Tilsed from South Africa. Ronny was a youth team goalkeeper at Arsenal when they won the double in the 1970–71 season and had also played for England at the European Youth Cup in Prague in 1968 when they beat the Soviet Union in the final in a penalty shoot-out. He had gone to South Africa with a number of other English professionals at that time to play out his career. While the South African league was a professional competition, it was not recognised by FIFA for political reasons, so we were able to get players from South Africa without paying a transfer fee. It was a lucky break for us and handed the club a much needed lifeline.

Ronny was an excellent goalkeeper but had probably not been in the right environment to succeed in England. He was at Arsenal in the era of Charlie George and the glamour and fame of the team probably didn't help him concentrate on playing football. I always thought he needed to have someone like Mark Bosnich sitting on the substitutes' bench to make him play at his best. He was invaluable for the Canberra team in those early years in any case.

I should pay tribute to Ronny because he has been a great mate of mine ever since my time at Canberra City. Although I have met thousands of people through football in my lifetime I have struggled to regularly stay in touch with most of them. But Ronny and I have remained firm friends ever since Canberra and I probably see more of him and my old Socceroos team-mate Adrian Alston than I do of anyone I met through the game. Adrian played a few matches for Canberra City as a guest player during the 1977 season and he was a very similar character to Ron. I can remember driving with Ronny to the Canberra Airport to meet Adrian and I said to him, 'You'll like this bloke, Ronny.' As they are both very outspoken, life-of-the-party characters they hit it off immediately.

A day after Adrian arrived at the club in 1977, I drove him and Ronny down to the New South Wales town of Griffith for a coaching clinic. When we drove into the town there was a huge crowd of journalists and reporters milling around the hotel we were staying at. As soon as we saw them, Adrian piped up, 'You could have warned me, Johnny. I wasn't expecting this much media for my arrival'. Of course, the media were actually in Griffith covering the murder of prominent anti-drugs campaigner Donald Mackay but I'm sure Adrian would have liked to think that his arrival at Canberra City could create such interest!

I remember Ronny taking me aside one day at training and telling me about a player he knew that was playing in South Africa who would be a great addition to the team. This sort of thing tends to happen a lot in football and it never seems to work out but, because Ronny was an experienced player, on this particular occasion I took his word for it. The player in question was Tony Henderson, the very same Tony Henderson who would go on to captain Australia. Not a bad signing when you consider I had never seen him play and the club didn't pay a transfer fee. Tony is probably one of the best two-footed players I have ever seen. His technique for hitting long balls, passes and shots was amazing. I don't think I have ever seen a player as consistent as he was in striking the ball. As soon as I saw him playing I realised he was the type of player around which a team could be built. (As I had done at the end of my playing career, Tony later scored a goal with his last kick in football, albeit a penalty in a penalty shoot-out win for Marconi over Sydney Croatia in the 1988 grand final.)

After Tony arrived, we signed other players. Ivan Gruicic came from Melbourne Croatia and John Stoddart came from St George. John's brother Brian also came out from South Africa bringing another player John Brown with him. We then managed to get Roy Stark on a free transfer and persuaded Jimmy Cant, who eventually went on to play for Australia, to sign. Bit by bit we put a team together. It was a slow process and I was still desperately trying to get players from anywhere and everywhere but, by the time the first game came around, I was confident that I had a competitive line-up.

The team's first game in the new National Soccer League, and my first game in charge, was played at Manuka Oval in Canberra against West Adelaide in front of around two thousand people. We lost the game 3–1 but were pleased with the crowd and how the game had been played. Throughout the entire season our goal was to make sure we were competitive and although we eventually finished second from the bottom of the league I was still happy considering our preparation. We were never easy beats or out of our depth.

It wasn't as if the league was a poor standard of football either. In those days there were no Aussie players going overseas to pursue more lucrative football careers, so all the country's best players were playing in the national league and most of the clubs had very stable playing rosters. This was exactly how people like Alex and Frank had envisaged the new football competition when they formed the league. However there was still a definite pecking order. The big clubs like Marconi and Sydney City held an advantage over the rest of the field in terms of finances, structure and support and they dominated the competition as a result. That was probably why no one ever really expected us to finish in the top half. In the end, the results themselves were not as important as getting the club started and making sure we were a competitive team. I knew we had achieved that objective after our first year.

Things were more stable at Canberra City in the 1978 season. One of the big differences was that the team began playing at the new Bruce Stadium. When I had first arrived in Canberra I had not really believed the guys who told me a new stadium would be built, because these projects tend to have a way of dragging out past their anticipated date of completion. However they were spot on in this case and a wonderful new stadium was ready for us to use in the 1978 season. It turned out to be the perfect home for the team and amazingly our first game at Bruce drew seven-and-a-half thousand people. This turnout was incredible for soccer in Canberra and demonstrates the importance of having good facilities. Suddenly everyone was talking soccer in Canberra.

I tried to boost the playing strength of the team by bringing out three boys from Argentina and exploring every possible avenue for introducing new talent to the club. I ended up with a mix of players from everywhere. I can remember my house may as well have been a hotel because I had players staying with me the entire time I was with Canberra City. The club simply couldn't afford to put them up in a hotel and so I would simply take them back to my place. I can't imagine it happening today but there weren't many other options at the time. Luckily, my responsibilities as director of coaching hadn't lasted long because the board soon realised how much effort was required to coach a national league team. Because of the time involved, I simply wouldn't have been able to do both jobs at once.

Throughout my time in Canberra I always realised that I was probably two or three players short of having a side that could make the finals. Unfortunately, there was just never enough money or anyone who was willing to put their hand in their pocket to allow me to buy the extra quality that the team needed. Quality players simply don't come cheap and I guess all small clubs realise that fact very early on and try and make do with the best players they can find with their limited resources. It is frustrating though when you know your team is reasonably close to success. As it was, the team drew eleven of its first thirteen games in 1978. It was a remarkable record but while we were not losing, the fact that we were not winning either meant that it was an extremely frustrating period for everybody concerned.

Our home match against Marconi at Bruce Stadium was the perfect example of our season. A great crowd of around ten thousand people turned up because Marconi was clearly the best team back then, with Roberto Vieri, the father of current Inter Milan star Christian Vieri, running their midfield. But we played some inspired football that day and were in control for most of the match. The crowd really got into the game and when the chant of 'Canberra, Canberra' went up I thought the whole stadium was going to fall in. It felt like I was in South America for a moment. However, regardless of the emotion of the crowd we couldn't convert our dominance into points. We had all the possession and played well but could still only manage a 0–0 draw. I guess that's just the way football goes and it summed up our season. Even with the disappointment of the result it was still a big day for the club. The team played well, there was a big crowd and the atmosphere was electric.

The Canberra City team's performance just fell away in the last twelve games of the 1978 season. One of the reasons was that we didn't have a large enough squad. Any good team needs depth to cover injuries, suspensions or any other unfortunate circumstances and we didn't have it. When we lost Danny, Mike and Steve to the Young Socceroos for six weeks it disrupted our performance on the field and affected the team's performance as a whole. While I was proud that we had the highest representation of any national league club in the Young Socceroos, losing three players for six weeks cost us. I know other clubs have suffered a similar fate in more recent times.

What often happens when smaller clubs enjoy some form of success is that the big clubs begin sniffing around their players. It happens all over the world and it began to happen to Canberra City in 1978. Marconi became extremely interested in Tony Henderson and several other Canberra City players started receiving offers. Even I was approached by Sydney City and South Melbourne to take up a position with their club. These offers require careful consideration and they are always distracting to players and I'm sure these circumstances conspired to take away the team's focus and concentration during the later part of the season. The team simply lost its way and finished the season badly.

My record at Canberra City actually pales in comparison to what I achieved at St George but the funny thing is that I still feel I did a better job at Canberra. I won two championships in two years at St George yet my performance as coach was far superior at Canberra City. It sounds strange but I guess that's what makes judging a coaching career so subjective. Looking at results on their own is superficial. Performace comes down to a whole range of factors that aren't always apparent from a points table. At Canberra I had to deal with players not getting paid. I had to try and attract players from all over the world to a team with only limited finances. I had to play my boys against far superior teams. I had to ensure the club was built on strong foundations and ensure it became a club worthy to compete in the national league. It is one thing to be a good coach when you have good players, but you really are tested when you are facing teams with better players. That is a new and different challenge all together. So when I reflect on my time at Canberra I look back with pride at the role I played in getting the club up and running.

It was a mutual decision of mine and the Canberra City board for me to leave the team at the end of the 1978 season. The board decided that they wanted me to abandon all the promotional and public relations activities that I had been involved in for the past two years and simply concentrate on coaching the team. I wasn't too happy with the proposal because I had spent a great deal of time building up the profile of soccer in Canberra and I thought the board were trying to undermine my position in the local community. The situation was slightly awkward for me at the time because I was primarily negotiating with two board members, Charlie Perkins and Theo Moulis, both of whom I considered close personal friends. Things also became more complicated when I was offered a position by Sydney City. In the end, Canberra City and I simply decided it would be easier for us to go our separate ways. There was no acrimony. It was just a case of both of us heading in different directions. I was quite happy to see my assistant and good friend, Vic Fernandez, take over the coaching job at Canberra

City and my own move back to Sydney would eventually prove to be the right decision for me.

Canberra had been a great experience for me though and I still have a soft spot for the city. I felt like I was leaving the club in good shape and so I wasn't worried about leaving anyone in the lurch. I had been the manager, the public relations man, the media man, the promotions man; I had provided a home for many of the players and acted like a father for some of the younger guys. It had not simply been a case of turning up for training a couple of nights a week; it was an all-encompassing commitment to the team, the club and the region. I don't think I could have given any more of myself.

I always felt happy with the effort I had put in to nurture the region's talent. There were now three international youth players around which a team could be built and the club's organisational structure was well established when I left. At the end of the team's second year in the national league, the local basketball officials approached the club to ask our advice on setting up a club for their own national competition. They wanted to follow the same model that soccer had and I took it as a real compliment to the club and the code. The crowds were solid at that stage too and the future looked fairly bright. Perhaps I would have liked another shot at taking the team to the finals but all things considered I was comfortable with my decision to leave. It was quite an ironic decision though because as soon as I moved, the property I had my eye on in Canberra at Gold Creek came onto the market and I decided to buy it. It was a beautiful piece of land on the rural outskirts of Canberra. I simply fell in love with the place. My decision to buy the property with my brother Geoff was also a business move. Geoff and lifetime friend John Chewgyn and I thought the place would be an ideal venue where junior coaching clinics could be held.

The early years of the national league were fantastic times to be involved in Australian soccer. Match attendances were good and I think the Australian public got a real insight into why soccer is so popular overseas. They were now watching a higher quality, well-supported and properly administered competition and it was proving to be compelling entertainment. The league was a truly national concept and areas such as Newcastle, Canberra and Adelaide really broadened the previously dominant Sydney/Melbourne focus of the game.

There always seemed to be something new happening back then in terms of teams trying new marketing ploys and strategies. Some teams brought out famous international guest players, such as Malcolm Macdonald, Charlie George, Bobby Charlton and Kevin Keegan, and they were a huge success. At Canberra City we managed to get Peter Marinello, the first million-pound player in Britain, to come and play for us. Peter was labelled as the next George Best when he left Motherwell to play for Arsenal but, as is often the case, he never made the most of his potential. He was a big star though because he was crafty, fast and exciting. I can remember Ronny Tilsed telling me one day that we should try to bring him out to Australia because he would draw a big crowd. We did and it worked beautifully. It was that sort of time when everyone was excited and trying different things to capitalise on soccer's newfound stature.

Unfortunately though, the impetus created by the new national competition didn't last. I don't have all the answers to the problems that have beset the league since but I think the downhill slide began when the administration became a bit complacent. They stopped updating the concept and allowed the competition to stagnate. Soon it was being overtaken by competitors copying its original ideas. Soccer had been an innovator and a pace-setter, but when it needed an injection of new life, nothing happened.

14

The New York Cosmos

⚽ BACK IN 1975 I had teamed up with Socceroo coach Rale Rasic to start a series of soccer coaching schools in the school holidays. Coaching schools where parents paid for the services of high-profile coaches were very much an accepted thing in the United States at that time. Rale and I were the first people to introduce the concept in Australia. There had certainly been coaching clinics for kids in Australia before 1975 but in those days there was no cost involved. The players participating in the clinics simply didn't charge to attend functions, to sign autographs or to coach kids. It was just considered part of soccer players' involvement and role in the game.

Rale and I actually started from the same perspective but gradually realised it was time to implement coaching on a commercial basis. It wasn't so much due to a need for compensation for our time and effort but really because our primary goal was to deliver a better service to young, aspiring soccer players. We knew that with some money coming in to the clinics, we could offer a properly structured course which covered aspects of the game that weren't normally properly taught to young Australian kids such as technique, tactics, fitness, prevention of injuries and the history of soccer in Australia and throughout the world. We wanted to go beyond just being a child-minding course, as many soccer courses had been treated by parents, and provide a real football clinic.

Our clinics were soon being held at Englefield stadium in Dural, Sydney, during school holidays. We would invite players from the state competition, and even current and former Socceroos, to help out so the kids could meet some of their heroes and to lend the program some added prestige. The strategy obviously worked because hundreds of kids attended and the clinics continued, in one form or another, for another five years. I gained a great deal of enjoyment out of the clinics and I felt like I was helping to improve the standard of play in Australia and strengthen the game's popularity at grassroots level. After a time though, Bill Englefield, the man who owned the stadium, wanted to take the idea further. He was keen to invest more money to develop extra facilities at the stadium, including residences where the kids could stay while they attended the clinics. Rale was supportive of this extra investment but I was cautious about investing my money into building facilities that were located on land that I didn't own. So when a decision had to be made, I decided to leave Rale and Bill to push forward with their plans while I went my own way.

After leaving the partnership with Rale, I established my own school holiday coaching courses that would continue to run from the late 1970s right through to the early 1990s. I teamed up with my former Socceroo teammate Ray Richards and he helped me establish the 'Johnny Warren Socceroo Academy'.

While the coaching camps were initially based in Sydney, they later expanded to Canberra. Over the years, I had more than ten thousand kids attend the camps and stay at my rural

Gold Creek property on the outskirts of Canberra I had bought in 1979. I held coaching camps there between 1980 and 1992. I don't think anyone could have asked for a better place to go to learn about soccer and enjoy some country living. The course was designed as a combination of soccer coaching and a week-long farm holiday. We would train three times a day but there would also be barbecues, bonfires, sheep shearing and kangaroo-feeding. Many of the kids had never enjoyed these sorts of outdoor things before and it meant they had an excellent adventure for a week because the focus of the camps was not on soccer twenty-four hours a day.

The average day would begin with a physical training session before breakfast and then move on to a technical session before lunch, concentrating on soccer skills and tactics. In the middle of the day we would visit different tourist attractions in Canberra, such as the War Memorial, the Mint or Parliament House, and then in the afternoon we would split the boys into teams and have a mini World Cup. The boys would use the facilities at the Australian Institute of Sport every night and then come back to the property to watch videos of great players like Pelé and Maradona. It was usually their first introduction to some of the world's best players and the other coaches and I decided to encourage the kids to watch these players so that they would gain an appreciation of the importance of skill and technique. We thought it was important for them to realise at a young age that without skill you couldn't become a top soccer player, so any videos or footage we showed were always of great players and their abilities with the ball. On other nights we would discuss the Socceroos or the history of the game around a big bonfire. I always tried to make sure I provided a fun environment in which the kids could learn about the game.

There were some very talented kids in those camps and several times we arranged for the best two players to be taken on the trip of a lifetime to the Pelé Coaching Camps in the United States. Not only would they get to attend the famous coaching camp in upstate New York but they would also be taken to places like Disneyland and Knott's Berry Farm for a bit of an adventure. They were even lucky enough to be given a helicopter ride over New York City. It was a very big deal for the kids and it was always great for me to see how much they enjoyed it.

The first time we decided to award such a trip to the two most talented kids things didn't quite go according to plan. I had about five coaching centres running at the time and I was really busy moving between all the centres and trying to give them all equal attention. It meant that I would get the other coaches together to choose the winners and they would let me know who they had chosen when it was time to announce it. One of the names that I was told on the first occasion we awarded the trip was 'Okon'. When I got up to announce the winners to all the kids I looked down the list for the name and found 'Klaus Okon'. So I went straight ahead and called out the name. As soon as the name left my lips though I realised that there was another Okon just below Klaus on the list. That other Okon just happened to be the future Australian captain, Paul Okon.

The coaches had obviously spotted Paul's talent very early and decided to award him the prize. I had mistakenly called out his brother Klaus. Even though Klaus was a superb player, it was already apparent that Paul, who was only eight or nine at the time, was going to be something special. Even at such a young age he had everything needed to make it as a top player. Once I had made the mistake though I didn't have the heart to renege on Klaus's prize. It just wouldn't have been fair. Little did I know that Paul would go on to play all over the world and captain Australia. Looking at the situation now, I'm sure Paul won't mind that his brother, who has helped him in his career got the trip anyway. Hopefully he won't demand that I take him on a helicopter ride over New York! Needless to say, I checked the names a bit more thoroughly after that.

The coaching camps were very demanding and, like most things in soccer in Australia, they were always underfunded. I never made a great deal of money out of them but I always hoped they helped a lot of Aussie kids enjoy the game and become more skilful. I like to think they had some influence on the game's current standing in Australia which is something far more important to me than financial rewards. I have always felt that it is important to instil the right technique in players at a young age and give them an appreciation for the intricacies of the game. There have been countless occasions when adults have come up to me and said they came to one of my coaching clinics or I visited their school when they were young and it still gives me a thrill because I have always wanted to give something back to the game. Many clubs now run their own coaching clinics and I take pride when I think back that Rale and I, and people who gave us their invaluable assistance and support, were really the pioneers.

During one of my visits to the Pelé Coaching Camps in New York, I was introduced to Pelé's personal coach and manager, a fellow Brazilian called Professor Mazzei. He was a lovely guy and I got on very well with him. Pelé was no longer playing for the New York Cosmos at that stage but he was still associated with the organisation and during one of my conversations with Professor Mazzei he told me that the Cosmos were coming to Asia in 1979 to play some friendly matches. He thought I should try to organise a game for the Cosmos in Australia as it would be no problem for the team to hop over for another match while they were in the region.

The thought of bringing the Cosmos to Australia immediately excited me because they had such a huge profile in the late 1970s. It is quite amazing now to think that twenty years ago they were drawing massive crowds and fielding some of the world's best players in the United States, a country people don't immediately associate with soccer. They were even averaging more than fifty thousand fans for their matches at Giants stadium at one stage. I realised this was a great opportunity to show the Australian public a really big team full of international stars. It was the sort of chance that the Australian public didn't get very often.

Although Pelé had retired, the Cosmos still had one of the world's biggest stars on their playing list—German World Cup hero Franz Beckenbauer. There were not many bigger names than him in world football so I knew his name would attract interest just on its own. The team also had the Italian Giorgio Chinaglia, the Englishman Dennis Tueart, the Brazilians Francisco Marinho and Carlos Alberto, the Iranian Andranik Eskandarian, the Dutchmen Wim Rijsbergen and Johan Neeskens, the Yugoslav Vladislav Bogicevic and the American Rick Davis. It was a tremendous mix of international talent and I really thought it would appeal to Australia's mulitcultural make-up.

When I next met Professor Mazzei he took me to meet with representatives of the company that owned the Cosmos, Warner Communications. They were quite keen on adding Australia to the itinerary because it seemed to make good business sense given they were already touring Asia. They explained that it would cost fifty thousand US dollars plus travel and expenses to bring the team out to Australia. It was a large amount of money in those days and my initial optimism was immediately dented because I knew it would be difficult to find someone willing to take that sort of financial risk in Australia.

When I returned home from New York I was working for NSL club Sydney City. I wasn't there in a coaching role but the owner Frank Lowy had wanted me on board after they changed their name from Hakoah to Sydney City to help ease the transition from a so-called ethnic club to a so-called Australian club. Frank had realised that the club needed to change their support base to attract the mainstream and I was brought in to help promote that change. Hakoah was a

Jewish-based club but the support they enjoyed after the immigrant boom was simply not being renewed in the late 1970s. I can remember Frank saying to me, 'John, our biggest problem is that our support is literally dying out. We have more supporters in Rookwood Cemetery than we do at the games.'

During my time at Sydney City the club actually ran a very successful competition in the *Sunday Telegraph* that gave the public the chance to enter suggestions for a new nickname. The winning entry would win a trip to the FA Cup final and we literally received thousands and thousands of entries. By far the most popular nickname was 'Slickers', so the team became known as the Sydney City Slickers. It was certainly a far cry from Hakoah.

Because I was working for the club I took the opportunity to approach Frank and his partner Andrew Lederer about the offer to bring out the Cosmos. Being businessmen, their predictable response was 'how much?'. When I told them the amount, they immediately suggested that I offer the Cosmos half that. It was again exactly what I had been expecting. The problem for me was that I knew it wasn't a negotiable deal. The Cosmos were a highly professional organisation and they weren't interested in doing deals. The fifty thousand US dollars was a flat fee and they didn't travel for less. When I broached the subject again with the team's management I wasn't surprised when they explained that the fee wasn't negotiable.

I wasn't completely deterred though and I went to see Australian Soccer Federation president Sir Arthur George. I wasn't really too surprised when he said it was too much money for the federation to risk but I was still disappointed. I thought the event would be a sure thing. How could matching up some of the best players in the world against the Australian team fail to attract a large crowd in Australia? No one seemed to share my confidence though and, in the end, all I got from Sir Arthur was his blessing that the federation would support me if I could set the match up. Other than that, I was on my own.

After meeting with Sir Arthur I had really run out of options with the soccer administration so I decided to use the newspaper column I was writing in the *Sunday Telegraph* at the time to bring the situation to the public's attention. I explained why I thought the event was a sure-fire success and lamented the fact that no one in Australia was willing to fork out the money to bring the Cosmos out here. It was really my last desperate appeal for support and I was surprised when I received a response.

It was about a week later that a German man named Ulrich contacted me. He explained that he was the catering manager at the Hilton Hotel in Sydney and was part of a group called International Artists. They were involved in staging all the international shows at the Hilton Hotel. There were four other people involved in the group, Ralph Lynch, Christine Finke, Ian Franklin and Ron Kitchen, and Ulrich explained that they had brought out many big-name entertainers to Australia in the past but were now interested in expanding their business to sport. The idea of staging the Cosmos had caught their attention.

I agreed to meet with them and was impressed by their enthusiasm and interest. I sensed that they would bring a different and more professional approach to staging the event. I then went back to Sir Arthur to see if the situation might change with my new associates in tow and we might get some financial support from the ASF but again all I left with was his blessing to arrange the match against the Socceroos. After that meeting I was left with the impression that if I could pull it off, I would have a job for life.

So I told International Artists we were on our own and we started organising the match. We managed to provide enough financing through the combined contributions of our contacts and it turned out to be one of the most exciting times I have had working in football. I was working with new people with innovative ideas and a fresh approach to staging a soccer match and it opened my eyes to how much more could be achieved in staging high-profile sporting events in Australia. I was there as a soccer person but these other people were from the entertainment industry so we were all learning from each other. It turned out to be the perfect combination.

I was able to drag in other people, such as my old school friend John Economos, to help promote the game with the ethnic press and the soccer community, while the others arranged mainstream advertisements, posters and promotions. Many of the methods of promotion were ones that soccer had never used before in Australia. I arranged and appeared in television advertisements with the Cosmos playing in the background, there were posters plastered all around the streets of Sydney, there were radio promotions and we even paid for advertisements in the newspapers, which was very uncommon in those days. We even employed famous publicist Patti Mostyn who had arranged tours to Australia for people such as ABBA to ensure stories about the match were given front- and back-page prominence in the mainstream media. It was all revolutionary stuff for soccer.

Having a publicist was of vital important because, although I was growing increasingly confident about the event, the soccer media were very negative about the match. They described the event as a circus and were adamant that it wouldn't succeed. Similar comments have probably been more justifiably made about more recent soccer events, such as the visit of Manchester United and the FIFA All-Stars, but the scepticism wasn't fair in the case of the Cosmos. We were intent on making sure the match was a first-class event, with all the top players competing and the event organised properly.

I think the media may have been sceptical because we announced that the game would be played on 24 October 1979 at the Sydney Showground. There was immediately a lot of bad publicity about the decision because it wasn't really a soccer ground and the media didn't think it was suitable for the match. Although they had some valid points, we had thought long and hard about where we would stage the match and the Showground was the best option. It must be remembered that there was no Sydney Football Stadium (SFS) in those days. The old Sydney Sports Ground stood in its place, running east to west on the site where the SFS now runs north to south. The problem with the Sports Ground was that it only had covered seating for three thousand people. We were already up for quite a lot of money bringing the Cosmos out and the decision to run the event in as professional a manner as possible had also required a hefty investment. We had made sure the Cosmos were put up at the luxurious Sydney Hilton, VIP lounges were set up at the game and even the dressing rooms were refurbished to top-class standards. It was pure luxury in comparison to my experience with soccer and it was simply unheard of in Australian soccer at that time. It meant, however, that we would be under extreme financial pressure if we could only pre-sell three thousand tickets because there was always the prospect of rain and we couldn't really afford rain insurance.

While considering our options the question came up, why not stage it at the Sydney Showground? Soccer internationals and club games had been played at the ground in the past but it was known as a poor arena from which to watch the game. The real problem was that the spectators were too far away from the field. It was a typical showground in the sense that there was a circular trotting track around the outside of the actual playing surface and this always meant that a rectangular soccer field was a long way from the crowd. Still, on the other hand, the real advantage of the Showground was that it had twenty thousand covered seats. The capacity of the Showground, at over forty thousand, was also much bigger than the Sports Ground, at around thirty-three thousand, so there would also be room for a bigger crowd.

The choice we had to make proved to be a dilemma and we went through every possible option before finally making a decision. Everyone knew it was a bit of a gamble but we thought that the majority of people would have a good view at the Showground if the pitch was turned on an angle so that it better suited the major grandstand. It wasn't a perfect solution but the critical factor was that the extra covered seating at the Showground would allow us to pre-sell far more tickets. Even pre-selling tickets to a soccer match was unheard of in those days and people were used to just turning up at the gate on the day. But, once again, the guys from International Artists decided to do things differently and give people the opportunity to pre-purchase a seat. There was a lot of money involved and they knew pre-sales would insure us.

Before we knew it there were twenty-six thousand tickets pre-sold. This was beyond our wildest expectations and gave us an immediate sense of justification in scheduling the match at the Showground. Now there are actually formulas that allow organisers to estimate what sort of crowd will turn up based on pre-sales but because this was the first such event for soccer in Australia there was, of course, no such formula. It meant we had no idea that selling twenty-six thousand tickets might mean we were going to have a problem with the crowd.

The night of the match was an unforgettable experience for me but unfortunately not because of what happened on the pitch.

The number of people that turned up to the see the Cosmos play the Socceroos that night still amazes me. It turned out to be an ideal evening, weather-wise, to be outdoors and the publicity campaign had obviously spread the word like wildfire. People seemed to descend upon the Showground from all directions. The police later told me that there was probably more than one hundred and fifty thousand people trying to get to the match. The mass of people had literally blocked the centre of the city and I was in shock as the game drew closer and more and more people kept turning up. Too many people turning up was one thing we hadn't anticipated when organising the event and this type of interest in soccer by the Australian public was unprecedented.

While there were turnstiles in some stands at the Showground to regulate the queues of spectators entering, there were other entry points manned by a lone ticket-collector. There was no barcode technology like there is today and it was a manual operation worked, for the most part, by old guys in grey coats. This inevitably meant it was a slow, arduous process getting people into the ground and as the crowd continued to build and the lines grew longer, those people who already had tickets obviously started to worry that they wouldn't get in to the Showground in time to see the kick-off. Soon the crowd started to push to make sure they didn't miss any of the action and a whole stream of people ended up literally bursting into the ground. Some of the gates were knocked over in the stampede. It was absolute chaos.

The entertainment background of the guys from International Artists meant they had an entirely different outlook on how the night should go. Instead of thinking of the match as a sporting event they viewed it as a night of entertainment and this meant putting in place a whole program of events, apart from the match itself, to entertain the crowd. The main aspect of this program was a spectacular fireworks display that was scheduled to go off about half an hour before the game. Fireworks have become stock standard at sporting events these days, but back then it was an amazing innovation.

When the lights at the ground were switched off so the fireworks would be better illuminated the entire place literally went black and provided the cue for the people lining up outside to surge forward. They must have thought the match was starting and the guys on the gates were suddenly under so much pressure that they simply had to give way to the hordes. It would have been dangerous not to and, in the end, people just pushed in to the stadium, whether they had a ticket or not. There was utter pandemonium.

When the fireworks display finished and the lights came back on the scene was incredible. Because the other organisers and I had been inside the Showground and not yet aware of what was happening outside I had to look twice to believe what I was seeing. The ground was just full of people. They were on the sidelines of the pitch, around the trotting track, in the stands, on the light towers and on the hill. There wasn't an inch of space remaining. From that moment on the rest of the night for me became a blur of doing interviews, taking complaints and trying to find out what had happened to cause this chaos. Every media organisation had a representative there and they wanted to know what was going on. What had happened? Were we going to refund people's money? Who was to blame? They were all legitimate questions but I certainly didn't have the answers at that stage.

To this day nobody knows how many people were actually in the stadium to watch the match or how many people turned away when they saw the crowds. Most people estimate there was somewhere between seventy- and eighty-thousand people. The seating capacity was forty-two thousand but the ground itself was massive and could fit in a great deal more people. The only thing I know for sure was that it was packed to overflowing.

I was disappointed I didn't get to sit back and enjoy the football because Jimmy Rooney, one of my teammates from the 1974 World Cup, had been named captain of the Socceroos for the first time. Jimmy was a terrific player, very skilful and dangerous in the midfield, and he scored the first goal. Unfortunately, I didn't get to see it. My old Canberra City player Tony Henderson scored the winner after Giorgio Chinaglia had racked up the equaliser for the Cosmos. It was a brilliant victory by the Socceroos considering the quality of the opposition.

All the other members of the Socceroo squad should be acknowledged for the part they played that night. They were

Greg Woodhouse, Ivo Prskalo, Peter Sharne, Mark Jankovics, Steve Perry, Joe Senkalski, Bobby Russell, Martyn Crook, Jim Tansey, Phil O'Connor, Ken Bowden, John Coyne, Gary Cole, John Nyskohus and a young Eddie Krncevic. The coach of the team was the flamboyant Rudi Gutendorf. Rudi came from the German school of football coaching and was a very good public relations man. He was a real character and is very similar in many ways to the popular former Perth Glory coach Berndt Stange. He will always have a place in Australian soccer history because, along with Sir Arthur George, he was responsible for getting Australia to the first World Youth Cup in 1979.

When Rudi had found out about the impending Cosmos visit, he was over the moon. He knew Franz Beckenbauer quite well from his days in Germany and thought the match would be a splendid boost for the game in Australia. So, in terms of helping us promote the event he was absolutely first class and was willing to do anything asked of him. One of the back page headlines from the *Sun* newspaper before the match read: 'Beckenbauer: I know how to stop him, claims Rudi', demonstrating how he helped get publicity for the match.

The media coverage the event received was absolutely amazing for a soccer match in Australia. The event even featured as the lead story on the front page of the *Sydney Morning Herald* the next day.

Unfortunately, the match and the success of the night were somewhat overshadowed in the mainstream media for the next few days by the problems at the gates and the trouble with the crowd. The back-page headline in the *Sun* newspaper after the game, 'Showground spoils soccer's big night', illustrated that focus in the media coverage. While it would have been more appropriate for the media to concentrate on the positive side of how many people turned up to the match rather than the negative aspects, I guess the attendance figures and the Socceroos' magnificent victory weren't sensational enough.

In the end, we had little option but to refund the money of those people who had bought tickets but couldn't get through the crowds to enter the Showground. People threatened to sue us not only for the cost of the tickets but also for loss of enjoyment. I wish I could have done the same for my loss of enjoyment! We immediately reimbursed those people but, of course, it meant that a night out of which we should have done handsomely financially, was not anywhere near as lucrative as it should have been. It is still hard to fathom now how having too many people interested in the event ended up costing us money.

We also got caught out financially by the Australian Taxation Office. After we paid the fifty thousand US dollar fee to the Cosmos, the tax office discovered that the fee wasn't being paid to the Cosmos organisation itself but was, in fact, being split between each player. Each member of the team was on a bonus for each friendly match they played and was paid accordingly. The tax office therefore decided that the players had actually earned money while they were in Australia and had to pay tax. As this hadn't been part of our agreement with the Cosmos, it fell to us to pay that as well.

I guess you could say the entire event, from start to finish, was a learning experience for me. Still, it remains a highlight of my football life. The people that were there at the match remember it vividly because it was such a unique, ground breaking event for the time. It remains the biggest one-off sports event Sydney has ever held, so I think I can rightly be proud of it. Although in some ways it was a disaster, it should ultimately be seen as an example of the latent soccer audience that exists in Australia. More than anything else, it reaffirmed my conviction that if you have a good soccer event and promote it properly, Australians will turn up in their tens of thousands.

The ASF were so happy with the response to the Cosmos match that they asked International Artists and me to promote the Socceroos next home series against Czechoslovakia in 1980. The Czechoslovakians were coached by my friend Joe Venglos and visited Australia as the European champions so it was a high-profile event. However, I only became involved in the promotion of the match being played in Canberra because of other commitments. We employed the same promotional principles that had been applied during the Cosmos match and some eighteen thousand people turned up to see the Socceroos get beaten 4–0 by the Czechs at Bruce stadium on 27 January. It was a record crowd for Bruce stadium at the time and was another roaring success despite the Socceroos' loss. It was an even better result because the Czechs clearly weren't as big a drawcard as the Cosmos. While they had a great team they didn't have the international stars and big names that the Cosmos offered.

Unfortunately, the other matches in Sydney and Melbourne weren't very well attended. The Socceroos' huge loss in Canberra probably didn't help matters because I think everyone had been hoping for a more competitive match-up. The Socceroos went on to lose 5–0 in Sydney before managing a 2–2 draw in Melbourne.

After that series I ended my association with the guys from International Artists. It was an amicable parting; we had made a huge success of the Cosmos and shown that adopting a professional approach to staging soccer in Australia can be tremendously successful. I think the event still serves as an example of what can be achieved in Australia if everything is done by promoters, or soccer's administration, to ensure that the event is professionally managed. As for that hope of a job for life with the Australian Soccer Federation, unfortunately it came to nothing. I wasn't particularly surprised.

15

Australia's Best Coach: SBS

⚽ SBS, SPECIAL BROADCASTING Service or, as it has been jokingly referred to over the years, 'Soccer Broadcasting Station' or 'Soccer Bloody Soccer', has singularly been the most influential organisation on the development of football in Australia. From youngsters first being introduced to playing the game to internationals strutting their stuff in the most celebrated competitions, SBS has enhanced the knowledge and understanding of the world game in Australian fans and players alike.

Football has brought me into contact with the entire Australian world of migrant life, and one of the best examples of this is my relationship with Les Murray and with SBS Television. Les Murray's story from his early days in Hungary as Laszlo Urge to his status now in the Australian soccer community is one of thousands of migrant stories that have played a signifcant role in building modern Australia. The name 'Les Murray' has, indeed, become synonymous with soccer in Australia.

Growing up in Botany, I hopscotched my way through childhood in blissful ignorance of the unrest occurring on the other side of the world. I was part of the next Anglo–Australian generation, and my life was made up of backyard test cricket matches, street games, youth groups, selecting which school I would attend and, in my own naïve way, rebelling. At the same time, Europe was still smouldering from the devastation of the Second World War and countries such as Les Murray's Hungary were politically oppressed and poverty-stricken. Hungarians, by and large, had been accustomed to a healthy standard of living and had been a progressive people, so were suffering greatly under the authoritarianism of the occupying Soviets. In 1956, the Hungarian revolution—the uprising by the Hungarian people against the Soviets—was born. The Soviet tanks swiftly rolled into Budapest to crush the insurgence that resulted. For a few weeks during that time though, the borders, which had hitherto been closed, were briefly opened. Les's family, feeling that the revolution was doomed and that the communist government would return and continue the oppression, decided it was time to leave Hungary while the borders were still open.

Leaving before dawn, the entire family rode on the back of a truck to the railway station before taking a train to the border; a trip that was to take three days. Constant questioning along the way and troopers' queries over Les's parents' 'funny' identification papers made for a staccatoed journey. At one point, his father was taken off the train and interrogated for five hours before returning to his panic-stricken family. There were Soviet soldiers everywhere, and the confusion and fear in the air were palpable. As the family approached the border in the dead of the snowbound night, they were terrified that the noise of the snow crackling underfoot would alert a sentry to their presence and he would shoot in their direction. Finally, they made it across the border safely. It was December 1956 and they spent the next six months in a series of Austrian refugee camps.

In Australia, Hungarian refugees were keenly sought after because many NATO countries saw the political mileage to be gained by taking in refugees who had opposed communism. Australia was the first to accept the Urge family and in May 1957 eleven-year-old Laszlo and his family arrived here.

Les's family's first home in Australia was the Bonegilla migrant hostel in Albury. Les describes it, with shuddering emphasis, as a concentration camp. The family's first move within Australia took them to the New South Wales city of Wollongong. Les's father secured a job in the Port Kembla Steelworks and the family settled in the Illawarra. All week long, Les and his brothers went to school, unable to speak English. Understandably, they felt like outsiders. At work, his father was thought of dismissively as a 'wog' and seen almost as sub-human by the 'Aussies' at work. Les's mother would try to shop for the family but without any English, couldn't order potatoes or other staples and, for the most part, certainly wasn't assisted by unsympathetic shopkeepers. These were some of the hostilities migrants had to face every day. This was the experience not only of Les and his family, but of an entire generation of new Australians. As a kid and teenager, I was probably also accepting the adage that people like them were just wogs. Theirs was a different Australia from mine. Les may as well have still been in Europe, such was the contrast between our Australian teenage lives. Were it not for football, I probably would never have had the opportunity to cross paths with migrants like him.

Around the same time, 1957–58, the Sydney soccer club, Budapest, was born. The ethnic clubs that sprung up around the time of the migrant boom virtually became weekend havens for migrants. Football clubs eased the way, and provided safer passage for migrants into mainstream society.

Les first experienced the Budapest football club when it visited the Illawarra from its base in Sydney to play one of Wollongong leading teams, Corrimal. You can imagine the feelings of Les and his brothers when they turned up and saw this team, Budapest, made up entirely of Hungarian players. Suddenly, they were confronted with a crowd of three or four thousand supporters who were almost all Hungarian. They hadn't seen such a familiar gathering since they'd left Hungary. For a couple of hours, Les and all the other Hungarians felt at home. Naturally, they all kept going to the Budapest games and after graduating from high school in 1963, Les moved to Sydney with his family where they became weekly Budapest followers.

I had since made my own move from Canterbury and joined St George Budapest. Les's dad was on the committee of the club, although at first I didn't know who he was. He was always at the club with his three sons. Les and his two brothers, Andrew and Joe, used to kick a ball around and watch us train. That was the first time our paths crossed.

The access that Les had to the team, via his father's official status at the club, meant that it wasn't long before he and I started to mix socially. I spent endless hours in eastern suburbs cafés (the Hungarians were doing the al fresco coffee thing decades before the latte set twigged to the fun) with people, including Les, from the St George Budapest club.

Covering football in the media was something to which Les took an early shine, working particularly with the Hungarian-language newspaper in Sydney. By the time Les left to work in England as a journalist, our acquaintance was well and truly established. Upon his return, I found myself working full-time with the St George licensed club in a public relations role. Part of that job involved the booking of entertainment. As Les also moonlighted as a part-time musician I had occasion to book him and his band 'The Rubberband'. I think he still owes me commission for that gig!

Les hadn't returned from England to pursue a music career, but to take up a position with Channel Ten. While he had been in London, the NSL had just been established in Australia and news reached him that the NSL's host broadcaster, Channel

Ten, was doing the rounds looking for talent. He organised to perform an audition, from London. Calling English first division football matches from the grandstand seat for which he'd paid, Laszlo recorded his commentary into a pocket tape recorder. He sent the tape back to Channel Ten and, upon learning that his audition had been successful, returned to Australia to commence work with the network. Peter Skelton was the television executive responsible for bringing the young Laszlo back from London. It was the same Peter Skelton who, at the network's NSL launch and just before introducing his newfound talent, hurriedly informed Laszlo that he should probably do something about his name. 'What can we tell them your name is? We can't use Laszlo Urge. Is there an Anglicised version?' asked Skelton. 'Tell them it's Murray, Les Murray,' came the self-assured reply.

As it was to turn out, Ten didn't go the distance with soccer. As a result, Les ended up in the labyrinthine world of SBS where he worked in a part-time capacity, subtitling Hungarian language programs. One day, Peter Skelton, who was now also at SBS, bumped into Les in a corridor. After a huge sigh of relief, and some colourful exclamations over his luck at running into Les, he proceeded to ask, 'What are you doing Sunday? Do you want to call the soccer for us this weekend?' It was 1980 and SBS was going to air with that season's NSL grand final in which Sydney City was playing Heidelberg. It was Friday and the game was to be played two days later. Les didn't take long to accept the offer. It was the start of his SBS on-air career and the start of Australia's football revolution. It was the first weekend of SBS transmission and the commencement of the SBS mission to convert the pagan world of Australian sport to the one true sporting god—football.

Because I knew Les and because of my playing career and associated activities, I had my own public profile and was invited to sit alongside Les for the commentary of that match at the Bruce Stadium where Heidelberg beat Sydney City 4–0. It was some twenty years ago now, and our friendship has remained ever since. Soon afterwards, I was contracted by SBS and the 'Captain Socceroo' series began. It was the first television program dedicated to coaching football. The 'Captain Socceroo' shows featured the best footballers doing their most brilliant work. It was intended for young and aspiring players who wanted to learn more about the game and more about improving their own skill. It set SBS apart from other networks because it helped build the football product in Australia, rather than merely broadcasting games, as other networks did with other sports. All the while, Les and I would commentate on the football matches together. With SBS, the ratings were not an imperative. The mission to educate Australians about soccer was under way.

The allure of SBS for me was its commitment to football. The great thing about SBS is that all the people involved behind the scenes are committed football people. The editors, producers, researchers, studio crew and people from every level of the operation are spellbound by *jogo bonito*—the beautiful game. It has made working there very easy for me. SBS has always treated the game with respect and likewise, has always tried to treat the viewer and the fan with the same respect. SBS recognises that the fans don't want someone coming on air laughing and making jokes at the expense of one team over another, as I've seen happen on other networks. Les has coined the phrase 'The World Game' which has been tattooed onto his personality. It is perfect Les, economy of phrase yet right to the heart of the matter. SBS is a network with viewers from all sorts of backgrounds and allegiances. Even when an Australian team has been playing, objectivity has had to be maintained at all times. It is always natural to want Australia to win but that emotion has never been permitted to descend into denigration of opponents. Such an ethos has been an integral part of SBS's delivery of football to the Australian community. For the people at SBS, communicating football is more a mission than a job.

Credit is especially due to former SBS Head of Sport, Dominic Galati, who has always fought for soccer in Australia and who was instrumental in picking up the World Cup broadcast rights to Italia '90, USA '94 and France '98. Blanket coverage by SBS of World Cup football has given the game in Australia huge impetus.

The result of not having ratings pressure meant that Les and I were given latitude to package football in accordance with the way we both viewed it. We are pretty satisfied with the fruits of our labour. Philosophically and ideologically, Les and I are on the same wavelength and I admire his professionalism. Les is a first-class presenter whose love of football stems from the beautiful style of football the Hungarians advocated in the 1950s with the great Hungarian team of the Puskas era. In many ways, because of our common ground, we look at football through the same prism. Our partnership, through SBS, has been a very happy one. He is a beautiful writer and I often marvel at how it is that people with English as a second language can express themselves so well. Football has been fortunate to have had Les as its presenter in Australia.

Les and I have been everywhere, at all sorts of odd times, talking and broadcasting football. The amount of time we've spent in airports, planes, and studios is almost countless. The conversation between us has never waned. There has always been too much to talk about, too many football opinions to share and too many games to analyse. At Italia '90 we would get home after an early start and an exhausting day where we'd be on set until about two each morning yet we would unwind with a good hour's chat about the football we'd seen during that day before hitting the sack. One of our funniest memories of travelling together happened while we were working in Italy. It became our custom to eat at a particular quaint restaurant at a piazza near the studio. We became such regular customers that we got to know the waiter really well. We called him Diego, because of his resemblance to Maradona. The restaurant was frequented by local businessmen and their wives and/or girlfriends and/or secretaries. During one lunch, a huge row erupted at the table next to us. A very smartly dressed executive was dining with a very attractive, and much younger, female companion. The heated exchange—all in Italian, of course—became so intense that Les and I were sure the argument must have been over something to do with their private life, such was the passion and vigour of the drama. We called Diego over and asked him what was going on. 'Oh,' he said, 'they are arguing over the Azzurri [Italy's national team]. She says Roberto Baggio should play midfield and he says Baggio should play as striker.' It was a great example of the passion that football inspires in Italy in people from all walks of life.

One of my highlights during my time at SBS was in El Estadio da Luz in Portugal for the 1991 World Youth Cup. No other Australian media interest was there yet the calibre of the young players representing Australia in that magnificent tournament was world class. Our young Australian team played in front of one hundred and twenty-nine thousand people against the tournament hosts and the ultimate champions, the same Portugese team of modern-day superstars Luis Figo (recently the world's most expensive player and 2001 World Player of the Year), Manuel Rui Costa, Joao Pinto, Fernando Couto. SBS was there, no one else. We felt like crusaders. I remember reading the player bio of Paul Okon, a young Aussie playing like the great Beckenbauer himself, who listed as his favourite television show, SBS's 'World Soccer'. That was a special match for all of us at SBS. Young Aussie players are products of an era of access to a broad range of football, thanks largely to SBS, which has provided footage and educational programs on football from all over the world. Essentially, SBS has been the best coach of young Australian players since the 1980s.

There have been other World Cups as well as the Youth World Cups, European Cups, Continental Championships from Asia, Africa and South America as well as Australian soccer we've covered. Ungodly hours spent in the SBS studios, covering matches from Europe has all been par for the course. The mad month of May, as it has become known, has had us virtually camped out at SBS with pre-dawn starts watching the games coming in live via satellite, sitting out the back in the 'Lizard Lounge' compiling our notes, laughing at each other's one-liners and enjoying both the football and the company. I have been privileged to work with people who feel such a connection with the game and who get so totally and indescribably excited by watching matches being played across the world, even when they have to watch them with wearied and bloodshot eyes prised open by matchsticks.

As Les sees it, I have grown up as a dinky di Aussie as well as someone who can also relate to the people who imported soccer to Australia. I find that to be a humbling endorsement. According to him, though I wasn't born in Europe and while I may 'put tomato sauce on my hot chips', when it comes to football I am as European as he is. To be perceived as having a cosmopolitan football appreciation is gratifying to me. To have been part of the SBS push to allow all Australians to also appreciate soccer from all over the world is a source of pride for me.

SBS has impacted on Australia's sporting landscape and put soccer on our cultural agenda. For SBS, football is a true charter item in the sense that it is international with a huge following, it is the game of the communities, and it reflects the cultural diversity of modern Australia.

The Australian version of the game has changed due to SBS's exposure of world football. It has provided Australian viewers with unfettered coverage of the best football from all parts of the world. Media people from other countries are unanimous in their admiration for what SBS represents. The France '98 World Cup was testament to SBS's commitment to broadcast every game, live and in its entirety. Our English colleagues couldn't fathom such coverage, particularly considering the absence of the Socceroos. I remember production teams from other countries unplugging their whole operations at the very moment their team was out of the competition. We were almost knocked over in their rush to depart. But, throughout the entire World Cup, SBS was there beaming pictures and stories back to Australia. The international media that SBS has engaged to help its coverage have jumped on board the SBS mission in a mighty way. I think of the likes of Martin Tyler, in my view the best football commentator in the English-speaking world, whose opinions of the work SBS does with football are rapturous. (I remember being in awe of Martin, the first time I worked with him. He is a giant of a man with impeccable professionalism. He has a worldly appreciation of football and a wonderful feel for the unique problems of Australian football.) People like Martin Tyler, and his compatriots Gary Bloom, Paul Dempsey, Gerry Harrison and Ian Darke are all well respected, worldly football identities whose endorsement of the SBS product has been a big part of football's acceptance in Australia. Australians can see that it's not just 'wogs' carrying on about football, but also those 'blessed Brits', who consider football a way of life and think that the Australian contribution is a worthy one. SBS has also opened the way for our own quality commentators. Of these, Paul Williams is outstanding and, after Martin Tyler, the best commentator in the English-speaking world there is.

SBS has really been Australian soccer's de facto marketing partner although I don't think this has ever been recognised as it should. Since losing the broadcast rights to Australian football, SBS's obligation to cover the local game has been made redundant. The fact that programs such as 'On the Ball' have continued in this vacuum is a huge credit to the dedication of the network. I think of the entire loyal football crew who put the show to air, so admirably hosted by Kyle Patterson. Kyle is a real football-loving journo. He is not afraid to ask the hard questions for the sake of the game and I am full of admiration for him. There is a wonderful support cast, who give the fans insight and coverage into the game. It is a difficult job to do, in the midst of so much controversy and inertia at local level. 'On the Ball' tries to make some sense, for the disenfranchised fan, of the struggles Australian soccer is facing. Yet often the show is criticised by people in the soccer administration of this country as being too negative. SBS has never criticised the game. The question that critics should ask is simple—where would the game be without SBS?

Other players in the media market, vis-à-vis commercial television networks, are now realising what SBS has known and preached for eons—football is the world game and that any media organisation that purports to be global must embrace football. I am happy to have been identified with Les Murray, as people synonymous with soccer in this country. Walking together towards the Hindmarsh Stadium in Adelaide for a game one day, legendary Adelaide soccer journalist Allan Crisp called out, 'Here comes Mr and Mrs Soccer' although I don't know who was mister and who was missus. All I know is that we've become known as the soccer couple and that's fine with me.

16

My Latin Love Affair

⚽ Over the years I have been accused of being a Latin lover. I make no apology for it because in the next life I hope to be a Latin, particularly a Latin of the South American variety—preferably Brazilian. My everyday life is full of reminders of my love for South America and its football. My email address starts with 'zico10'; Zico being one of the greats of world football often called the 'white Pelé' and who, like all key players in South America wore the number-ten shirt. My property in Jamberoo is called Maracana after Rio's world-famous stadium. My two Angora goats are called Zico and Diego (after Maradona). My grandchildren, though only babies, call me *abuelito*, meaning small grandfather. For the past twenty-one years, after a trip to South America every year, I have worn the lucky wristbands of *Senhor do Bonfim da Bahia*—the Saint Bonfim of Bahia (Bahia is a city on the Brazilian coast)—bands in various colours that symbolise health, well-being, love and so on. You tie them on your wrist with three knots, making a wish when tying each knot. The bands are never to be removed and your wish is supposed to come true when they fall off, which often takes several years to happen.

As SBS television viewers would know, over the years I have been a great admirer of South American football and the benefits that accrue to Australian football from it. However, there was no South American influence on me while I was growing up.

I can remember going to the movies when I was young and seeing a twenty-second black-and-white film of the FA Cup final on the newsreel shown before the feature. It was the only view of overseas football that I ever saw when I was growing up and I would often go to the movies simply in the hope of catching this glimpse of British football. British football was all I would see in the media of the way the game was played overseas, through magazines and the occasional newsreel. However, my introduction to football in Australia was very multicultural. The players in Australia during my youth came from all over the world and the soccer teams were representative of many varied cultures.

It was this first-hand experience of multicultural football that gradually moved me further and further away from the British game. I have already mentioned the influence that the arrival of the four Argentinians, Victor Fernandez, Hugo Rodriguez, Lorenco Heredia and Salvador Isaac, had on my early career at St George Budapest and my views on the game. I was also fascinated by their stories of Argentina and of what football was like over there.

It was probably my great friendship with Victor Fernandez that really kick-started my love affair with South America. We became good mates while playing at St George. Our friendship was further strengthened by coaching together, both at St George and at Canberra City. On the field, he consistently reminds me of Maradona in his appearance and the way he played. He was all left foot and loved bending the ball and taking free kicks. He even wore the number-ten shirt like Diego. Off the field we became very good friends and I served as the best man at his wedding to his wife Sandra in 1965.

Since he retired from playing, Victor has probably been the unsung hero of youth soccer in Australia. He has taken on the role of assistant coach in various Australian youth teams for many years and has always done a wonderful job in promoting the nation's young talent. Our various links to the game have taken us in different directions in recent years and it has been more difficult to catch up but we're still great friends and I really have Vic to thank for sparking my passion for South America and its football.

In recent times I have become particularly close with my former teammate from my early days at St George, Salvador Isaac, his wife Carmen and their children, Graciella, Jorge and Mario, who live in Buenos Aires. Of course, every year part of my South American trip is to catch up with them for a *parilla* (barbecue) for which Argentinians are justifiably famous and to see a football game, whether it's to see River Plate at the Monumental Stadium or to see Boca Juniors at the famous Bombonera Stadium. These are special times with my former teammate, who married in Australia while he was here and whose daughter was also born in our country.

One of the other important factors that first intrigued me about South America was the phenomenal success its ten nations have enjoyed in international competition. I was amazed that South American football was played so differently and yet had always been so successful. Of the sixteen World Cups played to date, teams from South America have won eight. That a tiny country like Uruguay, with a population of only three million people, has won the World Cup twice and Olympic Games gold twice is simply incredible, and everyone has always appreciated the amazing performances of Brazil and Argentina in international competition. The bottom line is that when you consider there are more than two hundred nations affiliated with FIFA, the track record of the ten nations from South America is remarkable.

Even with most of the best South American players playing for European clubs, club teams from South America have dominated the Toyota Cup, which is the unofficial world club championship and is played between the champion of Europe and the champion of South America. Of the thirty-eight Toyota Cups played to date, South American clubs have won twenty-one. Argentine clubs have won eight of these titles, Brazilian clubs six, Uruguayan clubs six and a Paraguayan club has won the remaining title. Again, it is a remarkable record considering the might of European football throughout the years. Unfortunately, South American clubs have won only one of the last six Toyota Cups, which is a sign of the increasing number of South American players being lured to Europe by lucrative offers.

It wasn't until 1981, long after my playing career was over, that I first fulfilled my wish to travel to South America and explore the continent for myself.

Brazil had never really been a football idol for me when I was playing, like it is for many people now. While I can remember seeing some black-and-white footage of the Brazilians playing in the 1966 World Cup and knew of the great players, I was at the time probably more interested in Argentina because of my own experiences with my Argentine soccer friends. Believe it or not, I wasn't even really a fan of Pelé at this early stage. While I had heard of him and knew about his amazing feats, he was really a mystery man. But, all this changed as more and more televised images and reports of the Brazilian teams and players became available in Australia. Their amazing success, and the way they played the game captured my imagination.

There were two specific reasons why I decided Brazil would be a good place to start my personal journey into South America. One was that my fourteen-year-old god-son and nephew, Jamie, was showing a lot of promise as a player. He had played in representative teams for the Illawarra and New South Wales for many years and desperately wanted to be involved in full-time football. He wasn't interested in school and it was his dream to be 'like his uncle', working full-time in football. I decided that if he really wanted to become a top player then I should take him to the best training ground, Brazil. So Jamie and I set off on our adventure together.

Apart from my desire to help Jamie's career, I had also become increasingly intrigued by Brazil's performance on the football field and was very keen to uncover the secrets behind their success. Why was it that the Brazilians played the game better than anyone and how were they able to produce players with better skills and technique than anywhere else? Brazil is certainly number one in terms of individual skill. This has allowed them to play the game with the unmatched art and beauty that has so often thrilled the world.

What's more, Brazil is able to produce a prodigious number of great players. They have so many top-quality players that they could probably field twenty teams capable of winning the World Cup. It is no coincidence that many of the developing nations of world football, particularly those in the Middle East, Asia and Africa, have turned to Brazilian coaches to lead them into the future.

I thought my trip would be a perfect opportunity to find out how this Brazilian production line worked. Was it the way players were trained? Was it the junior development program? Was it the beach football? The music? The culture? Or was it just something in the water? I had always thought, and still think, that embracing some of Brazil's methods would be beneficial for the Australian game. I believe the early years of football in Australia were overly influenced by the English game, with its lack of emphasis on developing skill in the individual player, so I hoped that gleaning some information from the masters of skill might help change the situation in Australia.

My dream trip to Brazil started out like a nightmare. My first impression of pollution-choked São Paulo, a city of twenty-four million people, was particularly uninspiring. The city can be a magical place but it is daunting even for experienced travellers, let alone the uninitiated visitor.

I wanted to find somewhere that Jamie could learn about the Brazilian game. I thought perhaps he could train with a youth team and they could help his game by identifying some areas where could improve and show him some training techniques. But obviously I needed to make some connections within the Brazilian football community.

We eventually decided to leave São Paulo and fly to Rio. I can remember sitting in the hotel room after we had arrived and trying to figure out what my next move would be. I was in a strange city with my fourteen-year-old nephew, I didn't know a soul and I didn't speak the language. I was seriously considering packing our bags and just heading home.

Luckily though, I decided to ring the governing football body in Brazil, the CBF, to see if they could help us. It was a long shot but we had few alternatives. I explained my situation and to my amazement I was immediately invited to the CBF's office in Rio. When I got there, I was further taken aback by how friendly the people there were. I would later realise that such warm hospitality is a trait common to all the Brazilians I have met, but at the time I thought I had simply been extremely fortunate. The staff were sympathetic to my predicament and immediately arranged for someone to come and help Jamie and me.

Not long after arriving at the office I was introduced to Brazil's FIFA representative Carlos Alberto Pinheiro who was extremely helpful and introduced me to a man called Professor William Lawson. It is a peculiar trait in Brazil that just about every coach in the country is called professor but, at the time, I thought he must be a football-loving scientist. The country places such an emphasis on football that there are specialist schools that offer courses in football coaching. When coaches graduate they become a professor in the science of football. This system is simply another demonstration of how important football is to the people.

William immediately took it upon himself to act as our chaperone for the rest of our trip. I later found out that the CBF had given him the express job of taking care of us, without any consideration of a charge or fee. It was an incredibly benevolent gesture towards us because we had literally just turned up on their doorstep. I spent hours and hours talking about Brazil with William as he showed us around Rio and gave us a unique insight into Brazilian football and life; an experience that simply wouldn't have been possible without William's local knowledge. I am eternally grateful to him for that.

One of the first places William decided to show us was one of Rio's biggest football clubs, Club Regattas Flamengo. Most of the clubs in Rio are known as Club Regattas because they started as rowing clubs. Flamengo is quite unique because it is considered to be the club of all the people of Rio. Their opponents say the only time it is safe to go to Rio is when Flamengo is playing because all the city's crooks are at the match! Having been to matches in Rio several times I can certainly vouch for the fanaticism of the Flamengo supporters. I still clearly recollect seeing a destitute man lying in the gutter in Rio all kitted out in his Flamengo shirt and shorts. Incredibly, his little dog, lying in the gutter next to him, was also wearing his own Flamengo gear.

Flamengo has seen many star players wear its colours in the past such as Zico and Romario. It has a tremendously competitive record. I was quite amazed at the size of the club headquarters and the array of facilities it offers. It has tennis courts, futsal courts, a basketball stadium, volleyball courts, an athletic track, swimming pools and facilities for several other sports, such as bocce. It also boasts souvenir shops, coffee lounges, restaurants, club rooms and trophy rooms. The headquarters also have club rooms and bars so families can go there for social activities. It offers something for every member of the community and is an integral part of the life of every Flamengo fan. It also has spectacular views of Rio and is close to the city's wonderful beaches. There is simply nothing like it in the Australian soccer world.

The football team play at the famous Maracana Stadium but their training ground is at the club headquarters. It is known as the Gavea and it is located in a spectacular setting with the statue of Christ the Redeemer on the towering mountain, Corcovado, in the background. I have always thought that it must be a truly inspirational place to train. The training sessions in themselves are amazing spectacles, always packed with hordes of fans and media.

During our stay, William took Jamie and me to games at the Maracana Stadium, always in VIP seats, and led us on tours of the trophy rooms at the CBF and Flamengo. The South Americans are very big on trophies, particularly large gold and silver ones, so their trophy rooms are cavernous places that are treated with great reverence. There are wall-to-wall trophies and the prestige and history that exudes from these rooms takes your breath away. I have experienced nothing like it in Australia.

The boss of Flamengo at the time of my first visit to Brazil was Mario Zagallo. He is one of the biggest names in world football having won two World Cups as a player, one as coach and one as assistant coach. You can imagine my awestruck excitement when I was asked if I would like to meet him.

Zagallo had actually been to Australia in 1977 as the coach of the Kuwaiti team that beat the Socceroos in their 1978 World Cup qualifying campaign so he was familiar with our country. As would so often be the case when I met high-profile Brazilian football identities, Zagallo turned out to be extremely down-to-earth. He talked about his experiences with Australia and asked how our football was progressing. I was surprised at how friendly he was considering I had turned up unannounced. This surprise quickly turned to amazement when, at the end of the conversation, he offered Jamie the chance to train with the youth team. My nightmare trip was suddenly becoming the dream trip I was hoping it would be.

After about five weeks in Rio, Flamengo were impressed enough with Jamie to ask him to stay on and play for the youth team. It was a major step for Jamie and he ultimately ended up living and training with the team in Rio for six months. Jamie's experience helped give me an insight into Brazilian training methods. He would attend an American-run school in the mornings before meeting up with the youth team at the Flamengo headquarters in the afternoon. They would then travel by bus to one of the three official club training grounds. The trip took around an hour and the players were always singing samba songs and clapping and banging the seats. Jamie would sit next to Djalminha, who now plays a starring role for Deportivo La Coruna in the Spanish Primera Division. He and Jamie became friends because Jamie would help him with his English homework. Jamie must have done a fine job as an English tutor because Djalminha ended up topping his class in English and even now Jamie still takes a special interest in his career.

The ground the youth team usually trained on was in the middle of some banana plantations and the mosquitoes in the area were so enormous that the players were supplied with rub-on alcohol to keep the insects away. There were about forty players in the Flamengo youth squad so the competition for places was fierce. Even though the players were friendly, there was always an undercurrent of strong rivalry for places in the starting team. There were usually several bad fouls committed in the eleven-a-side training matches and Jamie told me that it was not unusual to see several players with their shirts completely ripped off during a match. However, the training sessions placed an emphasis on developing skills. Drills to improve passing and dribbling; running while juggling the ball; stationary and non-stationary heading, and shooting were all regularly practised to enhance players' ability with the ball. Everyone was also encouraged to practise using both feet in order to become a more complete player.

At the end of the training sessions the players would do a warm-down, and then be given one or two sandwiches to eat and a flavoured milk drink. Every player in the squad was weighed prior to every session and the players who were considered under-weight were given two cheese sandwiches instead of one. Jamie was considered underweight but would usually only end up with one sandwich after giving the other to one of the other players. He was never sure whether some of the others had enough food as some came from extremely poor backgrounds.

Jamie hurt his right instep while practising shooting for goal at one training session and two weeks later discovered a large boil in the exact same spot as the original instep injury. The injury was extremely painful as was its treatment. Jamie still remembers the immense pain he was in at the time. He was also bitten by a dog while doing a six-kilometre training run along the famous Copacabana Beach with his teammates. He needed to have a series of rabies injections and still claims that the dog must have known somehow that he was the only *gringo* in the group.

William Lawson, who was looking after Jamie, thought Jamie's bad luck might be the result of someone using voodoo on him. So William asked Jamie to write his name down on a piece of paper and went off to see a lady with 'special powers' in Rio. When William gave her the piece of paper with Jamie's name on it, she was able to describe Jamie's appearance exactly, including the recent problem with his foot. She told William that another member of the squad had placed a spell on Jamie in order to get him to leave Brazil. To overcome the spell, she advised that Jamie needed to go through a series of bathing rituals and prayers. So, for the next three days, Jamie bathed in a pot full of boiled garlic. While he was bathing, he had to rub the garlic leaves all over his body. For the next three days he had to bathe in onions and for three days after that in the leaves of a Brazilian plant with special properties. It didn't end there though. Every day, after Jamie had bathed as per instructions, he was told to go to a local street corner and place seven ten-cruzero coins in a circle, light a candle and say a prayer telling the bad spirits to go away. Then, after nine days of these rituals, he had to take all of the leaves from the garlic, onions and the special plant and throw them into the ocean. Only after all of that and another prayer stating that the spell had been defeated was Jamie free of the evil spirits! Not a common experience for a fifteen-year-old Australian kid.

Unfortunately, Jamie broke his leg twice after coming back to Australia and playing for St George so he didn't continue with his football career. Rio, and Flamengo, showed Jamie what was involved for *cariocas* to survive in football. It is an exacting regimen. It was the sort of once-in-a-lifetime opportunity that other people only dream about and while I'm certain it taught him a great deal about football, I'm also sure that Jamie learned a great deal about life as well.

One highlight of my first visit to Brazil was being introduced to a game called futsal. Watching futsal for the first time was like being let in on a national secret because it was the one thing that immediately struck me as being unique to the football culture of Brazil. Up until then, what I had seen of the Brazilian training of young players was nothing out of the ordinary. The way the young players played futsal, though, left a major impression on me.

While the term 'futsal' literally means salon football, the game is probably best described as court football. Everyone seems to play it in Brazil—every school has a court, which is not only used for futsal but also for tennis, volleyball and basketball. All kids are brought up on it and see it is as part of everyday life from a young age. At a senior level, the game is professional and so it also offers many kids a means of escaping their poverty. The game is played with a fierce passion as a result.

I was lucky enough to be taken to the São Paulo junior futsal championships. The sight of little kids expertly using the sole of the foot to control the ball—which is heavier than a soccer ball and doesn't bounce—and improvising and making do with the limited space was a real eye-opener. I observed that the young players were literally forced into using the proper kicking technique and playing with their heads up by the very nature of the game. Everyone was constantly in motion, making runs to support their teammates. I began to appreciate that all the amazing skills of the senior Brazilian players, all their wonderful dribbles and feints, come from having to play pressure games when they are young in an area restricted in space. If they can't dribble and find their own solution to the limited space in futsal they simply don't survive as a player.

I was convinced then that the game was a large part of Brazil's senior success. From a technical point of view, the game develops skills like no other. Players like Ronaldo and Romario were forced to work out their own solutions to the problems they faced on a futsal court and I think that's why they are such amazing and unpredictable football players in terms of their skill level. I was convinced that my visit to the futsal courts had helped me uncover one of the major secrets of Brazil's success on the football field.

Ever since my trip to Brazil I have encouraged kids back in Australia to play futsal to increase their football skills. The game is slowly growing in popularity in Australia. I have only recently returned from the world championship in Guatemala and the experience confirmed my conviction that futsal will become one of the great entertainment sports of the twenty-first century. FIFA has already put in place a policy to actively push futsal because they can see its potential international value.

By the end of my first trip to South America I had also fallen in love with Rio and its people—the *cariocas*. The *cariocas* give the city a magical quality by their warmth. They seem to be always dancing, enjoying music and playing football. Having to spend the rest of my life there wouldn't worry me at all. There's something happening all the time and it doesn't cause any distress that the girls are all beautiful either. The beach, in particular, is always a hive of activity and there is always football being played. It is normal to see old men hanging around kicking a ball because in Brazil absolutely everyone plays *futebol*. You don't see the same thing in Australia. I can remember watching a group of kids playing a game just off the beach using an empty Coca-Cola bottle as the ball. The beach is floodlit at night and competitive matches continue until dawn. The highlight of the morning is the Hospitality Cup, which brings out teams from all the bars, clubs, restaurants and hotels along the beach. It is the most valued prize of all the competitions played in Rio because the prestige for restaurateurs or hoteliers that goes with having the Copacabana Beach Football Championship Cup displayed in their restaurant, club or bar, is unrivalled.

The Brazilians erect big screens up on the beach when there are big matches at night-time so that everyone gets to see the games. On one trip I was lucky enough to see the World Futsal Championship and the World Beach Football Championship in Rio. Two twelve thousand-seat stadiums were constructed on the beach for the event and there was free admission to the matches. As a result, the atmosphere was pulsating. The officials would bring out big hoses at half-time and hose everyone down to keep them cool. Just the experience of being in a culture that lives and breathes football is exhilarating for me and it is why I have travelled back to South America over twenty times since my first visit.

There is a saying in South America: *pobresa pero feliz*. It means 'poor but happy'. I think it nicely sums up the Brazilian culture. People talk of the South Americans as the *mañana* people, because they are supposedly always putting things off until tomorrow. But I think Australians are really more the *mañana* people. While many people here plan to enjoy themselves when they retire or go on that holiday next year, the South Americans seem to live for the moment and take advantage of life's beauty. Of course, their passion for football is a great part of this because it is an overwhelming part of their daily existence. When Brazil plays, the entire nation stops to watch. Fireworks light the skies every time Brazil scores so those people who are not at the stadium will always know how many goals have been scored. You might not know whether the team has won, but you will always know how many goals have been scored.

Football is just such an integral part of the culture in Brazil. Everyone has an opinion about football and their general knowledge is simply astounding. In Australia, the politics of the game often overshadows the game itself but in Brazil the minutiae of the game dominates all else. I was particularly impressed by the football knowledge of the women in Brazil. When I asked one lady why the women appear to know so much about football, she responded, 'If you want to get a man in Brazil you have to know about football.' The amazing thing I found was that the women I met seemed to have a much better understanding of the game than most Brazilian men.

I'm lucky enough to have made many Brazilian friends throughout my career in soccer. One of the people I met during my role as football ambassador for the Sydney 2000 Olympics was Professor Neto Espezim. He is a qualified coach, a former journalist and now runs the Brazilian Football Academy out of Rio. He was the right-hand man of international soccer heavyweight Joao Havelange for many years and has always been a very respected figure in Brazilian football. He is a real character with countless stories and knows everything that is going on in the game around the world. Spending time with him is always such an enjoyable experience because of his knowledge and passion for the game and his friendly nature. In many ways he sums up Brazil for me.

I can still recall asking Neto whether it was possible to get a one-on-one television interview with Dr Havelange for SBS Television. I have always been a great fan of Dr Havelange because I believe he revolutionised world football when he became FIFA president in 1974. Besides introducing development, coaching and sponsorship programs that helped develop the game in Asia and Africa he established an education system for the world's best young players by introducing the various Youth World Cups and by ensuring that the Olympic Games remained at the under-23s level. He also supported and promoted futsal, beach football and, more recently, women's football. Getting a one-on-one interview with him was a big deal because of how highly he was regarded in the international football community.

In answer to my request Neto told me that Dr Havelange didn't give one-on-one interviews to anyone. I wasn't surprised and, because I knew it had been a long shot, I just left it. He was the president of FIFA after all. But, after I had finished eating dinner with Neto that night, he casually said, 'By the way, your interview with Dr Havelange is at ten tomorrow morning. Don't be late.' It summed up what an amazing friend Neto is.

Another person that comes to mind when I think about Brazil is Denis Menezes. He used to be one of the top radio journalists with the Il Globo radio station and I can remember him taking me to the Fla-Flu, which is how the locals refer to the derby match between Flamengo and Fluminense. It's one of the great derby games in world football and there were some one hundred and twenty thousand people at this particular match. Denis took me down behind the goals at the Maracana with all the other radio reporters while the match was in progress. All the reporters had to stick their microphones through the goal net when a corner was being taken so the listeners could hear what was going on in the goal box. Following Denis around opened my eyes to how tough a job the football reporters in Brazil actually have. They interview the players before the game, during the game, at half-time, in the showers after the game—literally everywhere and anywhere they can. Still, when Denis took me down to the dressing rooms I was amazed at how down-to-earth the players were. There was none of the histrionics that goes on with top athletes in other countries. All the players had their families around them, because the game is very much a family affair over there, and they always appeared happy to chat to the reporters.

I first met Denis in 1988 when I was employed by the ASF to travel to Brazil to find out about the Brazilian team that was coming to the Bicentennial Gold Cup. The CBF president at the time was Otavio Guimaraes. He was also heavily involved with Formula One motor racing and was a wonderful larger-than-life character. He has since passed away but he was so helpful to me on that trip that I remember him fondly. When I arrived he set up a meeting for me with the Brazilian coach, Carlos Alberto da Silva, and I was able to learn all about the young stars that Brazil was sending out to Australia. It included the likes of Muller, Romario, Jorghino, Taffarel, Branco and Giovanni and I was not surprised when they eventually won the tournament by beating Australia 2–0 in the final.

During the Bicentennial Gold Cup I also bumped into Carlos Alberto Pereira again. He was coaching Saudi Arabia in the tournament and it was during this time that I became good friends with him. I was extremely pleased when he took the Brazilians to the 1994 World Cup because it vindicated him after all the criticism he had received in the lead-up to the tournament for being too defensive and not producing enough winning results.

I was lucky enough to have lunch with Carlos at the

Fluminense club on my last trip to Brazil and was overwhelmed to think that I was sitting with a World Cup-winning coach. Carlos has always been interested in what is happening in Australian football and when I told him that Soccer Australia was searching for a technical director, he said he would be interested in that position. I passed his expression of interest on to Soccer Australia but, to my knowledge, they have never been in touch with him. Maybe they are looking for someone with better credentials...

I have been back to Brazil every year since my first visit there. My usual routine is to fly to Argentina and catch up with my old St George friend Salvador Isaac before heading on to Rio. The experiences I have had in the football stadiums of Argentina during my time there have been particularly unforgettable. Watching Boca Juniors play at the famous Bombonera Stadium, or the Chocolate Box as it is known, is simply mind-boggling. Boca are the team of the people and its fans are known as the *descamisados* or 'the shirtless ones'. This is because most of the stadium is full of young guys with their shirts off, waving them above their heads, chanting and cheering. The stadium is usually packed to capacity an hour before the game and the crowd entertains itself by chanting wildly and throwing confetti. There are no dancing girls or rock bands to entertain the crowd like there often are in Australia. Usually there is just a boy who walks about the pitch juggling a ball for up to an hour before the game. Maradona used to do it when he was young. The crowd never appears to pay close attention to the kid but if he ever lets the ball drop everyone in the crowd certainly lets him know they've noticed by cheering madly. All things considered, I would probably rate the Bombonera, alongside the Maracana and the Azteca in Mexico, as one of the best stadiums I have ever been to.

The more I see of South America the more I love it and I never tire of visiting. Although my focus has probably always been on Brazil and Argentina, I have also travelled to many other parts of the continent, including Chile, Colombia (which is one of the most beautiful places I have ever been to), Uruguay, Ecuador and Venezuela. They all offer their own unique football cultures and have all provided me with great experiences and friendships outside of football.

When it was announced that Australia had been given the World Youth Cup in 1993 I decided to travel to the South American qualifiers in Colombia on a working holiday. I knew I would be helping SBS with its World Cup coverage so I thought visiting the qualifiers would give me all the inside information on the teams.

At the time, I had also been thinking about trying to get the Brazilian youth team out to Australia to play a series. I thought the Australian public would respond enthusiastically to their international status and I knew a series would offer the Young Socceroos some invaluable preparation for the World Cup. I thought the Brazilians would also appreciate it as good preparation for their World Cup quest.

When I met the Brazilian team manager Carlos Alberto da Luz at my hotel in Medellin I took the opportunity to ask whether arranging a tour was a possibility. Carlos, who was also to become a great friend of mine, immediately invited me to training to meet the Brazilian coach Julio Leal and his brother, and assistant coach, Jairo. They were both keen on my offer because they realised it would provide an advantage over the rest of the competition if the team qualified for the World Youth Cup. Playing a tournament in Australia would allow their team to become familiar with the conditions and the facilities and would also provide them with the opportunity to organise training venues, accommodation and other administrative requirements well ahead of every other team.

In the end, Brazil won the qualifying tournament for the World Youth Cup ahead of Uruguay and Colombia and before I knew it I had been invited to fly back to Brazil with the team so I could meet with the CBF and arrange the Australian tour. Once again, the Brazilians amazed me with their hospitality. During the trip to Brazil I was fortunate enough to get to know the team very well, including current stars such as Savio, Dida and Jardel, as well as the coaching staff and I really enjoyed their company.

When I heard that the Brazilian youth team were preparing for another tournament in Venezuela at which Australia was also playing, I decided to stay on to watch. It proved to be a good decision because not only was it a memorable tournament, with Brazil winning and Australia making the semi-finals, it also further cemented my relationship with the team and the management. So much so that when I returned to Australia I was confident the tour to Australia would be a success. I had spoken to Dominic Galati, the Head of Sport at SBS, and to Les Murray, and they were tremendously supportive. SBS had the broadcast rights to the World Youth Cup and without its support the series against Brazil would have never have got off the ground. They immediately saw the advantages of promoting the event and threw the whole weight of the station behind it. In fact, the series was called the 'SBS Youth Challenge' in recognition of the television station's integral role.

The public response to the Brazilian youth team's four-match tour to Australia turned out to exceed everyone's expectations. The crowd in Perth for the first game was more than fifteen thousand-strong and people had to be turned away from the last game at Marconi Stadium in Sydney. I had people pleading with me to get them into the ground. There were television screens erected in the car park and in the club just so fans wouldn't miss out on the action. Once again, my belief that the public would support top-class football was vindicated.

Apart from being the initiator and promoter of the event, my job was also to look after the Brazilian team. As a result I spent a great deal of my time with the players and the team management. I became good friends with most of the staff, including the team medico, Dr Jordi. I still try and catch up with him whenever I visit Brazil and he always takes a look at my leg to see how the old knee injury is looking.

The entire team's professionalism and attitude was outstanding. The coaching staff was intent on using the trip as a learning experience and while there were some opportunities for the team to become upset, particularly after some questionable refereeing decisions, they always showed great diplomacy. The coaches wanted the players to learn about discipline and how to cope in unfavourable situations because they knew it would make their players stronger in the long run. As a result, winning was never the sole objective for the Brazilians on that tour. Preparing for the World Youth Cup was always first and foremost on their minds.

At the end of the fourth match in Sydney, the series was tied and needed to be settled by a penalty shoot-out. It was a particularly nerve-racking shoot-out for me because of a little slip-up I had made prior to the match. Before the team's last training session I had been asked by Julio Leal to find a place where the team could train that was near their hotel. He didn't want to have to go a long way and told me that he only needed goal posts. An integral part of all Brazilian training is practising penalties and free-kicks after training and this was doubly the case before a final (or any game which could go to penalties in the event of a draw) because at the end of training the team would select its penalty takers and prepare for a shoot-out.

I was assured by one of my contacts in the local soccer community that there was a set of goal posts at the Domain in the city so I told Julio to train there. Unfortunately, when the Brazilians arrived there were no goal posts to be found and Julio was understandably furious. He was forced to put down jumpers on the ground to act as makeshift goal posts so the team could practise their penalties. When I found out I was mortified. I think I was probably more nervous than the players during the penalty shoot-out because I knew if they lost that he would come looking for me. Luckily, for my sake, they won.

After the tournament I took Julio Leal and Carlos Alberto da Luz, the team's administration manager, to Adelaide to help them assess the venues for the upcoming World Youth Cup. They booked the best training facilities, checked the accommodation and ensured that every base was covered for when the team returned. It might seem trivial but it was a key part of their World Youth Cup preparations.

By this stage, I was feeling satisfied about how the tournament had gone and my own relationship with the Brazilian team. They were happy, SBS was happy and Soccer Australia was happy because the tournament had exceeded everyone's wildest dreams in terms of how the Australian fans had responded. The matches in Adelaide, Sydney, Canberra and Newcastle had all been well supported and well organised and had gone a long way to easing some fears that the World Youth Cup might not draw much of a crowd. In fact, the tournament was also critical in convincing FIFA and the IOC that Australia was capable of staging a big soccer tournament in the lead-up to the Sydney 2000 bid.

The final of the World Youth Cup between Brazil and Ghana was a great game; in fact probably one of the best I have ever seen. There was a full house of forty-three thousand fans at the Sydney Football Stadium and it was an exciting and tense atmosphere. Can you imagine any other sport attracting this sort of crowd to the final of a youth tournament where the host nation wasn't even playing? The skill level of the players was amazingly high and it seemed like the ball hardly ever went out of play. While Ghana looked the better team in the first half, Brazil somehow managed to shift up a gear after half-time to win. My view has always been that the best coaches have the ability to alter the course of a game at half-time; the time when they can sit down, talk to the players and make changes. Julio must have done that in the final because Brazil came out a far better side in the second half.

I actually think one of the special elements of Brazilian teams is an ability to lift when they need to. They have successfully managed to do it throughout their history and while I guess it is the sign of all true champions, I am sure their coaches have also had a lot to do with this ability. Of course, the expectation of Brazilian teams is always so great because they regard the silver medal as tin. Gold is the only medal that counts for them and their fans. That is why the Olympics irks them so much, because it is the one tournament they haven't won.

I was delighted with the performance of the Australian team, who had finished fourth and had quite clearly benefited from the earlier series against Brazil. The tournament had been great for the game in Australia and I was happy with the way everything had turned out.

The morning after the final I was invited to the Brazilian team meeting at the hotel. When I walked into the room I immediately noticed that the boys were all wearing their winner's medals. Julio called me up to the front of the room and said, pointing to his own medal, 'Half of this medal is yours, Johnny.' It was a special moment because I had not even received a telephone call from Soccer Australia to thank me for helping the Australian team to prepare for the tournament. I felt it had been a monumental contribution from myself and SBS to give the Australian team valuable preparation experience against Brazil. Which Australian team could possibly dream, at that time, of playing against Brazil four times in ten days? But not a word of acknowledgment ever came our way.

When I accompanied the Brazilian team to the airport for their departure, their striker Gian, who had scored the winning goal in the final, pulled me aside and gave me the shirt he had worn during the match. He had signed it for me and told me he wanted me to have it as thanks for my efforts. It was an amazing show of gratitude and I was stunned.

The next year when Gian made his senior debut for Vasco de Gama in Brazil, I was lucky enough to be at the match and was invited down to the change rooms. There were hundreds of people and media everywhere with cameras, microphones and cables all over the place. Players were being interviewed by the media wherever I turned. But in the midst of the masses Gian saw me and took off his shirt to give to me. Later he would write on it, 'To dear John, A great friend forever, No. 9.' I have since had both Gian's shirts framed because that is how much they mean to me. It is the sort of gesture of friendship that I will never forget.

Another example of the generosity of my Brazilian friends happened when I met my friend Carlos Alberto da Luz several years ago for lunch while I was in Brazil. He was carrying a paper bag when he arrived but I didn't think much of it at the time. During lunch he passed me the bag and told me to open it. Inside was a shirt signed by Ronaldo. Carlos told me that it was the shirt Ronaldo had worn in the recent Copa America, which Brazil had won. I was staggered when he told me it was now mine.

I guess it's moments like these that I remember when I think of my experiences with Brazil and South America. The Latins are such a friendly and giving people that my time with them always fuels my love affair with the entire South American continent, its football and its people.

After the Brazilian team had left Australia with the World Youth Cup under their belts, I was called by a Brazilian journalist who had been travelling with the team. I had met him during the tournament so when he said he needed to see me I invited him down to my farm at Gold Creek in Canberra. I assumed he wanted to talk about the Brazilian team but he took me by surprise when he said to me, 'John, I'm here on behalf of the entire Brazilian team. They want you to be their player manager.'

I didn't know what to say. I was completely dumbfounded and it took a while to digest what I had just heard. My first response was to explain that player managers or sports agents weren't established professions in Australia and that I had no experience. While sport management was big overseas, it was a little-known concept in Australia. I told him that I simply didn't know enough about this area of the game and I wouldn't know what I could actually do for the boys. But he stopped me in my tracks and explained, 'It doesn't matter, you can learn all that stuff. The boys want you to do it because they trust you.' I still regard his words as one of the biggest compliments I have ever received. It really meant the world to hear him say it. Unfortunately, I knew I couldn't take up the offer.

At the time I didn't like, and I still don't like, the principle of player managers and sports agents. They are probably necessary at some stages in a player's career, as I had discovered early in my own career, but I think in many respects they don't actually contribute at the grassroots level. However, it was obviously a tempting offer, especially when you think of some of the players in that Brazilian team. The likes of Dida, who played for AC Milan; Savio, who plays for Real Madrid; and Jardel, who plays for Porto and Galatasaray, would have obviously been lucrative players to manage. But sports management wasn't what I enjoyed about the game and I wanted my conscience to be clear.

When you think about Brazil you can't help but think of Pelé. My first experience of the great man came during the visit of Brazilian club team Santos during 1972 when he was a guest of St George Budapest—'the Saints'—at our club (Santos, coincidentally, means 'Saints' in Portuguese). I did not actually meet him properly until the Bicentennial Gold Cup in 1988. Pelé had been brought out to Australia to help promote the tournament and it didn't take long for me to realise that he was, in fact, a public relations person's nightmare. The problem isn't that Pelé is too demanding or melodramatic; it is rather that everyone desires his autograph or wants to share a few words with him. He is constantly besieged by fans. Crowds went berserk when he came to Australia and there was a near disaster in the Rundle Mall in Adelaide when he was practically mobbed. I don't know what those people who say Australia is not interested in football thought when they saw people stampeding to get his autograph!

When Pelé gives an autograph he does not just sign his name. He will write a heartfelt message, personal to each different fan. He is just that type of person and wants to give time to everyone.

There is one story I feel really illustrates his character. I was invited to a party at the Lord Mayor's office in Adelaide during the Bicentennial Gold Cup. I had taken my daughter Shannon, who was only twelve at the time, and had been assigned to the head table where the Lord Mayor and Pelé were seated. As people began eating, the Lord Mayor noticed that Pelé was still standing up. He said, 'Pelé, come and sit down,' but Pelé simply remained standing and replied, 'I'm waiting for the young lady to sit down first.' I quickly realised that the young lady he was talking about was Shannon, who hadn't yet been seated. I thought it was a tremendous demonstration of respect and humility from such a great sportsman.

The other anecdote that comes to mind involving Pelé was told to me by the Brazilian ambassador to Australia, Marcos Cortes at my fiftieth birthday celebrations. I had met Marcos during my frequent visits to the Brazilian embassy in Canberra when I needed to arrange visas for the players, coaching staff and officials of various Brazilian teams and I had become friends with most of the staff at the embassy as a result. Marcos has a very dry sense of humour and would often explain that while the worst football players in Brazil usually become goalkeepers, those that are particularly bad goalkeepers become ambassadors! Marcos told my guests that when Pelé had been in Australia he had spent some time mixing with the local Brazilian community. Towards the end of his stay, Pelé had approached Marcos and said to him, 'You know, Johnny does a better job of promoting Brazil than you do.' Marcos was actually the longest-serving ambassador to Australia in his country's history and the greatest figure in Brazil's football history told him that I do a better job than he does! It still makes me laugh. But I guess in many ways I have become an unofficial ambassador for Brazil in Australia. I just can't help it, such is my love for the country, its people and its football.

On Pelé's most recent trip to Australia, as part of a promotional visit for Mastercard's sponsorship of the 2002 World Cup, I was asked by SBS to do an hour-long interview with him. Although I had met Pelé many times prior to this, I was still quite surprised when he greeted me as an old friend. For someone who meets thousands and thousands of people in the space of a week I took his warmth towards me as a real compliment.

While all the other television crews came in with pages of notes and research to help them with their questions, I simply sat there and talked to him as one soccer player to another. It was a real pleasure for me and reinforced my pet theory that footballers are just footballers whether they play for Real Madrid or the Jamberoo Pub over-50s team. The interview was easy and enjoyable because it was just like talking to another player in the dressing rooms.

I believe Pelé was the greatest sportsperson of the twentieth century because he is generally acknowledged as the greatest player in the world's one truly global game. His message to everyone involved in the game that day, during our interview, was that no one is any better than anyone else in football and we are all lucky just to be involved in the beautiful game. I think it perfectly sums up the Brazilian attitude towards soccer and it's what makes Pelé, Brazil and South America so special.

17

The Olympics

My first taste of soccer at the Olympic Games came in 1956 when the games were staged in Australia for the first time. My older brother Ross, in what I still regard as a magnanimous gesture because he was nineteen and I was only thirteen, decided he would use his holidays to take both me and my cousin Keith to Melbourne to see some of the action.

I will always be grateful that Ross took us to the Olympics because it turned out to be a fantastic experience to see all of Australia's sporting greats in action, especially for a young teenager like me who really loved sport. One of the highlights was going to the athletics and watching Betty Cuthbert and Hec Hogan compete but, of course, the main reason behind our trip was to see the soccer.

There were no preliminary group stages in the soccer at the Melbourne Olympics. It was straight elimination so once a team lost they could pack their bags and start heading home. Australia's first match was against Japan at Olympic Park and the team included all my boyhood heroes, such as Bobby

Bignall, Ronnie Lord and Billy Henderson. I had followed many of the national team players at club level and it was a great thrill to see them playing for Australia at the Melbourne Olympics. They lived up to my expectations as well by beating the Japanese 2–0. The team really weren't expected to do that well but they were playing at home and I was excited about their chances after the first game. The victory over Japan moved them into a quarter-final match against India.

If there is one image that has stuck in my mind from the the 1956 Olympics it is of the Indian team lining up before their match against Australia without any boots on. I thought my eyes were playing tricks on me when I first saw them. They simply played with their feet bandaged! When I think back, it probably demonstrates how fair our boys were in those days because the Indians didn't suffer any serious injuries during the game. You can imagine teams playing now against opponents with no shoes on. It would be like a war zone. It didn't seem to make much difference to the Indians though because they ended up beating us 4–2. It was a disappointing day because had Australia beaten India, the team would have had a medal chance.

The final between the Soviet Union and Yugoslavia was played just before the closing ceremony and was watched by the biggest soccer crowd in Australian history. The player that still stands out in my memory is the great Soviet goalkeeper Lev Yashin. He is still considered one of the all-time great goalkeepers—some people still say he was the *best*—and it was something special to see him play. He was nicknamed the 'Black Panther' because he always dressed in black. At the time, he seemed larger than life and I would not have believed it if anyone had told me that nearly fifteen years later I would put a goal past him when I took the field for New South Wales against his Soviet club team Moscow Dynamo.

The Melbourne Olympics were not my first experience with international football. I had seen the Yugoslavian club side Hajduk Split play Australia at the Sydney Showground with my father when I was about six and I had been to see other international teams, such as Austrian club side Rapid Vienna, after that. If the Olympics had any lasting effect on me it was to fuel my interest in all things sport and my desire to represent Australia.

My memories of Melbourne and the wonderful spectacle of the 2000 Olympics in Sydney make me regret never competing in an Olympic Games. I would have loved to represent the country and try to win a medal. Although after 1956 I would go on to travel the world playing soccer, Australia did not enter a team after the 1956 Olympics until the 1988 Seoul Olympics. Of course, Australia was banned from international competition from 1957 to 1963 because of the dispute over financial arrangements concerning the transfer of foreign players into the local competitions, so we were not allowed to compete in the Rome 1960 Olympics. But, even when Australia was allowed back into the official international soccer community, the Olympics had become the sole domain of amateurs. Because the players in Australia received some payment for playing, we were considered professionals or at least *not* amateurs, and we were not allowed to compete. Olympic soccer was usually dominated by Eastern European teams up until the 1984 Los Angeles Games because most of their players played in army teams, employed by the state, and were therefore not considered professional. In reality, they were far more professional than we were.

By the time the Seoul Olympics came around, the International Olympic Committee and FIFA had decided that any football player could now play, professional or otherwise, and Australia decided to enter a team once again. Australia could technically have entered a team for the Los Angeles Olympics but had simply not got its act together in time. Of course, at this stage, the great player drain from Australian

MBE, 1974. After my comeback from injury and subsequent to Australia qualifying for the 1974 World Cup, on 1 January 1974 I received a telegram informing me that I had been awarded an MBE—the first time anyone had received the award for soccer. The Governor of NSW, Sir Roden Cutler, presented me with the MBE at Government House, Sydney.

World Cup '74 Socceroos. One of the many attempts to get the official team photo of the Socceroos in Germany, this shows the typical camaraderie and good-natured skylarking between teammates. Our base camp was at the Hamburg Football Club and it was the first time we had ever been afforded the luxury of being treated as professional full-time players, rather than the part-time players we necessarily were back home.

Proving the critics wrong. I'm followed onto the field in Hamburg by Ray Richards, Jimmy Mackay, Col Curran and Peter van Rjn, to the left. With our strong performance at the 1974 World Cup, the Socceroos proved the Australian and international critics of our chances wrong.

Fairytale finish. The last game of my career was played against Hakoah, a game described by Brian Mossop in *The Sydney Morning Herald*: 'The fairytale rise of reluctant coach John Warren ended in a dream sequence as St George Budapest carried off the 1974 Soccer championship at the Sports Ground yesterday ... Fittingly, it was a superbly executed goal by Warren that settled the issue beyond doubt ... as Warren walked from the field, the crowd of 10,883 stood to applaud a fine sportsman.'

The Sun Coaching Clinic. Thousands of kids around Australia attended coaching clinics I held. I really enjoyed taking the game to the kids because I felt like I was helping to improve the standard of play in Australia and strengthen soccer's popularity and profile. Everywhere I went, kids seemed to genuinely love the game.

Canberra City days 1978. As coach of Canberra City I had to build the team from scratch to play in the National Soccer League—a rewarding period in my football life because of the enthusiasm of everybody involved. Back (l-r): Billy Smith, Roy Starke, Jimmy Cant, John Brown, David Lindenmeyer, Ron Tilsed, Adrian Alston, Mick Milanovic, Oscar Langone, me. Middle: Keni Kawaleva, Brian Stoddart, Chris Tomlinson, Mick Black, Victor Fernandez, Tony Henderson, Ivan Gruicic, Nick Boskov, Danny Moulis. Front: David O'Connor, Allan Bourke, Greg Willets, Luis Salgado, Steve Hogg.

Canberra City supporter, 1978. Prime Minister of the time, Malcolm Fraser, our club's No. 1 badgeholder, learns some soccer skills.

This is Your Life, 1978. On my mother's birthday she invited me to Sydney with my daughter Shannon for her party. When I got off the plane from Canberra I was taken completely unawares by Roger Climpson who greeted me and took me onto 'This is Your Life'. The experience was a wonderful blur of friends, family and relived memories. Standing (l-r): my brother Geoff, my sister-in-law Nola, my brother Ross (Nola's husband). Front (l-r): My nephew Timothy, Mum, my daughter Shannon, me, Dad and two very tired kids for that time of night, my nephew and godson Jamie and niece Erica.

Football, family and friends. All the important people in my life were on the show and in the audience, not all of them pictured. Back (l-r): George Koi, Ray Baartz, John Chegwyn, John Watkiss, David Jack, Rale Rasic, Charlie Perkins, Dr Brian Corrigan, Uncle Joe Vlasits, Theo Moulis, Sir Arthur George, Mick Milanovic, host Roger Climpson, Steve Hogg, Peter van Rjn. Middle (l-r): Martin Royal, Atti Abonyi, Danny Moulis, Geoff Warren, Victor Fernandez, Laurie Hegyes, Nola Warren, Ross Warren. Front (l-r): Mum, Shannon, me, Dad.

My daughter. The highlight of 'This is Your Life' was host Roger Climpson announcing: 'And here's your biggest fan, three-year-old Shannon' as my daughter tentatively came out onto stage, blinded by the studio lights and a little confused at all the fuss. After the show, a dinner was held for everyone present on the show and in the audience, and there were many special and memorable speeches and toasts.

Pelé's New York Soccer Camps. My nephew and godson Jamie awestruck as he meets legend Pelé at the famous Pelé soccer camps in New York. The picture was later autographed for my young grandson 'To Riley, Best wishes, Pelé'. This photo captures the absolute warmth and generosity of this man who is quite rightly worshipped by young and old football fans, all over the world.

The Johnny Warren Soccer Academy. More than 10,000 kids stayed at my Gold Creek property in Canberra during the 1980s and 1990s to attend my week-long soccer camps. We would train three times a day and visit the Australian Institute of Sport but I would also make sure that the kids enjoyed a taste of country life with barbecues, bonfires, sheep shearing and kangaroo watching. At this particular camp in 1980 we had a special guest coach, Craig Johnston.

NSL Awards Night, 1983. Charles Perkins, Frank Farina, former Prime Minister Bob Hawke and me on the night Frank Farina was awarded Player of the Year in the National Soccer League. Several years later the award became known as the Johnny Warren Medal, soccer's equivalent in prestige as the Brownlow Medal is to Australian Rules Football for the players' player of the year.

Ice-skating champion. My daughter Shannon has always been a talented sportsperson but fell in love with ice-skating particularly and won state and national titles. I could certainly appreciate how little recognition she received for her efforts in Australia because like my time playing soccer, ice-skating was, in many ways, considered the wrong sport in the wrong country at the wrong time.

Canberra City Old Boys. My old friend Charlie Perkins got me to sign up to his team to play in the ACT sixth division competition in 1986. My stint with the Canberra City Old Boys turned out to be one of the most enjoyable seasons I have ever had—good camaraderie and winning results. Even though the total combined age of the team came to 595 years we won the league and cup double.

The young guns. Hopefully, when our current crop of young guns finish their careers they will have made the game better than when they entered it. Australia's chances for future World Cups will be improved by changes at an institutional level. Back (l-r): Harry Kewell, Brett Emerton, Craig Moore, Tony Vidmar, Shaun Murphy, Mark Schwarzer. Front (l-r): Kevin Muscat, Josip Skoko, Mark Viduka, Stan Lazaridis, Paul Okon (captain).

shores was only in its infancy and it was possible for us to select our best Olympic team from the talent actually still playing in Australia. I believe this 1988 team produced the best-ever performance by an Australian team.

The Seoul Olympics of 1988 was the first, and only, Olympic football tournament where all players were eligible to compete, irrespective of their professional or amateur status. Since 1988, Olympic Games football remains open to professional players, but FIFA has insisted that age restrictions apply. Their reason for this rule is to protect their own property, the World Cup, the largest cyclical event (whether sporting or cultural) there is. FIFA believes that to leave Olympic football as a fully open competition would effectively mean a 'world championship' every two years as each Olympic Games and FIFA World Cup are separated by two years, hence diluting the prestige of the World Cup. Realising the importance of football to the Olympics, the International Olympic Committee (IOC) later agreed to the compromise of an age limitation for Olympic football which is now a tournament for players under the age of twenty-three. The rider on that is for three over-age players to be included in each squad which is at the discretion of each coach and national association. But, for the 1988 Seoul Olympic football tournament, full national teams were in attendance. It was into this fray that the Socceroos entered.

Australia was drawn to play Yugoslavia, Brazil and Nigeria. Talk about a group of death! Nigeria, the Super Eagles, had burst onto the world football stage with a vengeance. (Indeed, Nigeria were to win the Olympic football gold medal in the very near future.) However, the draw first had us up against Yugoslavia, the aristocrats of central and eastern European football. Yugoslavia was still in its Tito conglomerate form; republics such as Croatia yet to gain independence. Consequently, the Yugoslav national football team boasted outstanding players from across the Tito divides, uniting prominent Croatian players such as Robert Prosinecki with

Serbian superstars such as Dragan Stojkovic. There were many others too but this football team, whose international diplomatic role was to cover up the cracks in the Yugoslav union, was excellent.

Socceroo coach Frank Arok's daughter was living in Yugoslavia at the time so he asked her to keep an eye out and tell him where the Yugoslavs were playing their warm-up games. She informed him that Switzerland was to be the location. Frank approached the ASF and told them that he wanted to go to Switzerland to find out what Yugoslavia were all about. They were to be our first opponents at the Olympics and Frank wanted to do the necessary homework. Frank was asked why he wanted to undertake such a mission. Frank, dumbfounded, explained that it was to give his team the best possible chance of beating Yugoslavia. However, the ASF didn't even want to contemplate such a fallacious notion as Australia beating Yugoslavia. An agitated Frank hit back with the assertion that 'of course we're going to bloody well beat them'. He told head office that he needed to go for only two days to see the practice game in Lausanne. The point was made to Frank that there wasn't any money to undertake such a trip, but I understand that Frank came away with the impression that if Yugoslavia was indeed defeated, his costs for the reconnaissance mission would be reimbursed.

Frank left for Europe and gathered the intelligence he felt was needed to unplug the Yugoslavian team. Frank was, in his former life, president of the Yugoslav Coaches Federation, so he was able to plot the downfall of the Yugoslavians extremely effectively. I think it remains Australia's greatest international result. The Olympic Games, no less. Frank plotted the victory and the boys executed it. Frank Farina scored the goal that sent howls of disbelief bouncing all around Europe, signalled the commencement of an inquisition inside Yugoslavia and propelled Farina on his own successful sojourn through professional European football. Back home, it was the day of SBS commentator Andy Paschalides' wedding and when news came through of the victory, all of us at the wedding erupted with sheer joy.

The next match was against Brazil in Seoul. It brought us all down to earth somewhat. Brazil won 3–0 with Romario scoring the three goals. Every time someone looked sideways, he'd score. The final group match was Nigeria and it produced another great result. John Kosmina scored the goal, Australia won 1–0 and moved through to the quarter-finals.

The quarter-final resulted in a 3–0 loss to the Soviet Union. That was a bad game for us; David Mitchell being sent off. Frank Arok recalled to me that the Soviets were 'kicking the shit out of him' and Mitchell, drained of patience, retaliated in view of the match officials so was summarily dispatched from the ground. As with the geopolitical makeup of Yugoslavia, perestroika was yet to envelop the former Soviet Union so their Olympic football team was an amalgam of talent from all the Soviet states and republics—a formidable combination of players. Ultimately, the Soviet Union beat Brazil for the gold medal. It is possibly some consolation that the final analysis shows that we were knocked out by the gold medallists. We came through the group of death. The Socceroos played against full national teams, in world-class competition, losing only to the gold and silver medallists.

I don't recall Arok ever receiving any reimbursement from the federation to compensate him for his endeavour that helped Australia perform so well at the Seoul Olympics.

Most people probably remember the performance of the 1992 team as Australia's greatest Olympic soccer achievement. The sticking point for me though is that by the time of the Barcelona Games the format of the soccer competition had changed again, so that it was now limited to players under the age of twenty-three. The Australian team was selected mainly from the successful side that had contested the 1991

World Youth Cup in Portugal, which meant that players such as Mark Bosnich, Ned Zelic and Paul Okon got the chance to grace the Olympic stage. The 1992 side had beaten a star-studded Dutch side with the help of a wonder goal from captain Ned Zelic to qualify for Barcelona. The goal forever marked Zelic in Australian soccer history and was critical in knocking out a Dutch side that included the likes of the De Boer twins and Marc Overmars. The Australian team then went on to make the semi-finals at the Barcelona Olympics and were unlucky not to win a medal so, on paper, they are far and away the team that has achieved the best result at the Olympics. It is only that the 1988 team were competing against the world's best professional players that makes me really exalt the performance of that particular team. Nonetheless, I am quite content to say that both teams were absolutely outstanding and again, showed the world *and* the Australian public just how great Australian soccer could be.

Results have been less kind to Australia since Barcelona. Certainly, the teams of 1996 in Atlanta and 2000 in Sydney have not performed as well in comparison. By Atlanta, the format had changed once again and now three over-age players were allowed to bolster the under-23s teams. This change doesn't appear to have helped Australia's performance though. I am not sure why. We certainly have talented enough senior players to come back and bolster the team and no one can question the standard of our youth teams. Still, just making the Olympics is an achievement in itself these days.

I was particularly interested in the 2000 Olympics because in 1991, I was approached by the bid team and asked to become their football ambassador. It was an honorary position that entailed helping the bid team convince the international soccer community that Australia was up to the task of hosting the Olympic soccer tournament. It was a role that became really close to my heart because it combined my love for Australia and my love for the game. The position saw me spend a great deal of time liaising with international soccer officials from all over the world. Some of these meetings took place in Australia but for much of my work I had to fly overseas to soccer tournaments and gatherings. I was given an allowance to entertain people and was encouraged to make as much contact with soccer people as possible. I took the responsibility of the position very seriously.

As part of my role as ambassador I flew to the under-17s World Cup in Japan, the 1993 Copa America competition in Ecuador and several other events in South America and Africa, including the under-20s World Cup African qualifying tournament in Mauritius. These trips were extremely important because everyone who is anyone from the world of soccer attends these types of events. They are like a smorgasbord of the international soccer community and not only was I able to liaise with people integral to the football world, I was able to push the Sydney Olympics bid and make sure these people knew that Australia was serious about staging Olympic Games soccer. Unfortunately, Soccer Australia never seems to have a representative at these gatherings and, especially after working as part of the Olympics bid, I have long stressed the need for Australia to have at least one person at these events to make sure our interests are being looked after within the international soccer community.

As football ambassador I presented a video of the 1993 World Youth Cup that was staged in Australia for worldwide distribution. This was essential in convincing the international community that Australia could not only stage an international football tournament but could also attract fans. As Australia has never been considered a hotbed of football passion it was important to convince the world that the community in Australia would turn out and support Olympic soccer. Empty stadiums were not what the IOC and FIFA wanted.

I really commend Rod McGeoch and the bid team for the excellent job they performed in bringing the Olympics to Sydney. They immediately realised that it was simply not possible to win an Olympic Games bid without recognising the vital importance of soccer to the success of the Games and so they attempted to ensure that a successful soccer tournament was a priority. They recognised two crucial elements. Firstly, they realised the necessity of calling the event football rather than soccer. (The word 'soccer' is a derivation of the term 'Association Football'—Assoc.—the sport's official name. Very few countries actually call it soccer but it has been acceptable in Australia because it differentiates the game from Australian Rules, rugby league and rugby union, which also call themselves football.) While FIFA would have ultimately ensured they called it football anyway—the game's global name—the bid team decided to keep referring to it as football when addressing the Australian community. It may seem a trivial point but it was critical in exposing Australia to the worldview of the game and demonstrating that we, as a nation, were willing to embrace this view.

Secondly, the bid team realised that because football is just about the number-one sport in every country around the world, Olympic officials are often football officials or supporters. The game is so important overseas that football officials hold tremendous sway and often double up as IOC delegates and officials. The bid team perceptively decided to focus on ensuring football was given a high priority because they realised it could impact upon the entire bidding process decisively. Ultimately, it is these sorts of decisions that can mean the difference between success and failure in terms of winning an Olympics bid.

In the end, it was an honour to be involved with winning the Olympics. Rod McGeoch was certainly a fine leader and I have nothing but praise for his offsider Bob Elphinston. Bob used to be the sportsmaster at Kingsgrove Boys High School when I was working as St George's public relations man so I had dealt with him in the past and knew he was an extremely capable person. Even though the bid was a real team effort, I think Bob was the unsung hero of the Games bid. There were so many people working towards the one goal that it was a tremendous experience to be part of and I look back on it fondly.

Despite this, it was not long after Sydney was awarded the Olympics that I became slightly jaded over the entire experience. Rod McGeoch was replaced and a new administration was installed. It seemed to me that the team that had worked so hard to get the Olympics to Sydney was now being given the back-seat once all the spadework had been done.

Soon after the bid announcement I became very ill. I contracted a viral liver infection in Ecuador in 1993 while I was working there in my role as football ambassador. The sickness really knocked me around and I drifted away from any involvement in the football tournament. SOCOG did not contact me in the interim and so by the time of the Olympics I had completely lost all contact with them. I wasn't even invited to any of the soccer matches and I wasn't sent any tickets. After all my efforts I didn't actually attend a single match of soccer at the entire Olympic tournament. Obviously, watching what I could on television wasn't as great as being there but I still enjoyed the football.

Two days before the official Opening Ceremony of the 2000 Olympics the MCG was completely packed to watch Australia play Italy—noteworthy considering it was an under-23s match. What other sport in Australia would pack the MCG for an under-23s game? Australia, a developing nation in football terms taking on Italy, one of the sport's giants was a sight worth beholding. It was the sort of David and Goliath contest that Australians relish. The game was televised live, prime-time. The teams were lining up for the national anthems. The emotion was palpable, even through the television screen. The camera started to pan across the Aussie Olympic football team—captain Emerton, Milosevic, Colosimo—for the national anthem and, at this significant moment of nationhood, the network broke for an advertisement. I found it disgraceful. Nothing like that happened when Ian Thorpe was on the dais. The impression is that swimming is worth national celebration, but let's not get too carried away with soccer. Never mind that the reality is that the national football team is more representative of multicultural Australian society than any other national teams and that no other sport has helped unite so many different communities and people of different cultural backgrounds in Australia.

Unfortunately, the Olyroos (their name created by the combination of the words 'Olympics' and 'Socceroos') became the first host nation to fail to progress past the first stage of an international FIFA competition when Honduras defeated them at the Sydney Football Stadium, finishing Australia's run at the Olympics. This is not the sort of record any nation wants to hold and it was a major disappointment because the team had had several years to prepare and played reasonably well during the tournament. Once again though, mistakes from normally reliable defenders cost us matches. Losing control of the ball at critical times, missing clearances and fumbling because of horribly miscued passes seemed to be mistakes so out of character for the calibre of the players involved that I couldn't help but think of the witch doctor from Mozambique and his curse again! The team certainly didn't play poorly during the tournament but, at that level, mistakes are usually the only thing that separate the teams. Australia seems to have learned this lesson the hard way on too many occasions. Still, while it didn't work out for the 2000 Sydney Olympics, I am confident that Australia will strike success in the Olympics in the future, once we are more experienced on the international soccer stage.

Apart from my own personal disappointments, I thought Australia's staging of the 2000 Games was tremendous. The entire event was first class and Australia was really showcased to the world as a great nation. The soccer tournament, in particular, was an outstanding success. The massive public support for the event simply reinforced what I have long known about the game in Australia—if a top-quality event is staged, the soccer crowd will be there.

The problem has always been that Australia doesn't stage enough matches that are of the highest international quality. Australia usually has two extremely important games every four years—the World Cup qualifiers—and the public knows it. Attempts to sell the public second-rate matches simply backfire. Events like the recent half-baked tour by Manchester United are actually harming the game in Australia because they leave the public disillusioned and feeling sceptical about the next big game. Few big-name players usually end up on the pitch because they are offered little incentive to come to Australia. Therefore, the contest usually has little passion or excitement because it is literally an exhibition game. Even the local NSL teams end up disadvantaged because they usually have to give up players for the Australian team because our overseas stars don't want to travel all the way back to Australia for relatively meaningless games. I believe the entire exercise is a damaging waste of time because instead of exciting Australian soccer fans, it leaves them feeling disappointed and unwilling to throw their support behind future big games. While it may be a commercial success for one businessperson, the public loses confidence with the sport and turns its attention elsewhere. That is why the Olympics were so important in regaining the public's confidence in international football.

The success of Olympic football should have helped clear up some common misconceptions in Australia about soccer and the Olympics. Many people in Australia believe that the Olympics are the biggest sports event in the world, but in commercial terms and by the number of worldwide television viewers, the football World Cup is a far bigger event. During my time working for the Sydney 2000 bid committee, I discovered that soccer attracts the largest percentage of paying spectators that attend the Olympics. Prior to the Sydney 2000 Olympics, on average, 36.7 per cent of all paying spectators to the Games were soccer fans. The figure from Sydney was somewhere around twenty per cent of tickets sold, or around

1.2 million of the six million tickets sold for the Games. It was only because Australia sold so many tickets to traditionally unpopular events in Sydney that the soccer figure was down in percentage terms on its usual average. In any case, the Olympics still relied on the soccer fan for a large portion of its popularity and commercial success.

This is why it staggers me when sections of the media and the public call for soccer to be removed from the Games. They don't realise that football will always be at the Olympics because the sport is so internationally popular and because football contributes so massively to paying for the Games through ticket sales. In the end, the Olympics needs soccer more than soccer needs the Olympics.

The soccer competition for the Olympics has undergone many changes in structure in recent decades but I personally believe it should now stay at the under-23s level. FIFA shouldn't diminish the importance of the World Cup by removing the age limit on the Olympics. The under-23s level reserved just for the Olympics fits in perfectly with their overall strategy of youth development. I think the current format should suit Australia too, even though we struggled in Sydney, because a large part of our success in producing new stars has been participation in youth World Cups and the Olympics. For the players involved, each level is a natural stepping stone which prepares them for the big time.

Overall, it was sad that Australia didn't do as well as we could have done in Sydney because to win gold or at least a medal would have really cemented a place for soccer in Australia's national consciousness. Unfortunately, winning a medal at the Olympics seems more important in the Australian sports' psyche at the moment than coming third in the World Cup. The Olympics have traditionally been an opportunity to showcase Australia's sporting talent to the world; to temporarily bask in the international limelight. The Australian public doesn't seem to realise how much greater the nation's reputation will grow overseas if we do well at the World Cup.

It will far outstrip any fame the nation receives from performing well at the Olympics. But until Australia can prove itself at the World Cup, the Olympics will remain particularly important to the future of Australian soccer. In many ways Olympic soccer is the future because it harnesses Australia's fixation with the Olympics and shows the nation what soccer means to the world.

18

The Mourning After

⚽ Now that we've missed the Korea/Japan 2002 World Cup, come Germany 2006 it will be thirty-two years since Australia qualified for football's Holy Grail competition. For supporters of the Socceroos they will have been thirty-two very difficult years. In 1996 Soccer Australia thought a saviour had been found in the form of Terry Venables. The atmosphere at the MCG in November 1997 was intensely euphoric, as the Socceroos seemed to stroll through their match against Iran to lead by two goals and be ten minutes away from France '98. The hope, the promise of qualifying for the World Cup was within our grasp. We were nearly there. Then, out of nowhere, Khodadad Azizi, the little Iranian master, bounded onto a majestic pass from Ali Daei through our advancing defence to be confronted by our last hope, goalkeeper Mark Bosnich. The crowd was hushed in suspended agony. Bosnich made himself as big an obstruction as he could. Azizi skewered the ball past Bosnich's outstretched left leg and it bounced determinedly into the now vacant goal. Most post-mortems of the match have looked to lay blame. But the way that second goal was conceived was just beautiful football carried out by an understanding between two top players who had benefited from playing many international matches together. The ninety thousand-strong crowd was silenced. Euphoria was replaced by nausea. The referee ended the match and ended our World Cup dreams, again. Somehow, working on the SBS broadcast, I had to make sense of what we had all just seen and give voice to the roller-coaster of emotions we had all ridden. Amidst the wreck of that roller-coaster ride, we had to be professional, to talk, to broadcast. Over twenty years in exile, and after watching the quality of the performance of the Socceroos that night, the way they dominated Iran after all the years of failure and the nearly-but-not-quite attempts to reach the World Cup and the thought that we were almost, finally, there... shattered. Back on air, live to the nation, Les Murray threw to me for analysis and I couldn't speak. It was all over. Nothing would come out. I cried on national television.

Qualifying for a World Cup is difficult territory for everyone, as of course it should be. The qualification competition is where the international pecking order of nations' teams is established. The World Cup is the pow-wow that elevates individuals, teams and nations to inestimable heights. Entry to this select group, by definition, should only follow an arduous series of tests.

I believe Australia's passage to qualification, largely through Oceania, is easier when compared with that of other confederations. At this stage in the development of the Oceania Confederation, of which Australia is now firmly a part, the level of competitive international football is extremely limited, with Australia and New Zealand easily out-muscling their co-confederate Pacific competition with little fuss. The New Zealand games aside, the World Cup cycle provides Australia with two big games every four years. Two meaningful games every four years means our team is all too often under-prepared and untested in important international matches. The collateral damage of this is that it leaves the Socceroos starved of the sort of competition that forges a strong identity for them and denies football the necessary opportunity to position itself prominently in the domestic sport hierarchy.

To further illustrate this point you just need to look at the scenario confronting Soccer Australia in the lead-up to the final qualifiers for Korea/Japan 2002. It was revealed in the *Sydney Morning Herald* that the matches involving the Socceroos in November 2001, a friendly match against World Cup holders France and the World Cup qualifier, would gross around fifteen million dollars. That figure was derived largely by projections that the MCG would be 'sold out' for both games. However, it was also revealed that the majority of that money was to go to the marketing partner of Soccer Australia, International Entertainment Corporation (IEC), in accordance with the contractual arrangements between the two parties. Furthermore, of Soccer Australia's remaining share, one million dollars had already been allocated to remitting outstanding Socceroos wages. The nett financial result for Soccer Australia was pretty uninspiring. Of course, all this is amplified by the fact that unlike rugby union's Wallabies, the Socceroos don't have an annual program of domestic test matches which fill stadiums and generate huge revenue. The Socceroos are consigned to one 'big' home game every four years. It is hardly enough to enable the sport to survive.

In purely pecuniary terms, the success of the Socceroos is directly related to the revenues available to the national team's program. The equation is simple—quality, competitive games build the profile of the national team and therefore funding is made more available to the Socceroos by Australian organisations. Funding is paramount to proper preparation. Apart from this, at the grassroots level, where future Australian sporting heroes are deciding which code of football they are going to pursue, the success today of the Socceroos is vital for the future success and growth of soccer in Australia. The quest for each World Cup is hindered partly because of the chronic under-funding that results from the disadvantaged market positioning of the Socceroos. The Socceroos, because of issues that have been both externally imposed as well as self-induced, are left like a shag on a rock in their attempts to make it to the big time.

Compare this with the life-and-death dog-fight that countries in South America (Conmebol Confederation) survive in order to experience World Cup glory. The representatives of Conmebol for Korea/Japan 2002 have played eighteen qualifying matches with the aim of finishing in the top four of the nine participating nations. Conmebol is a confederation where football is the lifeblood of the people. The national team's qualification is more important, for some, than life itself.

This situation is the same in Europe. Europe's confederation, known as UEFA, is divided into a series of qualifying groups. The competition for ultimate places is white hot. Along the way, some big teams fall. Holland for example, a European football superpower, finished third in their qualifying group and failed to qualify for Korea/Japan. France, the current World, European and Confederations Cup champions, failed to even qualify for USA '94. UEFA is divided into nine qualification groups, each consisting of five or six teams. For each World Cup cycle, countries are drawn randomly and placed into one of the groups. Some of the traditionally more powerful football nations are seeded so they are not drawn to play each other in the qualification competition. One seed is therefore placed in each of the nine groups. Inevitably, however, there are high-quality teams (such as England for 2002 qualification which was drawn with Germany, that group's seeded team) which will not be seeded. The result is an extremely competitive qualification process in each of the groups and from each cycle there are some noteworthy casualties.

Apart from Europe, there is also Africa and Asia, where football is also extrordinarily popular. Concacaf too, the confederation that takes in Mexico, Central and North America as well as the Caribbean nations, is another fiercely competitive developing region. Mexico, twice hosts of the finals, and the United States, the biggest sporting nation on earth, both flex their muscles in the Concacaf Confederation. Honduras too, is another formidable contestant, as evidenced when their Olympic team for Sydney 2000 defeated the Olyroos at the Sydney Football Stadium, ensuring that our boys finished the tournament, as hosts, without any joy at all. There is no such thing as a walk-up start for any finals aspirants, nor should there be.

FIFA, football's international governing body, has a membership in excess of two hundred national associations. For Korea/Japan 2002 there were only twenty-nine places available for qualifiers (France as holders gained automatic entry as did co-hosts, Korea and Japan). The politicking that goes on in world football is feverish. Elected representatives bargain to secure maximum finals' places for their confederations. For Korea/Japan, Africa had five direct qualifiers, UEFA had thirteen, Asia and Concacaf had three and Conmebol had four direct qualifiers. Thereafter, a series of play-offs determine the final places—Europe and Asia played off for one more spot and Conmebol and Oceania did the same. The Socceroos are at the whim of this political and convoluted process. As a result, a lot of teams miss out. Some countries will never make it to a World Cup. And, as we're all too painfully aware, Australia has only been once.

FIFA's geopolitics places Australia firmly in Oceania which is the weakest and youngest of FIFA's confederations. Oceania does not have direct qualification to the World Cup. It is the only confederation that doesn't. It is deemed too small and its member nations, in a football sense, too weak. The competition that Australia and New Zealand face is not strong enough to warrant direct qualification. Countries in Europe and South America hold a very firm line when it comes to the allocation of World Cup places that lie outside their respective confederations. They would both sincerely acknowledge that it is wonderful for the world of football to increase its interests down here in the South Pacific, but not at their expense. For FIFA to grant a direct qualification place to Oceania would mean another confederation losing one of their places. Oceania must earn its stripes and its member nations must demonstrate a level of football operation and achievement that wins the respect of FIFA's members. On-field success is what changes the attitudes of people within football and to date, unfortunately, Oceania and Australia have been limited by the qualification process in proving their mettle. Australia's various qualification series have been relatively easy when compared with the difficulties and intensity of other confederations. The final analysis for each quadrennial World Cup cycle boils down to a solitary, difficult, final opponent. Until then, the matches of the Oceania preliminary phases, aside from those against New Zealand, have invariably proven to be gross mismatches. The Oceania qualification stages saw Australia rack up world record scores, smashing American Samoa 31–0, for example. Socceroo striker Archie Thompson set an individual world record by scoring thirteen goals in that game. News of both the scoreline and Archie gained worldwide coverage, much of it derisory about the football of the Oceania region.

It is not necessarily the sole fault of the players that these series of final hurdles haven't been overcome. The system has failed them, failed all past players, and has failed the nation. That system has placed our finest players against opponents whose countries have implemented more sophisticated programs and methods to facilitate their entry into the World Cup. The national associations of other confederations have ensured that their national team takes its place in the finals. Their countries have realised that they need to be present at the greatest of all international expos.

In addition to improving its football, Oceania must use whatever political leverage it has to gain more international recognition. Indeed, Oceania has recently demonstrated that it has the potential to hold the balance of power in world football. The recent vote to determine the 2006 World Cup host nation was a case in point. Oceania's vote was the final determinant of Germany winning hosting rights. Oceania President Charlie Dempsey abstained from the final round of voting, for personal reasons, and his decision effectively handed Germany the victory. The result of Dempsey's decision caused great controversy. South Africa had been popular favourites to win the ballot, primarily because of the belief that the finals should be rotated around the confederations. Awarding the tournament to an African host would perhaps have signalled a new era for FIFA as Africa was yet to host the tournament. Supporters of rotation had tipped their weight behind the African bid also. Had Dempsey voted according to 'expectation', in line with the wishes of the other Oceania Football Confederation member associations, then South Africa would have won the right to host the 2006 World Cup. His subsequent abstention caused great turmoil in international football politics. While Oceania may be considered inconsequential in football terms, the political process is another matter and we should use this reality to our advantage. The Socceroos have suffered from this region's football underdevelopment. They should be assisted by the region's political opportunities.

Since 1974, the World Cup story of the Socceroos has been one of prolonged mourning. It does not merely describe the devastation felt after Australia's loss to Iran in November 1997 at the MCG and to Uruguay in Montevideo in November 2001. It is a tale of frustration and self-destruction endured in every World Cup campaign since we last qualified in 1974. The wider benefits of not attending the most prestigious football symposium have been lost for the country at large—that's where the hurt is. It has been a time characterised by periodic bouts of intense pain, gutless blame apportionment, confusion, pathetic inaction, anger and staggering denial.

There has been no obvious plan of action by Australia's soccer administration to try to solve the problems that have beset Australia's qualification chances. If there has been a strategy it hasn't been properly communicated to the soccer public. It seems that approaches have been reactive and ad hoc—there has never been a feeling that the soccer ship is sailing a steady course. We have all known the destination, but there's rarely been a feeling that the course has been plotted with flexibility for troubled times or unforeseen circumstances. The players and fans have been repeatedly dealt disappointment after disappointment which has produced the type of pessimism and cynicism about soccer that is evident in many Australian people's attitude to the sport.

Then, hope has grown from the onset of each new campaign until the Socceroos are once again defeated by circumstance before they have a chance to reach their full potential.

There have been three World Cup campaigns where our qualification hopes were butchered rather than it being a case of the opposition being too difficult. Argentina '78 was a qualification route which took us through the Asian Football Confederation (AFC) and was probably within our capabilities. The Spain '82 campaign was a disaster that saw New Zealand qualify and in 1997 we were back trying to qualify through the AFC. That still proved too much for us. We should have been good enough to overcome the fourth-best AFC team, as Iran was back then.

However, there were four qualification campaigns which did provide gigantic football opponents in the form of Scotland in 1985; Colombia, had we overcome Israel in 1989; Argentina in 1993; and Uruguay in 2001. The fact that Oceania hasn't been entitled to direct qualification has meant that it has had to share 'half' a qualification place with a team from another confederation. For that 'other' team, the play-off match against the Oceania representative was their second chance to qualify. For France '98, AFC had three direct places and one additional opportunity that would be fought out between its number-four team (Iran) and the Oceania representative (Australia). For Korea/Japan 2002, Conmebol had four direct qualification places and its fifth-best team, Uruguay, fought Oceania (Australia) for that remaining spot.

The politics of FIFA has resulted in these different qualification processes for the confederations in each World Cup cycle. Hence, for the qualifiers for Argentina '78 we shared a half place with Asia; for Mexico '86 it was with UEFA; for Italy '90 it was Conmebol; and for USA '94 (after Concacaf) it was with Conmebol again. This potted history demonstrates how Oceania has been inconsistently treated.

I am prepared to suggest that the failure for Argentina '78 hinged on an errant coaching appointment. Jimmy Shoulder, a twenty-eight-year-old Englishman who was the ACT Director of Coaching, was thrown into the position of Socceroos coach and, to my knowledge, didn't even apply for the position. I mean nothing personal against Jimmy who is a nice guy but in reality he was unsuitable because I don't think he was experienced enough. I also feel that he might have been too young for the role. Under thirty years of age, he was younger than a sizeable proportion of the team. As Director of Coaching for the ACT, Jimmy was responsible for coach education programs and junior development. There is a quantum leap between implementing how-to-coach programs and actually coaching the national football team.

The opening for Shoulder arose in 1975. Rale Rasic, the only coach to lead the team to the World Cup finals, left the position of Socceroo coach. Many people were agog that this had happened, but behind the scenes there had been deep enmity between Rasic and Sir Arthur George, chairman of the ASF. In Rasic's wake, Englishman Brian Green was appointed. Green, the new coach, left the job in a cloud of controversy surrounding a shoplifting offence. He had only been in the job for a couple of months.

Debate amongst the soccer public and soccer media raged over who should fill the breach. The arguments were soiling a domestic environment that was supposed to be ready for football's golden period. It was 1975, the year after the Socceroos had played at the World Cup, and the broader Australian community was now supposed to be ready to embrace soccer and realise its status as the world's most popular sport. Instead, the public was treated to a farcical situation where the darlings of Australian sport, following their football feats in Germany, were left isolated and coachless, after losing two coaches in quick succession. Soccer, through no fault of the players, was now the focus of negative media coverage for all the wrong reasons. The players and fans were left in a blundering wake.

The public wanted Rasic reinstated and was dumbfounded that there could be any doubt in the soccer administration about reappointing him. Rale, like everyone, had his opponents. Meantime, I received a call from Sir Arthur George. I was a young coach whose St George team had won the championship twice and Sir Arthur, who didn't want to be forced to reappoint Rale, wanted another coach to pit against him in the selection process. However, the state federations of New South Wales and Victoria wanted a Rasic–Warren coach–assistant scenario. Other states wanted Alan Vest, who was the Director of Coaching in Western Australia and is now assistant coach at Perth Glory. And then, of course, Jimmy Shoulder, the Director of Coaching for the ACT, was also billed as an alternative.

The appointment came down to a vote, which followed a process of elimination. Rale was eliminated first. 'I can't believe, I can't believe,'— his reaction still echoes in my memory. I went out second as a result of the other states voting against the choices of New South Wales and Victoria. In retaliation, New South Wales and Victoria then decided to vote against Vest, the candidate of their opponents. Both factions were behaving with eyes fixed firmly on politics rather than the relative merits of the candidates. With Vest out, only Jimmy Shoulder remained.

Jimmy Shoulder was Socceroo coach for the 1978 campaign and it simply didn't work out. It is wrong, and too simplistic to attribute all the blame for failure to the coach, even though I consider that he was an inappropriate choice. It was more due to a combination of factors. In some respects, the team itself never really settled. There were some significant names in that team including Alan Maher, Gary Burn, Peter Wilson, Col Bennett, Col Curran, Gary Morrochi, Jimmy Rooney, Peter Stone, Adrian Alston, Peter Ollerton and Atti Abonyi. There were seven from the 1974 squad in Shoulder's starting line-up. This should have been a powerful base from which to construct a successful assault on the World Cup qualification games.

But it was Iran who qualified in our stead. It was actually a harder campaign for the Socceroos than the qualification for France '98 because among others, the Socceroos had to play Iran, Kuwait and South Korea. These were all very difficult opponents. The Kuwaiti team was coached by Brazilian legend Mario Zagallo, a legend of World Cup history having won two World Cups as a player (1958 and 1962), been to another as assistant coach (USA '94, where Brazil were the champions) and two as coach (Mexico '70 and France '98). His assistant with the Kuwaiti team was Carlos Alberto Pereira, World Cup-winning coach of Brazil (USA '94). There was pedigree behind the Kuwaiti team, and petro-dollars too, hence the appointment of two such notable coaches. South Korea has been a longstanding international football rival of ours and they are always, regardless of the era, difficult to beat. But Argentina, the host country of the 1978 World Cup, was a destination we never looked like making. Iran represented our qualifying group. Australia was left at home to watch Mario Kempes dance through rivers of confetti and ripped streamers and claim the world title in front of a massive and adoring home crowd.

The 1982 World Cup campaign saw the appointment of flamboyant German Rudi Gutendorf in 1979. Rudi was an experienced coach with excellent credentials. Rudi's list of coaching jobs reads more like a travel itinerary with some fascinating stop-off points. As may be expected of such a world citizen, he was a very progressive coach. The Young Socceroos were born under his reign with players such as Eddie Krncevic, Steve Hogg, Graeme Jennings, Danny Moulis and Mike Milovanovic being some of the players of that first team. Another was Ian Rowden. (Rowden provides another example of the game never tapping into its most ready and valuable resource, the players. Soccer Australia shouldn't necessarily be run by ex-players, except where there is expertise, but there should be an input, especially where a player might bring some other skills to the management and administration of the game. As well as his football background playing for the Young Socceroos in 1979, Ian was tertiary educated and was already on a successful professional path in marketing at Coca-Cola. In his instance, the opportunity for Soccer Australia to employ his talents was even more powerful because Coke was deeply involved with football already—they owned the naming rights for the World Youth Cup. With his Coke links, football background and marketing nous, Ian was in a position to contribute enormously to soccer. As concepts, sport and marketing were yet to be connected. Soccer could have enjoyed a real advantage over other sports. As it was, Ian was never asked to do anything for soccer. Perhaps it should be mentioned that in those days Soccer Australia was a small operation run by a small office. Sports management and administration, and even sports marketing, weren't the industry and career choices that they are today. But I don't resile from my assessment that there has always seemed to be a reluctance by Soccer Australia to bring in knowledge. The result has seen the likes of Ian Rowden remaining distanced from the sport. Soccer's loss was Coca-Cola's gain.)

One of the hallmarks of the Gutendorf tenure was his great

aplomb as a promoter. He was the type of coach who couldn't help but attract attention. His Socceroo team (which included names such as Krncevic, Bertogna, Sharne, Rooney, Barnes, Tansey, Pruskalo and Henderson) started regularly playing friendly games. The opponents were worthy too: Greece, European champions Czechoslovakia (coached by Dr Joe Venglos), England, Northern Ireland and Mexico, which helped lift Australian soccer for a time. There was a great program of games.

The Spain '82 campaign began in earnest with a 3–3 draw away to New Zealand. This Kiwi team was obviously very talented as it was they who made their way to their one and only World Cup finals appearance. The key game for Spain '82 was at the Sydney Cricket Ground. The match ended 2–0 in the Kiwis' favour. It proved to be Gutendorf's Waterloo, and signalled his departure as coach. The Socceroos played through the other matches but the finals tournament was beyond them. Once we'd lost to New Zealand we were effectively out of contention. It was definitely a shame because the preparation of the team was comparatively good. The Socceroos had also toured Israel, Hong Kong and Malaysia before the games that counted. Also, all the boys were based in Australia, which meant that there wasn't a constant hassle assembling the team or problems with player availability.

The New Zealand game was the one that killed us. Nothing against Gutendorf, who was a worthy professional, but the New Zealand result was one of those dark pages in our football history. It's not something I like to revisit terribly frequently. So, for 1978 and 1982 respectively, we had a young coach followed by an older flamboyant version and certainly in 1982 the preparation was as good as it has ever been. But, in basic terms, New Zealand, our trans-Tasman foes, buggered us.

The late 1970s through to the early 1980s was an empty period for the Socceroos. Both the Shoulder and Gutendorf regimes had failed and the stocks of the national team were arguably at their lowest point. Scheinflug, Gutendorf's assistant, was given control of the team with the brief to extricate it from the quagmire in which it had found itself. However, in early 1983 the Australian team, with Scheinflug in charge, had played and lost both matches of a trans-Tasman series. It had now been some seven years since we had beaten the Kiwis. Scheinflug's tenure appeared to be on shaky ground. Simultaneously, Scheinflug was also coach of the Young Socceroos (involving Frank Farina) whose World Cup was to be played in Mexico in 1983. While away with the youth team, the senior team was scheduled to play a three-match series against England in Australia.

Frank Arok assumed the coaching position for the series. He was arguably the most celebrated coach on the local scene, and with Scheinflug away in Mexico, he seemed like the ideal person to play the role of caretaker. Meanwhile, tensions were rising between Scheinflug and Sir Arthur George who was not a Scheinflug fan. The relationship fractured irreconcilably at the Mexico Youth Championships over the embarrassment Sir Arthur George experienced due to the fact that the Australian team, drawn to play Mexico, the host nation, at the famous Azteca Stadium, arrived late to the stadium. George, a member of the FIFA executive, was forced into public relations damage control as kick-off for the match was delayed for an hour. One hundred thousand spectators were forced to wait. The delay of the Australian team was caused by horrendous traffic, something George had warned Scheinflug about. George requested that the team leave the hotel earlier than scheduled. A compromise was reached, but it was one that proved ineffective. George was furious.

Sir Arthur George had already been looking to remove Scheinflug. He was also becoming increasingly enamoured with Frank Arok's performance. The two had a great deal of mutual respect for each other. Adding to the appeal of Arok was the push coming from George's marketing man, Peter Sheean. Of Arok, Sheean was a huge fan. Again, Arok warmed strongly to Sheean. Both were energetic and big thinking men. Sheean believed soccer in Australia needed the Socceroos to be successful. The barriers that confronted the game would most effectively be removed behind a successful national team. Sheean became convinced that Arok was the man the Socceroos needed to be successful.

Scheinflug, however, was still officially in charge. Despite the groundswell moving with Arok, Scheinflug was still the recipient of considerable political support, most notably from the president of the NSL powerhouse Marconi, Tony Labbozzetta. Scheinflug's decision to travel to Mexico left the door open for Arok's appointment in a caretaker role for the series against England. Perhaps Scheinflug thought it was safer, in career terms, to avoid the confrontation with England. He had a choice between Mexico and the England series. He decided on Mexico, hence played into the hands of those who wanted him out of the national team. Success against England made Arok more desirable in the eyes of George and Sheean and cast greater shadows on the future of Les Scheinflug.

Scheinflug resumed his duties with the Socceroos from the moment he returned from Mexico and he took the team to the Merlion Cup in Singapore at the end of 1983. The team didn't perform well as Scheinflug attempted to reassert his imprint on the team. It was a forlorn task and Scheinflug's contract with the Socceroos was terminated in early 1984. The ASF board met to appoint a replacement. That meeting lasted five hours. The deliberations were highly charged and, for some board members, politically motivated. Eventually, Frank Arok was formally endorsed as Socceroo coach.

When Arok first came in, Australia was scheduled to play England on 12 June 1983 in Sydney. That team was comprised of Terry Greedy, Alan Davidson, David Ratcliffe, Charlie Yankos, Steve O'Connor, Graham Jennings, Joe Watson, Jimmy

Cant, Peter Katholos, John Kosmina and Phil O'Connor (the substitute was David Mitchell). Give or take one or two players, this time was characterised by stability. Frank didn't use many players. He kept the formula much the same. I believe this was the best era for our Socceroo team. Not because it was the Arok era, although I am an Arok fan, but because it was when all the boys were based here—with only Krncevic overseas. It was the era of the stable national team and of Club Australia, as Arok referred to it. Pride in the jersey was strong, team spirit was high, performances were good. Arok insisted that because the national team had so few opportunities to play serious matches, he must use the same players who would be familiar with each other's styles and habits as well as the team's system. 'Club Australia' wasn't a gimmick; it was a plan and its intent and output summed up so many of the things for which I admire Frank Arok.

As Arok's tenure commenced with the game against England, so too did he immediately mark his arrival with a change to the accepted format of the team line-up. The first game was started with a sweeper playing behind two 'policemen'. Five players were situated across the defence or midfield depending on what was required. Arok was slagged mercilessly for the tactics but the Socceroos picked up two draws with England and one loss. The Arok era of stability and of Club Australia was under way.

To the World Cup qualifiers and Australia squeezed through Oceania, past New Zealand and Israel, earning the right to face off against Scotland. The first leg was away in Glasgow at Hampden Park, the home of Scottish football. It was an amazing night. It was also a homecoming for many of the Socceroos expats such as the late Jinky Joe Watson, Kenny Murphy and David Mitchell—all who had healthy doses of tartan blood coursing through their veins. Striding out into the stadium that had held their footballing dreams captive, this excursion to Hampden was emotional and deeply spiritual.

The Glasgow game saw a solid performance. The boys were really up against everything. The crowd was vicious in their jeering. The mob was chanting all sorts of messages about the colonials' supposed love affairs with sheep. Although Australia left with a two-goal deficit to circumvent, there was a real feeling that the tie was still alive. There was still hope.

The return game in Melbourne was a spectacular game. It was almost superhuman what the Socceroos came up with that night. It was energetic, vibrant, cultured and committed. It was brave and brazen. They fought with a ferocity and played with a cohesion that was just fabulous to see. The final result was an amazing 0–0 draw. How we didn't score that night is something I still can't explain. The memory of that performance still captivates me. The whole crowd was mesmerised. Scottish football had some illustrious players too. Graeme Souness and the incomparable Kenny Dalglish are two examples. Sir Alex Ferguson was the coach and Scotland was a quality opponent.

The subplot to the return leg against Scotland was the debate over the venue for the tie. When the boys got home the question was, typically, is the game going to be in Sydney or Melbourne? For some reason, at that stage, Melbourne had a lot more clout. It was my feeling that when the boys returned to Australia, the match should be played in a situation that gave the Socceroos an advantage. My suggestion was that the game should be played in Darwin, in a warmer climate where the Scots would struggle to cope. I tabled the Darwin idea on SBS. Instead, in a variation of the theme that has so plagued the Socceroos, management decided that the game should be played midweek, at night, in Melbourne. As far as Sir Alex was concerned that was just bonny. Arok even asked for the grass to be kept longish so the Scots might tire but, lo and behold, the night before the game the grass was cut. With a score of 2–0 on aggregate to Scotland, the Socceroos missed out again.

The time between the Scotland episode through to the next campaign was perhaps the golden era of the Socceroos. The team played many games. The vast bulk of the squad was still locally based which made access to players easy. It also saw a new era of players such as Frank Farina, Robbie Slater, Graham Arnold and Paul Wade. It included the build-up to the 1988 Olympic Games, the Kings Cup in South Korea and games against Morocco, Egypt and Korea. There were home series against Czechoslovakia, a team that was a quality and extremely professional opponent. There was no sense of the Czech team being here on a promotional trip or end-of-season holiday.

The Bicentennial Gold Cup, a commemoration of two hundred years of European settlement in Australia, also featured in 1988. It was a tremendous home series that hosted Brazil, Argentina and Saudi Arabia. Romario topped the billing of the Brazilian team. Australia lost 1–0 in Melbourne to Brazil, but played a sensational game against the samba kings and football maestros. Romario slid a knife through Aussie hearts that night. One run, one touch, one goal. He seemed to stroll around the ground, hardly moving. He gesticulated wildly to his teammates and snarled arrogantly at the defenders. He sauntered his way through the game, barely breaking into a sweat. It didn't look like he gave a damn, then bang, he scored and won the game. He had a killer instinct, in the football sense.

Then it was to Sydney for one of Australian soccer's great nights. Perennial non-qualifiers Australia beat world football heavyweights Argentina, 4–1. It was an incredible night watched by a crowd in absolute disbelief at what they were witnessing. And Charlie Yankos let rip with a free kick which, from some distance, cut like an Exorcet missile through the air and flew into Argentina's goal. I still get goose-bumps when I think about it. That result, in conjunction with the

3–0 victory over Saudi Arabia who were coached by Carlos Alberto Pereira, rocketed Australia into the final to be played against Brazil. Brazil won 2–0 to win the Bicentennial Gold Cup. Romario had been at it again to score one of the goals; the other scored by Muller. No disgrace whatsoever by the result. On the contrary in fact, the tournament was a triumph for Club Australia and reaffirmed the ground gained by the national team under the stewardship of Frank Arok.

He was nicknamed 'the fox' by the Sydney media. He was always looking for ways to secure advantage for his team and was always a step ahead of everybody else. He wasn't a coach who just turned up for games; he used to research and study and scout. He was always trying different approaches—sometimes crazy, often unconventional but frequently successful.

Things were to get much better though for the Socceroos at the 1988 Seoul Olympics where they reached the quarter-finals. We haven't revisited those halcyon days yet. Perhaps we won't again. The days are gone when the members of the team were based domestically. I wouldn't go so far as to say that they played the best football because the boys were still very much part-time players but there was an aura about the Socceroos and a feeling that they were all something very special.

So began the campaign for Italia '90. New Zealand was slaughtered here 4–1 before the away game against Israel. That game was again marked by a Charlie Yankos free kick, another scorcher. Les Murray and I were commentating the game from our high vantage point. A free kick was awarded to Australia and what followed was one of the funniest moments of my experience as a commentator. Les uncharacteristically miscalled the action. Charlie bent his free kick around the wall. It looked for all money that it had gone out of play and into the goal's side netting. The deathly silence of the crowd supported our immediate belief that no goal had been scored. Indeed, that was how Les called it. That was broken by Les shrieking, 'It's a goal, it's a goal'. Hysteria broke out in the commentary box, which viewers wouldn't have known. Both Les and I were in a spin, our heads whirling in an attempt to mentally replay the sequence just to ensure that a goal had in fact been scored and at the same time carefully analysing each psycho-frame to check where we'd lost track of the ball's flight. It was an amazing thing, very funny and made special by the quality and result of Charlie's free kick. The result of the game, a 1–1 draw, made the visit to the Holy Land blessed indeed.

Then the disaster. We lost it in New Zealand again.

The day of the away game in New Zealand was just awful. The World Cup qualifier played as a curtain-raiser to a rugby union international. It was, I suspect, an attempt to have the game played before some sort of crowd. The fact that they were a rugby crowd and probably not at all interested in the real football contest seemed a point unworthy of consideration by the organisers. It seemed a strange piece of scheduling at the time. Even now, it is difficult to understand why it had to be so. In order to cater for the rugby, the kick-off for the football had to be midday, which was equivalent to ten in the morning Australian time for the Socceroos. It was an extremely awkward time to play. The whole day had a disarming air about it. The kick-off time was one thing, but it was more than that. There was a feeling of impending doom that morning in New Zealand. It turned out to be a disaster. It was a repeat of the 1982 scoreline. A score of 2–0 to the Kiwis, with Billy 'Pistols' Wright the scorer of both heartbreaking goals against us.

Les Murray, match commentator Mike Hill, SBS Head of Sport Dominic Galati and I walked straight out of the broadcast box and immediately left for the airport. We'd been to Israel where the hard job had been done. We had just had to win in New Zealand for the boys to be virtually there at the World Cup. It was such a shock result for us all. Nobody said a word to anyone else. Our flights were brought forward; we just wanted to get home to Australia. The result put the Socceroos behind, forcing them into a position where they had to play catch-up again.

Israel had to come to Sydney to win the group although they didn't have to win the game, just avoid losing. The onus was squarely on the Socceroos to beat the visitors and salvage the campaign. It was 16 April 1989. The football world had been rocked by the overnight news of the stadium disaster in Hillsborough—the FA Cup semi-final at which ninety-six Liverpool fans perished in a stampeding crush that resulted in the revolution of football operations in England. It was not a pleasant prologue for the Socceroos attempts to overcome their own problems. The Sydney Football Stadium, the venue for the clash, was absolutely packed. Nobody really expected such a turn-out, nor had they adequately prepared for it. It was the biggest crowd the SFS has ever had. That crowd is still listed as an official ground record. Furthermore, thousands were turned away.

Issues surrounding the team were taking on a modern complexion. It was the start of the problem for the national team of its overseas players. Arok brought back Yankos, Farina, Krncevic and Mitchell from European duty. Perhaps the overseas players never settled because they performed below their high standards. They were all terrific players accustomed to playing at a high level but upon return they didn't seem to adjust. Eli Ohana, who played briefly in the NSL with Sydney City, scored for Israel from a Yankos error. It was, in fact, a mistake that was completely uncharacteristic of Charlie. It's something that will probably haunt Australia forever. Perhaps the curse of the witch doctor was still at work. A young Paul Trimboli equalised almost immediately from the kick-off. But the damage had been done. I remember as the whistle blew for full time Arok running onto the field, with his hopes dashed, holding his wrist-watch, remonstrating with the referee for ending the game earlier than he thought was appropriate. In Frank's mind there was still time to score the winner. He was frantic. The team was crestfallen. It was a desperate sight. It was truly emotional mayhem.

For USA '94, Eddie Thomson replaced Arok as coach. The result of failing to qualify through Asia led FIFA to impose more onerous obstacles to Australian World Cup success. After topping the group last time around, Israel then had to play Colombia on a home-and-away basis before they could make it through to Italia '90. Israel failed at that point. However, the cumulative effect of Oceania's lack of progress was to reach its most acute zenith in the struggle to make it to USA '94. The last hurdle this time was to be the fifth-best South American team. A new Socceroo team was emerging. Ned Zelic burst onto the international stage with a performance of real substance against England at the SFS.

That game saw Alex Tobin win another scalp when he managed to defuse Gary Lineker, the star striker of English football and, as it would turn out, a World Cup Golden Boot winner. The team comprised a notable contingent from Adelaide City, including Socceroo record holder Tobin, Milan Ivanovic, Tony and Aurelio Vidmar and Robbie Zabica. The players on the Socceroo team were now extensively based in Europe. It was the start of the club versus country wrangling in Australian football. Frank Farina and Mark Bosnich, two high-profile examples, were forced into the middle of the debate.

The Socceroos' performances appeared to change too. The emphasis shifted to not losing rather than pushing to win football matches. This resulted in a string of dour games which achieved the desired result, but failed to inspire. Goals started to flow in the World Cup qualifiers for the Socceroos but that was primarily reflective of the weakness in the other Oceania teams. With the small island nations dispatched, progression from Oceania boiled down to Australia against New Zealand, which on the home-and-away basis, ended with the Socceroos racking up four unanswered goals.

The qualification path for the Socceroos this time around was through Conmebol. Furthermore, it was deemed for USA '94 that the Oceania winner would have to play off against a Concacaf qualifier before they could meet the South Americans and then make it through to the finals. The reasons for this resulted from the ever-present conundrum facing FIFA of how to accommodate the often divergent imperatives of football and politics. The fact that the Socceroos were drawn to play a member of Concacaf before they could earn the right to play against a member of Conmebol en route to a finals appearance would have seemed as bizarre to them as it was to us. But that was what FIFA deemed had to happen. In attempting to address the problem of lack of place availability at World Cup finals, FIFA has, over the years, increased the number of teams at the finals. When Australia qualified in 1974 there were sixteen countries competing. That number swelled to twenty-four for Spain '82. For Korea/Japan 2002, as with France '98, the tournament is between thirty-two teams. But the finals can't keep expanding this way and therein lies a real dilemma for FIFA. Sepp Blatter, FIFA President, has mooted changes such as holding the World Cup every two years, but the initial responses to that have been that it would be too onerous on everybody's already full football calendars.

The Concacaf series tossed up Canada as Australia's opponent. The away game in Canada thrust Mark Schwarzer, who'd just won the NSL goalkeeper of the year, into the national team for the first time. What was to transpire would give Schwarzer his entry into Australia's sporting mythology. Robert Zabica, goalkeeper for Adelaide City was named in the starting line-up in the absence of Mark Bosnich who had 'retired' from international football following the club versus country stoush. Schwarzer was called up to serve as Zabica's understudy. He happily took his place in the squad, made the trip to Edmonton, prepared with the team and took his place on the bench to watch the match. Mid-way through the first half, Zabica was sent off for a challenge he made on one of the Canadian forwards as he attempted to round the Aussie keeper. Thomson made the requisite changes immediately, which included throwing Schwarzer in to keep the team's goal. Schwarzer quips that at the time he was gazing around the stadium, counting the number of Aussies in attendance. Naturally, he wasn't expecting to be needed—reserve goalkeepers don't. Zabica's sending-off automatically precluded him, via mandatory suspension, from playing in the Socceroos' next match that would be the return leg in Sydney. The number-one spot was now Schwarzer's. Canada won the first leg 2–1.

The return leg was played at the SFS. It was such a tense afternoon. Australia seemed to squander a host of gilt-edged chances before golden boy Frank Farina scored with an overhead kick. The aggregate scores were now level, but with Australia having scored in Edmonton, the away-goals rule gave us the decided edge. If the Socceroos could only hold on, they would book their fight with the fifth-placed South American team. Canada managed to stall the party by scoring a goal of their own. It was Canada who now had an outright aggregate lead, 3–2. To survive, Australia needed to score once more. The opportunity fell to Mehmet Durakovic who was the first to a high bouncing ball and, with bloodstained and bandaged cranium, managed to head the ball over the advancing keeper and send the game into extra time.

The period of extra time came and went with no goals and the aggregate score locked at 3–3. Away-goals were equal too. It was time for the penalty shootout. Enter Schwarzer. With the fortunes of the campaign resting on his rookie shoulders, with Mark Bosnich watching from his self-imposed exile, with Zabica cooling his heels in suspended silence, with the stadium abuzz and the next stage of qualifying beckoning, Schwarzer emerged as hero of the day with a duo of saves that sent the

Socceroos and their supporters into raptures. Canada out, Australia through—an example of the quasi-religious redemptive capacity of sport, for it was Schwarzer who claimed responsibility for one of Canada's 'normal time' goals.

Of immediate concern to Thomson and his team was the identity of the South American opponent. One can only imagine what went through Thomson's mind—and stomach—when it became apparent that Australia's play-off would be against Argentina. Probably only Brazil could offer a more gigantic hurdle. Of some limited consolation was that by finishing fifth in their group, the Argentinians were apparently not their usual polished selves.

In the last match of the Conmebol qualifiers, Argentina was thrashed, at home, by Colombia in a 5–0 humiliation. For proud Argentina, it was a shattering result. Losing at home for countries such as Argentina is one thing, but to be on the wrong end of 5–0 almost defies imagination. Argentinians had been treated to the unique national euphoria of winning a football world championship on home soil in 1978 but were now, care of the result against Colombia, in the absolute depths of despair. These were arguably the darkest hours for Argentina's football. In the aftermath of the calamity came the clarion call to bring back the great man, Diego Armando Maradona. Sadly for us, he answered his country's call.

There has been but one Maradona. It was reported by some that Maradona's contribution was negligible in the Sydney match. But those people failed to appreciate what it is about Maradona, the player and the leader, that really makes him special. He was the real leader of his team. He was the inspiration behind their triumph at Mexico '86. Indeed, Argentina minus Maradona led to the 0–5 Colombia catastrophe which precipitated Argentina's showdown with Australia. Maradona's presence was pivotal to the game. I can testify to the power of his presence. I met him during the Argentinian team's stay. When introduced to him I literally went weak at the knees. I am an unashamed fan of his. I followed his career right through from his involvement in World Youth Cups up to and beyond his conquest of the football world. I used to have a videotape of him called 'Goals of a Champion' that I would take around to show at schools and at our soccer camps so that as many kids as possible could see what the great Maradona could do on a football field. I found the criticism in Sydney of him offensive because I thought it had more to do with his life off the field rather than his performance on it. The difficult transition from poverty to stardom was a path Maradona had travelled, but probably few of his critics had. The people of Argentina however, knew and loved Maradona for what he had given them in football and national pride.

In any event, at SBS we edited a collection of absolutely brilliant little touches he performed in his Sydney match. Admittedly, there was nothing like the wonder goal against England at Mexico '86, but the subtlety and elegance of his entries into the game, the manner in which he attracted attention to himself whilst freeing up others, the effectiveness with which he released teammates and included them in the game and the difficulty his opponents had in countering him was imposing. On top of this, he supplied the pass for Argentina's goal which, by the way, was another Australian World Cup defensive mess. Milan Ivanovic, such a cool and accomplished player, lost the ball in circumstances in which he had found himself a million times previously in his career and from which he had successfully negotiated safe passage. He was such a safe and wonderful player, an outstanding Socceroo. But the ball ended up with Maradona who delivered his pass when required with exactly the prescribed measure and Argentina took the lead.

In reply, Socceroo Aurelio Vidmar scored from a cross supplied by brother Tony and Australia drew level, at which score the Sydney game remained. The away leg was always going to be a momentous occasion for the team; I think probably more so than the away match against Scotland those few years earlier. More so, I believe, because it was the second leg and there was no return for the loser, whoever that would be. The Socceroos were terrific in the match, they gave absolutely everything but lost by the solitary goal—another entry into the catalogue of Socceroo misfortune. It was an own goal by indomitable skipper Alex Tobin. The same magnificent player who has marked so many of the world's top strikers, and successfully so. The own goal, just one of those things, an accident, a ricochet which couldn't have gone any better for Argentina—it looped, high under the cross-bar and inside the post. It was a pure and unadulterated fluke and another unfortunate example of the fickle world of football fortune and, perhaps, the curse on Australian football.

The decision of our soccer administration to play the first leg at home remains a mystery to me. By far the most popular option that is taken around the world is to play away games first and home second. I still can't believe that we offered to play at home first. FIFA didn't even have to arbitrate. I have heard all the stories about FIFA getting heavy on the decision-makers but I can't swallow them. I believe the real story was our soccer administration was petrified of the Socceroos copping a walloping away before returning home to what would effectively be a dead rubber. The game's coffers were empty again and the home tie first against Argentina, with everything even, would drop a nice bundle into the till. Again, it is the players whose hopes and dreams are subsumed by the game's continual financial plight. It is the players who constantly pay the price, largely because of poor organisation and management within our soccer administration.

In my view, the performance of that 1993 Socceroo team was even better when you consider the magnitude of the assault that Argentina made on USA '94. Up until Maradona was summarily excluded from the competition for failing a drug test, Argentina was the best team on show. The fact that the team wilted in the wake of Maradona's departure speaks loudly for the impact that he had on the team.

It was this team that Australia had to play in their quest to make the finals. They were up against a real force in the world game, twice winners and twice runners-up of the World Cup. The Socceroos had to play their away leg in a country immersed in football culture; a nation manically driven by the fortunes of the football team. The air was heavy with tension and expectation. The experience of the stadium that night will never leave me.

There was movement in the players' tunnel. Something stirred that sent an eerie hush through the noisy throng of supporters. Actually it wasn't as much a hush as a dulling of the roar. Maradona walked out onto the pitch and the crowd went completely berserk. He entered the playing arena and just walked around. He then walked off before the rest of the Argentina team came out and started their warm-up. The Aussies followed soon after. You can imagine the welcome they received! It was even worse for the referees who were next out. Anything that wasn't tied down was hurled in the direction of the referee and his assistants. It was a totally intimidating atmosphere. The crowd knew what was at stake and providing the intimidation was their preordained role in getting their boys over the line. In the world of sport there are challenges and there are challenges. Playing Argentina away, in a sudden-death, final-straw World Cup qualifier is in another stratosphere altogether. On this occasion, the Socceroos faced the added problem of Maradona—the football god and national hero who had taken on the role of a modern-day, male version of Eva Peron. Maradona, the opiate of the Argentinian masses was now also, unfortunately, Australia's World Cup nemesis.

Australia played very well that night in Buenos Aires. Despite the enormity of the task with which they were faced and the intensity of the daunting atmosphere, the Socceroos were very composed and competitive. It was another demonstration of the Socceroo tradition of playing well away from home. I believe that if Maradona hadn't returned to the team we would have beaten them. It took a deflected goal off one of Australia's celebrated defenders, Alex Tobin, to settle the tie. The luck went with Argentina. Once the Argentinians got on top it was going to be a big ask for the Socceroo lads. Too big an ask as it turned out, that night at El Estadio Monumentale.

Thommo remained coach in the initial phase of the France '98 expedition but he left midstream. His last competition was the Atlanta '96 Olympics. Thommo commented to me that he felt his end was nigh because of the so-called 'failure' of the Australian squad in Atlanta. Some members of the new ASF board, which was now under the chairmanship of David Hill, were not people steeped in knowledge of the football tradition of the Olympics and they seemed to believe—as most of Australia also seems to believe—that when it came to the Olympics, irrespective of the sport, Australia should be pushing for, if not winning gold. Football gold is arguably the hardest gold to win. The 1996 Olympic team qualified for the quarter-finals but got no further. We didn't win gold but I don't think it could be considered a failed campaign. However, Thommo was under the impression that there was a push to remove him as the Socceroo coach so he took the opportunity to further his career elsewhere. In effect, he decided to jump before he was pushed. Thommo accepted a good offer to coach in Japan's professional league.

David Hill then moved swiftly with his coup de grâce; his appointment of Terry Venables as coach of the Socceroos. The Venables appointment is the flag by which Hill is remembered, although his tenure was a tumultuous one for other reasons. I agreed with many things Hill set out to achieve. He was a very popular appointment. He was a breath of fresh air and a new face—and we desperately needed a new face. He was a fine media performer. Indeed, we at SBS outspokenly supported his campaign for the chairmanship of the ASF which, incidentally under him, became Soccer Australia. He attempted to contemporise some of soccer's labels; for example, registering the NSL as the A-League. The name-change brought Australia's professional club competition into line with some of its regional neighbours such as Japan whose professional competition was known as the J-League. While not earth-shattering moves, these initiatives were indicative of some much-needed lateral thinking. Hill also publicly set out some of the problem areas football was facing in Australia. He pinpointed the need to improve the standard of administration, recognising that soccer in Australia had been run by 'a lot of goodwill and not much else'. Although Hill's diagnoses weren't necessarily original, he succeeded in bringing them to light in the public forum. In particular, Hill, as a guest on SBS Television, highlighted the pivotal importance of the national league to the health and vitality of Australian soccer. On ABC Radio he stated that the NSL was, according to his measure, 'worryingly invisible'. His public performance was admirable and he crystallised a sense of hope for the fans. Making general statements, as he did on ABC Radio, that Australian soccer needed to 'extend its support base from exclusive ethnic communities', primarily, as he saw it, because 'in the increasingly professional world of Australian soccer, it is costing more money to run a club and unless the support base is broadened the (NSL) clubs will die' was the easy part. Up to this point, consensus was high. His stance was non-confrontational and generally, it was universally palatable. Even at those 'ethnic' clubs, there was (and is) a realisation that the life expectancy of their clubs is partly dependent upon them becoming popular and accessible outside of their own communities.

Hill began encountering problems when he turned his attention to the NSL. At the time of his ascension to the chairmanship, the NSL had been a fourteen-team competition. The 'feel-good' environment he had so far generated evaporated with his efforts to make the NSL a 'mainstream' pursuit. Two NSL clubs were cut, Parramatta Melita and Heidelberg, teams traditionally supported by Sydney's Maltese and Melbourne's Greek communities respectively. Simultaneously, Hill targeted the logos and names of some other NSL clubs, which he saw as anathema to his idea of 'mainstreaming' the competition. Crucially, Hill made a political enemy in NSL powerbroker and Marconi head, Tony Labbozzetta, by insisting that Marconi divest its logo of its Italian references (the colours of the Italian flag were represented on part of the club's logo) as part of his campaign to broaden the appeal of the club beyond the Italian community. A stoush then developed over logos and club names. Soccer then headed for the courts where Melita and Heidelberg sought an injunction against the NSL's 1996/97 competition commencement.

These were issues of change management. Most people realised that change was necessary. But Hill lost support in the game for the manner in which he went about instituting this change. In my opinion, his approach was without the support of a detailed plan which could have outlined what was required for the NSL and how it could be achieved. I disagreed with what I viewed as his jackboot style of management of some of the people and issues in Australian soccer. These were sensitive issues and his method of dealing with them provided ammunition for his opponents.

In terms of the NSL, success stories of the Hill regime are Perth Glory—whose performance on and off the field gives all true believers hope—and, to a lesser extent, Northern Spirit. Unfortunate postscripts to the Hill impact on the NSL, I believe, include the failure of the much vaunted 'mainstream' clubs. Collingwood Warriors and Carlton were two of the new teams that were born as a result of the Hill regime and were supposed to herald a new era of broad-based appeal for the NSL. Both have been expensive failures and, as a result, have further scorched the very important sports' market of Melbourne. The demise of Collingwood and Carlton can't be pinned on Hill but what is revealed by the whole affair was the dearth of research that was undertaken to find out what was required. What can be said is that the NSL and its clubs were struggling to access sustainable revenue streams. The NSL's market position was clearly troubled. Merely putting two new clubs into an already troubled market proved not to be the answer to the league's 'invisibility' after all. It showed that while rich on rhetoric, the impetus of the Hill regime lacked a quantifiable plan.

The appointment of Venables during this time was, in my mind, controversial. I fought the appointment because I felt the job should have gone to an Australian. I have spent much of my time in soccer fighting for young players and I also believe in fighting for opportunities for young Australian coaches. I had nothing against Venables, the man, at all. There was never any point where I took issue with his coaching record which boasts outstanding achievements. My arguments against him were on other grounds. He had legal problems in the United Kingdom where he had been barred from holding directorship of football clubs. There had been trouble resulting from his time as manager at Tottenham Hotspur. But, more importantly for me, I think he had too many different projects going all at once, consuming his time and interest. Yet, here he was, coaching the Australian team. I don't believe he had a good knowledge of Asian football, which was the pool from which our final opponent for the '98 World Cup qualifiers would come, and so I felt we really should have had a local coaching the Socceroos. I believe the job should have gone to Zoran Matic, coach of Adelaide City who is now the most experienced coach the NSL has ever had and was then, arguably, the most successful NSL coach there had ever been. Besides this, a large chunk of the Socceroo team had played or were playing for him at Adelaide City—Alex Tobin, Tony and Aurelio Vidmar, Milan Ivanovic, Ernie Tapai and Craig Foster.

Furthermore, there was the potential for public perception of a conflict of interest with Venables' dual role of Socceroo coach and his involvement at Portsmouth Football Club in England. The appearance of Venables using the national team of Australia as a stable for potential players for his club interests back in the United Kingdom was risky. There ended up to be a trail of players who followed Venables to English clubs—Craig Foster, Robbie Enes, Hamilton Thorp, John Aloisi to Portsmouth and then Craig Moore, Craig Foster and Nick Rizzo to Crystal Palace. This gave people room for cynicism and an opportunity to cast aspersions on the game. In my view, there was an obvious conflict of interest in this case.

Of course, the game didn't need this sort of innuendo and publicity. Just prior to Venables' appointment as coach, Australian soccer had been drawn into a public inquiry that focused on the netherworld of player transfers and associated skulduggery. Front-page national headlines and articles centred on these dealings, as Justice Donald Stewart tabled his report into the inner workings of Australian soccer which, among other things, he labelled as 'mafia-like'. The Stewart Report led to a Senate Inquiry which was headed by Senator Michael Baume. It was a very uncomfortable time for the sport. All of a sudden, Australian soccer had pricked the interest of mainstream media for all the wrong reasons. The dust had hardly settled on the public interest that was generated by Justice Stewart's report when Venables was appointed and Aussie players were being contracted to his English club. The game just didn't need any further controversy.

On the football side of the World Cup trail, I didn't see much focus from our new national coach. There was a six-month hiatus in games before the crucial match against Iran in Tehran. Iran wasn't scouted. Indeed, we didn't know the opponent was to be Iran until late in the piece. Reconnaissance on opponents was undertaken by one or both of Venables' assistants, Raul Blanco and Les Scheinflug. I still find this incredible because from my perspective, I don't care how good my assistants are; if I am committed to the job of coaching, then I am going to put in whatever effort it takes to see what my team will be up against. I didn't understand how a full-time coach didn't have time to watch his team's next opponent himself.

However, the actual football the team produced under Venables was very attractive. He had an unbeaten run of results including, ironically, the Iran series. The Socceroos were the only team not to qualify for France '98 while remaining unbeaten in the qualification rounds. The series against Iran was lost on the away-goals rule (the match was drawn 1–1 in Tehran and then 2–2 in Melbourne and with no aggregate winner, Iran progressed by scoring more 'away' goals). Venables attracted enormous attention to the game and performed charismatically in the media. Aussies really identified with the touch of the scallywag in him and appreciated his anti-establishment air. The players liked him too and respected his experience and expertise.

Perhaps people got carried away with the string of successes the Socceroos had under Venables. We definitely had good players but was it really a good team? There was an article I wrote for the *Sun Herald* about Socceroo Aurelio Vidmar who was then with Tenerife in Spain. Aurelio hadn't played for three months, the result of a falling out with his club's coach. As a result, one of our key players was trapped, unable to play football for another club, unable to prepare for the World Cup. My article pinpointed the need for Vidmar to be at least playing somewhere so he would be prepared for the World Cup qualifiers. I suggested that Soccer Australia should go through FIFA and expedite Vidmar's temporary return to the NSL, as a guest, to allow him half a dozen games to get back into the swing of things. It didn't happen and the national team suffered, I feel, because one of its main touch players was not, through any fault of his own, at his peak.

I commented prior to the final qualifier that the team was under-prepared. They beat Tunisia who had qualified for France '98. Tunisia was the Socceroos' only game in the six-month lead-up to the Iran matches. Before then, the Socceroos had beaten Hungary and Macedonia in friendly matches. But too many of the Australian players in the Iran match were out of match condition and had not been playing, for whatever reasons, on a regular basis with their clubs. It's one thing to be contracted to a European club but it's another thing entirely to be a regular playing member in that club's top team. I don't think enough of the boys had been playing regularly.

As for the Iran game itself, it is perhaps the first time, certainly since 1974, that all of Australia has stopped for a football match. The MCG game versus Iran has been etched so deeply into the psyche of Australians that people are able to recall, book and verse, where they were and what they were doing as the MCG drama unfolded. It is, most definitely, part of Australian sporting legend. I remember mentioning in my broadcast, as Australia was leading 2–0, that it was a very dangerous time for our team. There can be a tendency, at 2–0, for a team to take its foot off the accelerator and before anyone realises, the lead is reduced to 2–1. Suddenly the game takes on an entirely new complexion. The momentum swings to the chasing team; the team with the lead gets the wobbles. I recounted in the broadcast how this worked in Australia's favour in 1974 when we stung South Korea away in exactly these circumstances. We were down 2–0, with the Korean crowd going berserk, when we suddenly scored a goal and it became a different game. We got the second goal we needed to dislodge our hosts and send us through to the 1974 finals. Here we were, twenty-something years later, witnessing the same thing but with the tables turned.

There are a multitude of views as to what went wrong. I subscribe to two. The first is the loss of rhythm because of Peter Hoare, the serial pest (infamous for also disrupting the funeral of INXS lead singer Michael Hutchence, the Australian Open tennis tournament and the Melbourne Spring Racing Carnival) running onto the pitch, swinging on the goal and delaying play because repairs had to made to the goal's netting.

My second contention is that Venables did not do his job

properly during the delay. There were eight minutes where he had an opportunity to call the players to attention and ensure that their focus was on the job at hand. He needed to get among the players and ram home some truths about the situation; call on his experience as a big-time coach to steer our Socceroos through the unwelcome distraction and home to France '98. From what I saw, he didn't do that. Here was an opportunity to talk, soothe, exhort, strategise, plan. He didn't take it and I believe it was to our team's detriment.

No one will convince me that Venables' attention was with the job. It wasn't a mission for him, it was only a job, and there is a big difference between the two approaches. I think it is fair to say that it was the easiest draw the Socceroos have ever had. It was a golden opportunity to qualify for the World Cup. We only had to beat Oceania, then the fourth-best Asian team. There was no Scotland, Israel or Argentina this time around. Japan, South Korea and Saudi Arabia were already through and if we couldn't account for the fourth-best team in Asia then perhaps our football stocks weren't as plush as we'd all led ourselves to believe.

The undoubted positive about Venables and Hill was the promotion they gave football. They had us on the back sports' pages of the newspapers, mostly for the right reasons, on a refreshingly frequent basis. David Hill's public stance, when criticised about the degree of spending by Soccer Australia, was commendable. Hill stated that it was vital that the Socceroos were given every possible chance to qualify, lest anyone be accused of allowing the campaign to fail because of money. Hill was accused of being extravagant and cavalier with Soccer Australia's budget. After observing generations of Socceroo teams struggle because of lack of resources, I was happy that this could not be said for the 1997 squad—it was a well-resourced campaign, without being ostentatious.

The Socceroos didn't qualify for France '98. They failed in their mission without even losing a match through the qualifying games. The ramifications of Iran's escape act were felt right throughout Australia and have lasted, even fermented, in the period since. The same tragic sense of loss I felt after the game when I cried on national television resonated throughout old and young Australians alike. One of the many letters I've received throughout my life from kids who love the game showed this shared sense of loss:

> Dear Johnny,
>
> I am writing because I saw you when the Socceroos lost the world cup game, you looked very very sad. You looked even sadder than me, I hope you are feeling beta now. I watched the gaim with my dad. He says that Iran are cheaters. He says that they should get the biggest cheaters in the world award. What do you think? Are you friends with Les Murray? Who is your faurit player? Can I have your pitcher?
>
> Lots of love
>
> Lynet

Such has been the impact of the 1997 Iran failure that the Uruguay series became eagerly anticipated. Directly proportional to the anticipation is the sense of loss after failing to qualify for the 2002 World Cup after our games against Uruguay in November 2001. It is a feeling known all too well by the Socceroos and their supporters. The mourning for our lost World Cup chances will only stop when we eventually qualify for the World Cup finals.

Qualification for the World Cup of football is a trying process. It involves far more than the players. Supporters of the Socceroos and lovers of the game are an integral part of the voyage. Their emotions are as deeply entwined in the process as the players. Failure cuts them just as deeply. The sense of loss, especially as a result of the 1997 Iran series, most definitely flowed outside the sport's 'normal' boundaries. It was as though, finally, the intuitive sporting instinct of Australians had been tuned to the reality that the World Cup is the big-time competitive event. Australians want to be competing with the biggest and best and to be doing so with credibility. Australians love a host of sports, but the fallout from the MCG in November 1997 told me that they now knew, en masse, that Australia had to be at the World Cup finals to realise the sporting mythology of our own nation. Anything less is unbecoming of a sporting nation. The Australian people are right. Competing at the World Cup finals puts Australia on the biggest platform. It opens a window to global audiences that are counted in the billions. The benefits to Australia, and not just its football team, are only as small as our imaginations.

19

The Young Guns

⚽ FIFA MAY WELL be football's governing body. FIFA may also be fundamentally configured along democratic lines. In real terms, however, football is indisputably an oligarchy where the real influence behind the game lies with the clout of Europe's big clubs. These clubs, aggressively market-focused and funded by massive amounts of television and merchandising revenues, are now formally organised under the intimidating banner of the G-14—a body comprised of the fourteen biggest European clubs that, in my opinion, seek to serve their self-interest at the expense of others. The intent of the G-14 is a real threat to football as it has existed to date. The plan of the G-14 is for a super-club competition where its members, Real Madrid, Barcelona, Bayern Munich, Borussia Dortmund, Inter, AC Milan, Juventus, Liverpool, Manchester United, Marseille, Paris Saint-Germain, Ajax, PSV Eindhoven and Porto would secede from their domestic leagues and form a European super league.

The G-14's desire to break away from domestic leagues will challenge the viability of those very leagues. The vast majority of sponsorship and television revenue would follow the big and glamorous clubs into their brave new world while the rest of domestic league football would be left to fade into obscurity.

The world of G-14 is one of significant influence and power. It is a world of heavy-hitting politics and mega-dollars. The G-14 is an organisation that wields significant political clout and lobbying muscle, both in the football and secular worlds. The driving force for these cross-border super leagues is pay television. Television companies envisage huge subscription revenues by creating competitions that have the biggest football clubs in Europe playing against each other on a weekly basis. The competition would resemble various domestic league competitions that currently exist, but would only be for the fourteen very elite members of the G-14 group.

The impact of the G-14 has already been significant. The European Champions League has replaced the European Cup. The European Cup had been in operation since the 1950s and was established to determine the top club team in Europe on a yearly basis. It was a knockout competition, entry to which was reserved for the champion teams from each of Europe's domestic leagues. To win the European Cup was the most prestigious mantle a club could attain. The European Champions League, which now exists in its stead, came about as a compromise between the G-14—whose members were threatening to break away from the traditional competitions—and UEFA, football's governing body in Europe. The Champions League offers more latitude to teams who have not necessarily won their domestic league but have finished at a high enough level to gain entry into the competition, depending on how many places are made available to the respective leagues. For example, Italy, Spain, England and Germany may be allocated three direct Champions League places, whereas France, Holland, Portugal and Turkey may be allocated only two places. Norway and Sweden may be allocated one place in the Champions League each and smaller football nations will have to play through the pre-season qualifying tournament. In my mind, it is a system that has been unfairly designed to ensure that the big teams from the major leagues are represented and that the smaller teams have reduced access to the competition. The number of places allocated to each league is dependent on the performance of clubs representing that league. Consistently strong or poor results over a number of years affects the standing of that league and hence the number of teams that will be able to represent it in the Champions League. Furthermore, instead of the straight knockout format of the European Cup, the Champions League is divided into groups. Teams play home and away against the other teams in their group. The top two teams from each group qualify for the second stage, which is also a round robin stage, after which the competition becomes knockout. It is more convoluted than the traditional competition and certainly more contrived. There are more games, which means greater audience numbers and bigger television revenues. There is dissension in football circles about this development, not as much in protest at the Champions League, but more because people are aware that the Champions League is, after all, a compromise to keep the G-14 wolf from the door of their domestic leagues.

The traditional experience of football, up until now, has been successfully based on local, inter-city and inter-regional rivalries played under the umbrella of national championships. It has been linked globally by international tournaments—the World Cup, Continental Championships, Confederations Cup, Continental and Inter-Continental Club Championships, and the Olympics. The depth of the relationship between the fan and his/her local club have kept the tribalism of football and the passion for the game alive. Local clubs have become powerful and valuable community reference points and assets. In many parts of the world they have been the very fabric and sustenance of communities. I fear that the ambitions and desires of the G-14 are antithetical to the community spirit of football.

The tentacles of the G-14 are also enveloping Australian players. Paul Agostino is a Socceroo who, born of Italian migrants and hailing from Adelaide, left Australia as a teenager to chase his dream of football fame and fortune. After stints in Switzerland and England, Paul found his way to Bundesliga club 1860 Munich. His German club is the local rival to football monolith Bayern Munich. Paul, a striker for 1860 Munich, made a promising start to the 2000/2001 Bundesliga season and managed to score enough goals to be near the head of the scoring charts—a remarkable achievement in itself.

About one third of the way through the 2000/01 Bundesliga season, Paul Agostino's phone rang. On the other end of the phone was Silvio Berlusconi, President of Italian giants AC Milan, self-made media magnate and the main mover and shaker in the G-14 group (and now Italy's Prime Minister). Berlusconi wanted Agostino to play for his Milan team and he was prepared to pay eighty million dollars to see that happen.

If someone had said to me up until recently that Australian players would be strutting this type of prestigious stage I would have called them crazy. I don't think, in the wildest dreams of even the most optimistic person associated with the game through its Australian history, that we could have believed what we are seeing now. Even Uncle Joe Vlasits and the pioneer coaches would be incredulous. But that phone call received by Agostino indicates the level of respect that Australian players now receive. Agostino is not the only one. Indeed, Berlusconi's advance notwithstanding, Paul is not hailed to the same degree as some of his more illustrious Socceroo teammates. This is the bona fide big time and Australia is handsomely represented.

This is the outcome of the evolutionary process in Australian soccer. No one can tell me that the likes of Ron Lord, Billy Henderson or Bobby Bignall—1956 football Olympians—

weren't good enough to play in Europe. Similarly, I can't believe that Baartz, Abonyi, Alston or Kosmina, Yankos, Davidson, Crino, or the era that followed given the opportunity of the current crop, wouldn't be achieving the same thing. In athletic terms, they would have to be on par with today's players but in bygone days there was no discernible career path for them and no other real playing alternatives. We played for our club and the national team and we tried to qualify for the World Cup, end of story. There was no youth development as such, no television, no Youth World Cups to play in. No academies, no Australian Institute of Sport and no intensive training centres. Australian footballers, as athletes, have always been good enough to succeed. The contemporary Australian footballers, as athletes, now have greater opportunity.

The fact that we can sit and watch Kewell, Viduka, Bosnich, Okon, Schwarzer, Tiatto, Aloisi, Lazaridis, Slater and Filan playing in the English Premier League, to list just one competition, is a scenario which is still very difficult to believe. To think that Australian players are now so sought after by European teams and that there are so many Australian players who earn a professional living in the big leagues of the world is remarkable. To see Kewell and Viduka play in the European Champions League and display a skill level that surpasses nearly every other player; to watch them play Real Madrid, the football club of the century, and for them to be amongst the best performers just blows my mind.

The story of the young guns is summed up in one word—opportunity. Today's players are benefiting from other people's ground work. The Australian team was something that used to be, quite literally, thrown together at the last minute. If a game was scheduled for South Australia, a team of crow-eaters would be formed to save on travel costs—the typical approach of Australian soccer many years ago. When the game moved to Victoria, the team would be reselected and filled with Victorians. The boys would meet each other for the first time in the dressing room before the game. That would sometimes be the extent of the relationship of the 'teammates'.

The players of today are products of a dramatically improved Australian system, one that has been refined over the years. They bear testament to the evolution of the local scene that was once an importer of talent and is now, in basic economic terms, an exporting nation with a string of clients queuing to purchase its football products: our worthy Australian players. It is an exciting achievement for Australian sport. The current generation of Australian footballers is the product of talent identification programs and has been developed by coaches using up-to-date training science. The players today are benefiting from a culture with an enhanced awareness of football. Many of these players have been exposed to, if not brought up on, the Coerver coaching method which through small games and repetitive skill practice and imitation trains the players in automated technique response and close ball control. Most players are also products of the much-maligned NSL clubs who have provided them with so much opportunity to develop their skills in competition and who have provided the platform for their careers. While I have been critical of the way this country treats soccer because I am impatient to see the day when soccer is embraced in the same way as rugby league and AFL, I have to admit that Australian soccer is doing something very, very right.

Of course, we have always had good players. The pioneer of overseas professional football was Joe Marston who was fifty years ahead of his time. Joe Marston was a name I first heard as a kid, when Dad used to take me to games. He began his career with Leichhardt in 1943 as a seventeen year old and left seven years later to chase his dream, playing for Division One team Preston North-End in England. Here was a young Aussie boy playing in the same team as Sir Tom Finney, a player whom many regarded as a better winger than the great Sir Stanley Matthews. He put in five very productive years starring for Preston and became a favourite son of the club.

He also played in the 1954 FA Cup Final (which his Preston team lost to West Bromwich Albion 3–2). During the five years he spent with Preston he scaled such heights that he was selected for the Combined English League team to play Scotland at Glasgow's Hampden Park. Having played so well in that game, the press reports acclaimed him as worthy to have played for England, were he an Englishman! Either side of his English adventure, he won thirty-five caps for Australia, captaining the national team twenty-four times. Sadly, Joe could not play for Australia at the 1956 Olympics because he was judged to have been a professional player, due to the money he had earned in England. It was amazing that this could happen in the days of 'shamateurism'; the days when Eastern Europeans were employed by the state, in their countries, to basically be professional sportspeople. They were still considered amateurs though, and eligible for the Olympics.

Joe Marston was ahead of his time inasmuch as a player really had to have a passion for the game to leave Australia back then. Ron Lord, another celebrated Socceroo who could easily have forged a career overseas, recalled that guys could earn more money here, in combination with their employment, than the players in England who were bound under maximum wage rules. Ron Lord was offered to go to England but because he earned more as a plumber here than he could ever hope for from football there, he decided to stay put. Joe was distinctive because he dared to dream about a career in big-time English football. He had a dream to 'make it' and to eventually play at Wembley. He was the first Australian to appear in an FA Cup Final and was acknowledged as one of the finest players in England. It was a massive achievement. The other point about Joe's success is that it was done at a time when the world was still a big place, not like today's globalised world. The English League wasn't the multi-national extravaganza of today. Foreigners weren't commonplace in football. Joe was a foreigner, and Australian at that, and Aussies weren't renowned in England as footballers. Joe certainly changed that perception. He became the target of a big transfer bid from London club Arsenal. Joe ended his time as captain of Preston, one of the powerhouses of English football back then. It was no coincidence that the club's heyday coincided with the contribution of Joe Marston. A couple of years back, the club historians selected Preston's best ever players. This roll call of former players included Sir Tom Finney, Sir Bobby Charlton, David Beckham and Joe Marston. Not bad company in which to have been included.

The other pioneer was Eddie Krncevic. He was the first Australian to go to mainland Europe. For many of those who followed, Krncevic helped a lot of players who were seeking to make their own way. He was a father figure to many of his generation, including Frank Farina, Robbie Slater and Graham Arnold and he was always there to assist the other Aussie boys in whatever way he could. Importantly, he also gave overseas clubs a good impression of Australian players. His own performances eased the way for other Australians who followed by showing that Australian players were viable alternatives to Europeans and worth considering as footballers. Indeed, helping other nations understand and appreciate that Australian players are talented was a very important role the pioneers of Australian soccer assumed. Krncevic's own career achieved this in mainland Europe.

The most recent Aussie who has made an indelible mark on international football is Harry Kewell. He is a phenomenal player and is so exciting to watch. Harry is one of the best dribblers of a football in Britain. He also possesses one of the best left feet I have ever seen in action. He is both a creator and scorer of goals, although probably more the former than the latter. He has all the talents of a world-class player in his vision, skill, long- and short-range passing, crossing, free-kicks and dribbling. But the biggest indicator of Harry's value is that he is a big-match player who rises to the occasion every time; a player who truly makes things happen on the field. I find myself watching him play for Leeds on the television, sitting with my brother, screaming at the screen to 'give the bloody ball to Harry'. His impact on English football has been so huge that there is unprecedented interest from British clubs scouring the Australian cities and countryside looking for the next Harry Kewell. That is quite a legacy for a player who has at least another decade of top-flight football ahead of him.

I first saw Harry playing in the qualifiers in Tahiti for the under-20s World Cup. He played left fullback. I was mesmerised; I couldn't believe what I was seeing. I said at the time that he was a better player than Brazilian star Roberto Carlos. To be heard saying that about an Australian kid—a footballer educated in Australia—you run the risk of being certified insane. But I truly believe he is a better player than Roberto Carlos and I know, equally, that I'm not mad. Those who watch Harry play know what I am talking about. Leeds United Football Club, his current club, also knows it. With Leeds, he often plays striker as well as left midfield depending on the coach's desire. But he's an all-round player. It is incredible that an Australian player is so good.

Harry has maintained a high-octane output, to the point where he is a keenly sought-after talent. Joining him at Leeds was compatriot Mark Viduka. Viduka's star has also shone; his performances so credible that after shelling out six million pounds to sign him from Scottish club Glasgow Celtic last European summer, Leeds face the advances of continental clubs offering cash in the vicinity of twenty million pounds—quite a tribute to the NSL, his local club Melbourne Knights and the Australian Institute of Sport. He is a delightful player, whom I describe in the same terms as Dutch artisan Marco Van Basten. He has impeccable touch and a skill level out of this world. But he is not out of this world; rather he is from Keilor in Melbourne's industrial west—a testament to the efforts of Australian soccer today.

The fact that these boys are doing so well in England is significant. If they were in Japan or Brazil they wouldn't be having the same impact locally. The English Premier League is one of the highest profile competitions in the world. The Australian media love the English Premier League.

For a long time there was no pathway for Australian players to that competition. The efforts of Joe Marston aside, there was never a proliferation of Australians playing professionally in England. Because of the success of the current crop of Aussie players over there, it will make it easier for the next generation of our footballers who pursue international playing careers. The better Australians do in England, the more coverage the press will give them in Australia. The exposure of their exploits will serve to spur on more youngsters to try and emulate them. I look forward to the day, in Australia, when the press reports the successful Aussies who are playing in Germany and Italy and Spain and France. There is already a large contingent of them, doing very well, but locally the media's measuring stick is whether or not they are playing in England. That will change, as the exploits of the players force Australians to understand more and more about football and its place all over the world. The reputation of Aussies as footballers has been enhanced and there is a clear path now into the big leagues of the world, and immense pecuniary reward for those who make the grade.

I think the most telling aspect of Australia's football development has been the impact of former FIFA boss Joao Havelange on football. His presidency commenced in 1974 and the ensuing years of his reign brought seismic change to the size and shape of FIFA and its showpiece, the World Cup. Prior to Havelange's term, Oceania, Africa and Asia had the grand total of one spot between them at the World Cup finals. Central and North America didn't have any places at all. Havelange took the game to the world. Under him, FIFA gradually expanded the finals tournament, giving more representation to Asia, Africa and Concacaf. By expanding the opportunities, he began to empower this new constituency, which has led to the decentralisation of the power in football from its traditional European and South American base. FIFA's membership increased such that today it has in excess of two hundred members—more members than the United Nations—and its democratic structure means that the national associations of the 'new frontiers', Asia and Africa, have the same voting power and rights as everybody else. That is, at the FIFA Congress, the votes of Senegal and Qatar are now worth the same as Italy or Brazil. The sheer size of the African and Asian confederations means they have become significant political power blocs.

It was Havelange who instituted the series of international youth tournaments. This was what he referred to as his education system—the under-17s and under-20s World Cups, the Olympic Games (which is an under-23s tournament with minor age dispensations)—which were all regarded as stepping stones to the world game. I remember asking him at the World Youth Cup in the Soviet Union in 1985 when it would be that Australia (Oceania) would get direct qualification to the World Cup. He told me, 'You have to prove yourselves. You've proved yourselves at kindergarten, you've proved yourselves at primary school and you're proving yourselves at high school. You now have to prove yourselves at university [the Olympics] and you have to prove yourself at Ph.D. level [the World Cup]. When you do that you will gain automatic qualification.' He made it clear that it was incumbent upon national associations to demonstrate to the world the types of improvements they were implementing in their own operations. Acceptance and respect in world football terms very much depended upon progression through each level of competition. That same mentality has pervaded the global football psyche ever since. National football associations and leagues need to prove their performances through a vigorous process of refinement before they will be seriously recognised. That process has been beneficial for everyone. The game is booming everywhere. The United States which, as I said, has never been considered a soccer country, will eventually become one, particularly because of the influence of its Latino population. Many predict that this influence will increase in the years to come. Along with their linguistic influence, Latinos will also spread their football passion throughout North America. That is a huge plus for football.

Havelange did a great job for world football by taking it to the four corners of the earth. We now witness the Africans playing in the World Cup, with five qualification places (also African nations have won the last two Olympic Games tournaments) and acknowledge how attractive their football is. Asia, with three direct qualification places and Concacaf with three also, demonstrate how the Havelange charter has embraced all the regions of the world. We should remember that when the World Cup was given to the United States in 1994 the decision was proclaimed by football people throughout the world as disastrous and the media coverage of the decision was largely negative. The crux of most of the criticism was that North America was not considered a soccer region and people believed that popular professional sports like gridiron, baseball, basketball and ice hockey were too entrenched for soccer to breathe, let alone thrive there. USA '94 turned out to be one of the big World Cup successes, a magnificent tournament. And the legacy for the United States has been brilliant, with a professional men's league (Major League Soccer, MLS) commencing soon after the completion of the 1994 tournament and a professional women's league (WUSA) having completed its inaugural, highly successful season. The United States is now a nation reported to have over twenty million registered soccer players, more than Australia's total population. Soccer has made such inroads into families in the United States that part of Bill Clinton's election strategy when seeking his second term as President was pitched to the 'soccer mum'. Though many feared the worst for USA '94, the decision to hold the finals there has been vindicated resoundingly. It was Havelange, the visionary, who was responsible for changes such as these.

Similarly, the Havelange legacy, which is still alive at FIFA, pushed heavily for China to host the Olympic Games as a means of taking top-class tournament football into the world's most populous nation. Beijing 2008 gives China this opportunity. There was also a big push within FIFA to take the World Cup to Asia, hence Korea/Japan 2002. These developments are largely the result of Havelange's work to broaden the base of interest and involvement in football throughout the world. In many ways Havelange anticipated globalism before the multinational corporations did. Indeed, I believe that globalised football, care of Havelange, was one of the first contributors to the phenomenon of globalisation. As Havelange said to me, 'We [football] want to conquer the whole world.'

Havelange also gave life to other forms of football. The Havelange era saw the birth and growth of women's football, futsal (indoor court football) and beach football. He took football to the stage where an international match could be played tomorrow between almost any two nations and the result would be hard, if not impossible, to predict. Expanding the World Cup also assisted FIFA by increasing the size of television audiences and sponsorship revenues, giving FIFA a bigger 'war chest' to realise its vision of world domination for its sport. Emerging regions, such as Africa, typically were huge supporters of Havelange, because he included and empowered them. The electoral support Havelange received in return guaranteed the longevity of his presidency and enabled him to enact his visionary plans.

Along with Asia, Africa and Concacaf, Australia is one of the major beneficiaries of the twenty-four year reign of Havelange. Virtually all of the current Socceroos have progressed through the ranks of the various youth teams to overseas professional careers.

In league with the Havelange development pathway, on the local scene, was SBS Television. No one will convince me that the role of SBS hasn't been pivotal in the development of football in Australia. The most effective football coaching takes place where kids imitate the players they watch on television. The current generation is the first to be brought up on SBS, and now pay television, watching televised football from every part of the earth.

SBS and multiculturalism have enhanced our football stocks and hence our place in the world. Twenty years ago, as a player, one was very much moulded by the ethnicity and culture of one's club and its coach. There was little cross-fertilisation of ideas and methods. So often in earlier days, the clubs were run as community meeting places or political forums and as such they rigidly adhered to a monocultural structure. This often manifested itself by the players, coaches, administrators and supporters of individual clubs being drawn from solitary ethnic groups. This is what David Hill set about changing. He wanted to encourage the NSL to view itself as a commodity that needed to be commercially viable and appealing to the Australian public in order to survive into the new century. These structures (NSL) needed to be opened up to embrace the wider community if the league was to be worth anything commercially outside its traditional boundaries. There have been varying levels of that same realisation for almost twenty years now, but the administrative, cultural and commercial challenges have proven to be a difficult row to hoe for the NSL and many of its clubs. In terms of player development, the isolationist nature of many clubs meant that the doors were closed to alternative playing and coaching styles. Clubs had their own style that reflected the history and culture of their ethnic backgrounds. While off-field reform, in terms of commercialisation of the clubs, has been painstaking and problematic, the football changes regarding players and coaches have, over the years at club level, been irresistible. In this realm, whether by design or the passage of time and generational change, the power of a blended football product is being realised. I rather think that the experience of soccer has, in this sense, been to endorse the value of multiculturalism. The power of blended football is that Australian soccer has taken the best methods of playing and coaching from the many and varied cultural influences that exist in its clubs. The United States has had much the same experience, but on a larger scale. The opportunities for such hybrid styles are enormous. I think much of the credit for facilitating this effective blending of football traditions and styles in Australia into its current powerful and unique form is due to SBS, which has heightened awareness of the world game through its broadcasting efforts.

Australian kids today have hours of images each week of the best football in the world from teams all over the world. They are so knowledgeable of the football world, of who's who and who does what. Television offers them a terrific grounding in the game. The kids can play football by themselves, refining technique, and imitating the stars.

I'm delighted that television has influenced the style of the young players and has taught them that style is based on skill. As a result, the Australian style of football is a beautiful cocktail of all the different nationalities that comprise modern Australia. That cocktail adds to the Anglo qualities which are inherent in Australian sport: the competitive nature, the never-say-die attitude, the tenacity, the physicality and the readiness to face any challenge. It's an aggressive style that seeks to take the game to its opponent and force them into error. The 'have a go mentality'. It is one that has been modified and improved by the mix of all these different types of Australians (South Americans, Europeans, Africans, Asians). And SBS has provided the images to produce football gold.

The first group of players to acknowledge that television had such a formative role on their football skills was the 1991 Young Socceroos. I remember the under-20s World Cup in Portugal as being the tournament that probably changed

Australian football forever. This was where a lot of our boys were spotted. Okon, Kindtner, Maloney, Trajanovski, Popovich, Bingley and Bosnich, Kalac, Seal, Stanton, Poric, Sorras and Babic were all attracting the attention of big-time European clubs. I remember that the team hotel was full of brazen agents, poring over the players with offers and expressions of interest. It was the real commencement of Australia as a target of poachers.

The Australian Institute of Sport has also played its part. I view it more as a finishing school, albeit a very good one. The players have already reached an elite standard before they arrive at the institute. Success in football originates more from parental involvement; mums and dads introducing kids to football and taking them to games. It originates from discussing football around the dinner table and sitting around the television watching football together. Mark Viduka owes more to his dad and his early years at the Melbourne Knights than he does to anyone else. He spent a year or so at the AIS but his talent was already there. Success in football requires a connection with the sport, starting off in the family or through friends; it's not something that is made in a year. Football is a visceral thing.

The talent identification system in Australian soccer is also highly effective. It may smack slightly of Cold War Eastern European sporting regimes, but trawling the playing fields in search of raw young talent has played its part in uncovering the bounty of brilliant players we have. Australia has proven very adept at training that talent by realising the importance of building players' skills. That is why I am so delighted with Kewell, Okon, Zelic, Emerton and Viduka, as examples, because what sets them apart from many other players is their skill. It's no longer size and strength that is the paramount concern on the field, but skill. It is skill that enables players to have time on the ball and execute their passing, dribbling or shooting options. It is skill that makes them so exciting to watch, because skilful players make things happen during a game. It is skill that so excites the Australian fans and has them clamouring for seats. It is the mastery of skill in practice and execution in matches that makes the game so addictive for players. It is skill that makes for *jogo bonito* as the Brazilians call it—the beautiful game. Overseas clubs have always liked Aussie players because they are so well disciplined and such good fighters. They are hungry for success because they know what it is like to be playing in Australia, where soccer has been a second-class sport compared to other football codes. But now our players have been given the opportunity to have lucrative playing careers overseas and have capitalised on this chance, because at home—here—there isn't the money to be made.

Credit is also due to the directors of coaching schemes. The days when the coach of the kids' team is the unfortunate parent who has drawn the short straw are lessening. Nowadays, people are taught how to coach, from basic through to advanced levels. Parents of kids involved in the game and other interested people can be coached on how to impart technical and tactical information to young players. More and more kids are benefiting from correct instruction. The weekend coach is now more likely to have played soccer him- or herself and so has a greater affinity with the game.

Football in Australia is also in better shape as a result of Eric Worthington. Eric is an Englishman who came out to Australia to establish the National Director of Coaching scheme in the early 1970s. This national scheme instituted instruction for coaches all around the country, from the grassroots level of football upwards. Eric was a professional footballer himself with an academic background. The structure Worthington has created with state directors of coaching has endured and credit should be given to the way these directors have ensured there is proper football education in the community. My only criticism is that for too long the coaching was too Anglo in focus. It took a long time for those in charge, most of them British, to welcome alternative views into the fold.

But for all the very real incursions football has made in this country, one of my biggest disappointments is that soccer has never used its best assets, its players, to promote the game. Australia is the one football country in the world where officials are probably better known than the players and where the sport's politicians have been the focus of media coverage over and above the exploits of the players. Football has been used by people to elevate and promote their own agendas and the players have been left in the shadows. The problem lies in the way the federal system of Soccer Australia deals with the issues and needs of its member states. Soccer administration in Australia has always been a numbers game where, until recently, there has been no room for independence by its members. Frank Lowy summed up the situation aptly to me one day when I worked for him at Sydney City. I asked him why he didn't take over the leadership of Soccer Australia. He responded, 'John, I'm an executive not a politician. I will make decisions for the good of the game but I am not going to spend all night telephoning people to make sure I've got the numbers for the decision to go through.' To me, that sums up the reasons why football hasn't advanced far enough in Australia. The politics of the game frustrates the fans, media and players. Until the focus of soccer shifts from the politicians back to the players and the actual game itself, the soccer stars of this country will be unable to promote the game to any meaningful extent.

I remember back to my playing days when we had the likes of Ray Baartz who was, and still is, an outstanding ambassador for the sport. He is a polished speaker, impeccably mannered and untainted by controversy. Adrian Alston is another player who can light up a room with his wit and presence, but who also has been relegated to cameo appearances at football functions and promotional events because of the way the politicians and administrators of the game have taken the spotlight away from players. In this day and age we have bona fide international football superstars with movie-star looks who have a magnificent presence. The likes of Bosnich, Zelic, Okon, Viduka and Aloisi are but a few. They are multilingual, cosmopolitan and classy. Unfortunately, they have not been marketed prominently in Australia like stars of rugby league, tennis and cricket have. As a result, the game's profile has suffered from a lack of media exposure. Improvements are starting to be made, but only gradually.

I believe that Australia's star players need to avail themselves to promote the game in this country. They need to be used much more to spread the gospel of football in Australia. Access to our star players is difficult because they are in Australia so infrequently and when they are in town, usually for important World Cup qualifiers, everyone wants a piece of them. It is a difficult balancing act, particularly for Socceroo coaching and management staff, and one that is made difficult by the four-yearly wait Australians must endure to see their Socceroos in live action.

I am disturbed by the increasing incidence of players requesting fees for promotional appearances and media interviews. In the *Sydney Morning Herald*, Bernie Mandic, Harry Kewell's manager, was reported as saying that Harry would be available for interviews but these interviews would incur a fee. I must say I was disappointed. The report did make the point that those fees would then be donated to a charity; a nice sentiment, but one that doesn't really help the development of the game itself in Australia. I fully support the right of a player to make money, particularly when it comes to purely commercial arrangements and endorsements, but I don't think payment should be requested for the media interviews that feed the football appetites of the fans. It must be remembered that it is the fans' love of the game and its stars that creates the very healthy remuneration packages for today's players. It is those same fans who deserve media access to their idols. The feeling I get that players are forgetting their football origins disturbs me. I feel that the role of the lady who worked the canteen at the junior soccer club to raise funds for the kids to play football should never be forgotten. And the role played by the much-maligned NSL clubs who, by and large, lose money hand over fist, but provide the opportunity for players to perform on a competitive platform shouldn't be forgotten either. You only have to go to the local soccer ground to watch the mums and dads and every Tom, Dick and Harriet working themselves ragged to provide a game of soccer for the kids. It is a massive network of people that continues to provide the foundation for a child's ascension to stardom. The soccer fans of Australia crave news of their Australia soccer idols and the least our star players could do for their supporters is to grant appearances or interviews without expecting a fee. It is the duty of our soccer superstars to bequeath to the next generation an improved football environment in this country. The players completely deserve their success and the rewards that come with it. All I ask is that they don't forget their football roots.

I don't want them to do as Craig Johnston has done, a player who could have had a major impact on the game here but chose instead to play for England. Johnston could have brought his professional experience to the Socceroos and it would have been a huge boost for them and perhaps it would be been enough to help us through against Scotland, for example, in 1985. While understanding why he couldn't play, it was very disappointing that he chose not to accept the chance to do something very special for Australian soccer. Not only did he knock back that chance, but he played for England, our arch sporting rivals. That really hurt everyone in Australian football. The disappointment was more acute when he commented that 'playing soccer for Australia is like surfing for England'. That comment was exactly the sort of perception against which we struggle here—that Aussies don't play real soccer. The future of thousands of young kids, who kick soccer balls are in the hands of our top players, such is their influence. What will be the legacy of today's Socceroos?

It is about the opportunity that has been afforded to young players that I had occasion to speak with the Wollongong Wolves boys about on the eve of the Oceania Club Championships, conducted in Papua New Guinea in January 2001. My address was on the day that we had all been to the Bomana War Cemetery, just outside Port Moresby. Inside the cemetery were some four thousand Australian war graves. No other nationalities, only Aussies. The lawns were beautifully manicured; the headstones fastidiously maintained. We took some time to stroll around, absorbing the atmosphere and reading the no-frills epitaphs—Bill Smith, 18; Fred Jones, 19—unheralded individuals who paid the ultimate price for their country. There were also numerous graves of 'unknown soldiers'. From the cemetery we then went to the children's hospital. One hundred kids to a ward, mums and dads sleeping under the bed, another four hundred kids outside who'd come down from the Highlands. A population with a high HIV infection rate, along with malnutrition, malaria and tropical diseases. The kids lay there, barely skin and bone, and the Wolves players gave out souvenirs—soccer balls and club merchandise. It really brought a tear to the eye. And we were there, in PNG, for a football match.

The keynote of the speech was about chance. The chance that avails itself in a game to score was part of the theme. However, the content reached far greater depths. Success in the PNG tournament would send Wollongong to the World Club Championships and to a competition where our NSL champions would play against the crème de la crème of world club football. As such, the tournament provided a chance that money couldn't buy. The really beautiful things about sport are those that can't be bought and to go and play the best in the world was one of these. Even more than the football chance though, was the chance that the boys have in life, the chance that had eluded those kids in the hospital. The four thousand graves and the sacrifice Australian soldiers represented also signified the chance they provided for others who followed them in peace, with opportunity they didn't have. That is why they offered themselves, to smooth and guarantee the way for those who followed. Without the sacrifice of war, Australia could well be a different place. A place with different cultural imputations. A place which didn't 'populate or perish', and hence a place without the benefit of post-war European migration. Perhaps this is the view of a history simpleton, but because of the diggers and because of the 'wogs' coming to Australia and bringing their football with them, those boys I was addressing, the Wolves, had the chance of a lifetime. It was a moving experience to address the team, who are an eminent collection of admirable characters. The circumstances of our day's excursion and the recognition of the opportunity that had been provided to us was a powerful emotional combination. In my career, I had a better chance than Ron Lord or Joe Marston, and Kossie (John Kosmina) had a better chance than me. Wadey's opportunities outstripped Kossie's and now it is Okon and his crew who are benefiting from the sweat of their predecessors while they simultaneously pave the way for the next generation of football players.

The development of Australian footballers will only accelerate and the future is bright. Apart, of course, from the stagnation that paralyses the local game, the Aussie players will continue to chase the dream overseas and, hopefully, the Socceroos will reap the rewards. We need to guard against youngsters racing off overseas too early. A much better path can be bedded down here with the NSL and adequate study, before leaving for overseas. Kids leaving in their young teenage years is something I find a bit alarming. For every success story there are many more kids who forego education in an unsuccessful search for glory. However, Brett Emerton is a great example of what I think is the most effective way of making the progression. He has a very supportive family that helped him plan every step of his football career. As part of their New South Wales Institute training, when they were teenagers, Brett, Harry Kewell and Wollongong midfielder Paul Reid went to Leeds United in England. Like Harry, Brett was invited to stay but chose to return to Australia. One of the reasons was to finish his education at home. He also wanted to develop his basic game. I think he has benefited from delaying his move overseas. He stayed in Australia up until Sydney 2000 and was captain during the Olympics competition—an honour he will treasure. He is an exciting player, like Harry; a player of whom much is expected when he gets possession of the ball. He has tremendous endurance, speed and power. He also has a very high skill factor and some of the tricks we have watched him execute in the European Champions League for Feyenoord are traceable to the Coerver training methods employed in his youth. He now epitomises the modern flank player and his best days are certainly ahead of him. His career hasn't yet been as spectacular as some of his contemporaries, but it will eventually get there. He is moving step by step from a very sound base. Emerton provides a good role model to aspiring Australian footballers. One of the scary aspects of the speed at which youngsters head overseas is the failure rate of young footballers. As far as I am concerned, Brett Emerton has shown a far better and more sustainable way to realise the dream of top-flight professional football.

As I look around at the young guns, I can't help but think of Uncle Joe. If he is looking down on all of this from the football stadium in the sky, he would be gratified that part of his message had been received—that skill separates players from the crowd. I am grateful for having worked under Uncle Joe and, similarly, if I hadn't come across the South Americans or

Frank Arok or Dettmar Cramer I would have been a far inferior player. I have developed a more global view of football and the world as a result of all these men's influence and learnt to appreciate the vital importance of skill.

The other part of Uncle Joe's mantra was for one to leave the game better than when one entered it. That's the only message I'd like to leave for the boys: leave football better. Open the way for the next generation to be better players and better people. I hope that from here on in the boys are able to evade the clutches of humanity's greatest scourge, greed. Football is enslaved by it and I hope that our boys don't give in to it.

I think back to the first time I saw Kewell play and the comparison I made of him with Roberto Carlos. I wonder if there are people scouring Brazil looking for talent and now using Harry, rather than Roberto Carlos, as their benchmark. I'm sure that scenario won't be far off.

20

Where To Now?

⚽ IT WAS 25 November 2001 and the score at El Estadio Centenario, Montevideo, was Australia 0, Uruguay 3. Sitting in the commentary box I was overcome with an awful feeling of déjà vu. It was about 5.45 pm local time and I was witnessing scenes of intense jubilation, Uruguay style. Their boys, 'La Celeste', the Sky Blues, had overcome significant odds and won through to the World Cup finals to be held in Korea/Japan in 2002. There was national relief and the strains of victory palpitated all around. Lying in the wake were the frustrations and dreams of the Socceroos and their supporters—again. Escorted from the field, barely able to walk unassisted, was the inconsolable Tony Vidmar, veteran of three failed campaigns. He was shattered. I think the pictures of Tony summed up how many felt.

It wasn't how things were supposed to be this time around. This was 'the finest' assembly of football talent ever to represent Australia. This was the first team to win the home leg of the deciding qualifying tie. To Montevideo these Socceroos took a one-goal lead, care of Kevin Muscat's MCG penalty in the 20 November game. This was the team that was going to consign previous failures to the dustbin. There was a vibe that it was Australia's hour. Alas, the records will show that by once more failing to qualify for the World Cup, we have made no progress as a footballing nation since those halcyon days of 1974. It is a harsh judgment, but perhaps a fair one.

The records will show what they will. It is our responsibility, however, to scrutinise the result of 25 November 2001 and discover the message contained therein. Whatever view one is to take on the World Cup campaign, the fact is that we lost a game of football 3–0, one in which we at least needed to score, if not actually win. Uruguay had not scored as many as three goals in an international for fourteen months, yet score three against us they did. Indeed, through this campaign Uruguay had scored only nineteen goals in nineteen games. The loss was the second biggest in our World Cup history. I think back to 1974 when, at the World Cup finals themselves we, as part-time footballers, lost 3–0 to West Germany, the eventual world champions. With far less heralded Socceroos teams, the scoreboards have been far more flattering; against Scotland and Argentina in particular. In relative terms, this team boasted playing résumés of greater repute than any of its predecessors. Questions must be asked about the outcome. Analysis must be conducted, scrutiny and criticism must get to the heart of the reasons for our failure and the results applied in a concerted effort to ensure our failure is not ongoing.

I found myself in a more objective mood post-Uruguay compared with the Iran match of four years ago. After Iran I cried on national television over the unfairness of it all. However, losing to 'La Celeste' was followed by the sober realisation of our inadequacies at the top level of international football. Uruguay's win certainly highlighted these. It is not a reflection on individual players, who were our best players and of whom we are very proud. I rated this team as having a very good chance of qualifying based on their performance in the Confederations Cup in 2001, where they beat both France and Brazil before finishing third in the tournament. They were a fully professional squad, many of whom were accustomed to big-match club football. Added to the list, of course, were Kewell and Viduka, who are both huge attractions.

For the first time, in my memory at least, logistics were in our favour. I think the draw decided upon by FIFA benefited us, for it must be remembered that Uruguay played their last game of Conmebol qualification on 14 November, at home against Argentina. They needed a result to ensure progression and the 1–1 draw enabled them to squeeze into the play-off against Australia by the most slender of goal-difference margins, heading Colombia on the table by a solitary goal. La Celeste then, immediately at the conclusion of the match against Argentina, boarded a plane and flew all the way across the planet to prepare for the 20 November match against Australia at the MCG. Despite the intense lobbying of Conmebol officials, FIFA refused to extend 25 November as the deadline for all final-round qualifiers. This put incredible time pressures on Uruguay. While Uruguay were enduring all of this, the Socceroos were holed up in the Crown Casino in Melbourne, in relative relaxation and five-star luxury. They had played world champions France on 11 November which was great preparation and in which the Socceroos performed very well, drawing 1–1.

I think we had the friendliest referees ever officiating a Socceroo match, particularly in the away leg. Certainly, the Socceroos have played under more trying refereeing circumstances. The penalty awarded at the MCG was a soft one. In Montevideo, the foul count tipped significantly the way of Australia, suggesting that it was the Socceroos and not their hosts who most tested the patience of the referee. In fact, Australia committed something like twenty-four fouls to Uruguay's sixteen but Australia received only one yellow card compared to Uruguay's six, of which one was for celebrating a goal and three for wasting time. It made a mockery of the pre-match Australian press about Uruguayan football being the world's dirtiest. I think Schwarzer could easily have been sent off for an incident with Uruguay striker Richard Morales. One Uruguayan player, Regueiro, was fouled by Australia on eight occasions. The fact that a yellow card was given for the second of these is an indication of the tolerance shown by the referee. These things just don't normally happen playing away games, particularly in South America.

Quite how Uruguay overcame the emotional and physical exhaustion they must have experienced amazes me. They flew across the world twice within a week, in economy class, with the enormous weight of their nation's hopes resting on their shoulders. The Aussies, equally desperate to qualify for the finals, had to fly only once and they did so in business-class comfort. In the world of athletic pursuits, these are massive considerations—a fact acknowledged by coach Farina when he declared his desire to play the home leg first, hence forcing his opponents into the double-travel scenario. But La Celeste is renowned for its fighting qualities and, as the national newspaper of Argentina, *La Nacion*, declared the day after the game, '*Uruguay: Es cierto, la celeste nunca muere*'—'Uruguay: it's certain, La Celeste is never dead!'

Let's be under no illusion, Uruguay was a huge opponent and perhaps we got carried away, expecting to qualify. Uruguay, with all its football pedigree, exemplified the chasm that exists between Australia and bona fide international football. This chasm, more so than the result, should be the real source of angst for us.

Apart from the first fifteen to twenty minutes of the second half, the Socceroos were running a distant second in this two-horse race. However, down 1–0 at half-time after star Dario Silva muscled past Shaun Murphy to shunt his low shot past Schwarzer into the goal, Uruguay could easily have had a greater advantage on the scoreboard—Recoba hit the post from a corner, Schwarzer saved brilliantly at the feet of

Magallanes, while Murphy, miraculously and acrobatically, cleared the ball off the goal line where, without him, a goal for Uruguay would have been certain. Farina's half-time address must have pushed some buttons with the Socceroos because the period immediately after the break was their best. They dominated the flow of the match and came close to scoring the elusive goal that probably would have been enough to dash the hopes of the hosts and catapult the Aussies to Korea/Japan 2002. I thought the fatigue factor was setting in and Uruguay were waning. The crowd sensed the same as they turned their ire onto the rotund figure of Uruguay's coach, Victor Pua, who paced his sideline area with discernible agitation.

But football matches turn on a dime. That is part of the game's attraction and I have to say that Pua won the tactical battle comprehensively. The crowd was right; Australia was reasserting itself in the struggle for the last available place at Korea/Japan. Pua reacted and, by doing so, effectively decided the game for his team. Magallanes was substituted for Morales, the tall, black striker from local club, Nacional. Only moments later Morales used his physical presence to bullet home a header, past Schwarzer, and ever so slightly released the pressure-valve on his team. Next, Pua substituted Regueiro, who had done his job brilliantly down the left wing for Uruguay. His pace and penetration gave his team inestimable momentum. Largely because of him, the Australian team were pinned in their own territory for longer periods than they would have liked. But with his job done, Pua changed him for the more defensive Del los Santos, who made his way straight for Paul Okon, the player exerting real influence for Australia from midfield. Pua, via Del los Santos, dealt with that threat. Finally, it was Morales again, who scored the third and decisive goal. The interesting subtext to Uruguay's result was that Alvaro Recoba provided Morales with both his opportunities in the game to score and both these players grew up playing in the same *campito* (playground) of their poor Montevideo neighbourhood.

Football is a game of opinions but unfortunately in Australia many within the game are scared of opinions. The criticism that I offer is to make things better and, in the aftermath of Montevideo, my suggestions are intended to make Farina a better coach. I have been an admirer of his since I first saw him as an eighteen year old playing for Canberra City. He was exciting; he used to electrify the crowd. He had great PR skills even then and he presented very well. He was always going to do well and be good for the game. He had something different about him, personality on and off the field—the 'star' factor. I openly supported his appointment as Socceroos coach. But I think that Frank would benefit with the involvement of a technical director. Frank's brains trust sitting alongside him on the bench—Graham Arnold, Tony Franken and Ange Postecoglou—were all promising but, at this stage, inexperienced coaches. I wonder who else Frank consulted about our qualification campaign? Did he approach any of Australia's South American football community for advice and input? Raul Blanco or Vic Fernandez?

There needed to be a grieving period after the game. There also should have been an inquest after our failure, yet I didn't see one. Instead, the effluvium generated by the press was mostly concerned with the politicking and positioning of coach replacements and the like. Amazingly to me, Frank was reappointed as Socceroo coach without having had a meeting with the board since his return from Montevideo. Futhermore, the advice of Soccer Australia's own technical director was not sought in Farina's reappointment. I find it hard to understand that something as fundamental as the national coach is not in the sphere of influence of the technical director. We won't have matured in football terms until the game is at liberty to conduct a proper post-mortem. For example, what level of research had been conducted by the coaching staff on our opponents for the Montevideo game? Frank expressed surprise at Uruguay's selection of Regueiro in the starting line-up for the game. His selection was so pivotal to the outcome and our people didn't really even know who he was! But perhaps the biggest conjecture surrounded Harry Kewell. It is either the case that Harry asked to be played as a striker and Frank agreed to this, or that Frank should take the heat for the tactical mistake, because it was clear that the Australian team was functioning more effectively when Harry played wide on the left, with Viduka being supported in the middle by either Agostino or Aloisi. The epitaph that 'we just had a bad day' is far from acceptable. The level of debate about our World Cup qualification performance needs to be raised and amplified. It is for the broader national interest that the Socceroos qualify for the World Cup, so where is the national scrutiny? Institutional Australia seems content to sit back and let football stumble, stagnate or wither away. Is it the sheilas, wogs and poofters mentality again? Australia at large, its media as well as its public and corporate institutions, should be tearing down the door of Soccer Australia demanding answers. 'It was just a bad day' is a completely unacceptable offering for our failure.

So it is from amidst this current wreck of non-qualification that diagnoses must be made and realities faced. The most obvious thing to me is that there appears to be no plan and no coordination of the activities of football in this country at a national level. I have been calling for years for the national body to appoint a technical director whose job it is to oversee the entire football operation in Australia, from junior development strategies to elite training and national teams. Throughout the course of this book I have nominated two possibilities—Joe Venglos and Carlos Alberto Pereira. Both are football experts—experienced coaches and managers, planners, developers and educators. Ideally, whoever the technical director is, the national coaching structure would be under his auspices. The technical director would not select national teams but in all other areas coaches would be answerable to him. He would establish the culture, construct the strategy, plan the program, set the goals and implement the model for football in Australia.

The technical director is the person who should oversee planning for all the national teams and establish a consistent playing style between those national teams. It is he who should appoint the coaches. His should be a long-term appointment, with a long-term view. He must be a person from whom all of football's constituents—the players, coaches, media and broader football community—can learn. He must be an international figure, to assuage greater interaction between Australia and the rest of the football world. Of course, Soccer Australia needs to acknowledge the need for the acquisition of such a football emissary. I have forwarded the names of both Dr Venglos and Carlos Alberto Pereira to head office. Nothing has ever come of either suggestion. Is it the case that Soccer Australia feels it can do without the assistance of such experts?

Other keys to Australia's football development are less directly affected by decisions at Soccer Australia, such as the inclusion of Australian teams in Asian competition. Simply put, Australia must engage its football neighbours in Asia, where massive opportunities exist. There are huge economies and populations which are, by and large, devoted to the sport of football. Australia wants and needs more trade with Asia, yet we foolishly do not pay attention to the most effective trade show of all, international football. Within the full range of Australia's diplomatic missions, football should have primacy. It is football that registers on the radar screens of the mass markets to which Australia needs access. Somehow, strangely, Australia's comparatively small population prefers to attempt to reprogram the Asian culture to make it more amenable to cricket, rugby or Aussie Rules than the world game of football. That is a huge task, much larger and costlier than harnessing football and riding its wave. Why ignore it?

Access to Asia through football will take work. It will take a lot of PR, as well as government and business support, to convince Asia we deserve their patronage. Some of the ground has been scorched already. The emergence of the 'Pauline Hanson' factor in the 1990s sullied our international reputation somewhat. There was also, in the mid-1990s, a program of exchange between Japan and Australia set up by me through Shun-ichiro Okano, the head of Japan football and boss of their 2002 World Cup committee. (Okano is the co-host of the 2002 World Cup, an IOC member and the most respected sporting official in Japan. I met him when I was captain of the Australian national team at which time he was the coach of Japan. I have remained close friends with this amazingly gracious man who has encouraged me in my mission to elevate Australian football onto the world stage.) It entailed the exchange of ideas and personnel, including players, coaches, referees and officials between Australia and Japan. It also involved a play-off between our NSL champions and Japan's equivalent, the J-League. The Melbourne Knights played in the first of these matches against the Kashima Antlers. I then handed everything over to Soccer Australia for continuation but nothing has ever happened from their end. Mr Okano has followed this up with me and it is very embarrassing to say that nothing has ever resulted from our efforts. Club teams from Japan, South Korea and China have been visiting Australia over recent years as part of their pre-season preparations. There has obviously been interest from them to be involved with Australian football, but it doesn't seem that Soccer Australia has been able to harness their advances. This level of operation is well below what is required of a national soccer administration to promote the game.

Already, former Soccer Australia chairman David Hill had attempted to include Australia in the Asian Confederation but was voted out at the FIFA congress 172 to 1 (his was

Australia's sole vote). Quite clearly, Asia doesn't want us yet. This should be the focus of inquiry in itself. In the meantime, the responsibility lies with Australia to make its football operations so impressive and professional that Asia can't help but welcome us. We must seek to be included in Asian continental championships—both club and international. It is the immediate way forward for us. It would give our national team more concentrated competition, more often. It would give our national league clubs access to large markets and television audiences, making them more attractive to sponsors desperate for the regional exposure. An Asian Champions League should be the aim. Imagine Perth playing Shanghai in front of one hundred thousand people—an irresistible proposition with boundless potential for football and Australia.

Important to football's future in Australia is the debate about direct qualification to the World Cup from Oceania. I can't agree that this is good. Australia would go from having two meaningful games every four years to having none. Direct qualification would be almost guaranteed, such is the gap in ability between Australia and its Oceania counterparts. Supporters of direct qualification argue that Oceania would receive a huge boost by having one of its teams directly qualify for every World Cup. However, unless the standard of football is improved in Oceania the results at each of those World Cups will potentially make for embarrassment. I don't believe we should earn our place through the political process of FIFA, but we should do it through our football itself, and show the world that we actually mean business. Furthermore, the contention that we would be able to access FIFA revenues through appearing at the World Cup finals is a vacuous one. Compared with serious interaction with Asian club and international competitions, FIFA appearance money is miniscule.

We'll certainly welcome it upon receipt, but please let's not make it the foundation plank of our business plan.

In many ways, it is the NSL that is the point of sale for football in this country. It is currently Australian football's ugly cousin, though it needn't be so. Australia will improve as a football nation when its national league is worth something more to both players and fans. When the stakes of such competitions are raised, as a corollary of professional operations, all aspects of football are positively impacted. Intense competition at a local level refines the playing standards and girds the mental strength of its participants—a more adequate preparation for the rigours of world football. From its vitality comes development, progress, quality, revenue, opportunity and results.

Australia, to its own detriment, ignores the potential of women's football too. It is already growing exponentially. Women's football is arguably the fastest growing sporting movement in the world. FIFA President Sepp Blatter stated at the completion of the 1999 Women's World Cup in the USA, 'the future of football is feminine'. Ninety thousand fans attended the final played out between the United States and China, which the United States won in a penalty shootout 5–4. The game's television audience in the United States alone was forty million—more than either that country's men's professional basketball competition (the NBA) or its men's professional ice hockey competition (the NHL) finals' series. The growth and profile of women's football in the United States is awesome. The inaugural season of the professional women's league of the United States (the WUSA), completed last year, performed well beyond expectations. The games were played before good crowds and the market impact of the league amongst young North American females was immense. Interestingly, the flag-bearer for women's football in the United States, Mia Hamm has reportedly surpassed Anna Kournikova in market worth in North America. Also interesting to note is that it was Australian Julie Murray—part of the national women's team of Australia, the Matildas—who scored a goal in normal time as well as the winning penalty in the shoot-out to deliver the inaugural WUSA Championship to her team, the Bay Area Cyberrays. The match was played at the famous Foxboro Stadium in Massachusetts in front of twenty-one thousand spectators.

We have also seen the bona fides of women's football on our own shores. Sydney 2000 treated the fans to football's sisterhood. Two of the highlights of the Olympics for me centred around women's football. One of them was the goal scored by Matilda player Sunni Hughes at the SFS against Brazil. It was a goal conceived and executed as if samba blood was coursing through her veins. Indeed, the great Pelé himself would have admired the effort. Here was an Australian woman doing to Brazil what Brazil has been doing to the world for the last fifty years or so. My second Sydney 2000 highlight was the gold-medal match of the women's football tournament, played between the United States (including Mia Hamm) and Norway. It was a memorable game because of the technical quality on offer as well as the sporting drama that unfolded. The United States was almost the unbackable favourite for the gold medal; Norway was supposedly making up the numbers only. Certainly, as the game unfolded, predictions and expectations seemed accurate. Team USA were awesome; athletic and skilful and really only matched by Norway's collective will plus their goalkeeper, who performed miracles that day. Somehow, in a manner that only football can contrive, the match went into extra time and the sudden death golden-goal scenario. It was a last-minute goal in normal time by the United States that had levelled the scores at 2–2 and taken the match to extra time. How Norway twice established and then held onto any lead is still, to me, incredible. However, the golden-goal was ultimately scored by Norway who, in any other sport, would have been out of the contest much earlier. Norway won the gold-medal match 3–2. Only football could dish up such drama. It was edge-of-the-seat exciting. It was classic football and it was female. Again, for Australia, women's football provides huge and global potential.

It is for this football culture, on a global scale, that I so desperately crave. It is this football culture that Australia so desperately needs. The loss in Uruguay was the latest instalment in the realisation that in football terms, Australia is culturally arid. Spending the days leading up to the 25 November qualification game in Montevideo I found it interesting and immensely disturbing to compare the press coverage of both nations with respect to the approaching game. Uruguay's newspapers were focused primarily on the football minutiae; the statistics, the injuries, the form, the selections, the personnel. Australia, on the other hand, seemed obsessed with non-football issues. Most notable was the incident at Montevideo's airport, where an unruly and orchestrated few disrupted Australia's arrival. Up until the game, this absorbed the interest of the Australian media. It was a minor incident and while being worthy of a minor news report, unfortunately became the focus for much of Australia. It was embarrassing in Montevideo to have to explain Australia's orgiastic consternation in response to the fracas at the airport. Worse still, the front page of Montevideo's major newspaper referred to Australian news stories: *'Reaccion de la prensa Australiana*—"Bloody Disgrace", "Animals", "Spitting and Abuse"' which showed Australia's small-mindedness in depicting the situation in Montevideo with such inflammatory headlines. It seemed to be the 'wogs' mentality again, referring to the Uruguayan people. I was flabbergasted reading it all. The Australian insistence to focus on security, rather than football, was mystifying. The ugly culmination of all this was seen on game day. The last place at the World Cup finals for 2002 was up for grabs. Australia's most important game of football was upon us, and a full-page spread in the *Sunday Telegraph* was headlined 'Escape Plan'. It seemed to convey the message, 'Forget about the football. How are our boys going to escape the "wogs" with their lives? In contrast, Uruguay's Sunday paper featured a full-page spread in sky-blue reading: *'Por el pueblo, Por el hincha, Por la celeste, Por favor!'*—'For the people, For the fans, For the Sky Blue, Please!'—an all-embracing message of support from Uruguay to its team. One newspaper issuing an exhortation on behalf of the nation, the other sadly reverting to type to ignorantly dumb down the significance of the match.

In my opinion, these are indications that our football culture is, at an institutional level at least, embryonic. Another example prior to the Montevideo game was the case of Australian media articles boldly declaring that soccer is about to enter the popular culture. This sort of stuff is wildly myopic. Soccer *is* the popular culture. It's the world's number-one game. It's fairly popular in Australia already too, although this sort of media content would have you believe otherwise. Then, in the rubble of the result at Montevideo, it was proclaimed that Aussies will never like soccer anyway, because it isn't gutsy or glorious and is therefore barely a sport. Wrong on both counts. An expeditious change of tack, not unlike a politician chasing a cheap vote at election time.

It is this sort of cultural resistance that must be overcome. This remains a pivotal issue in the nation's development and the game's vitality. I am reminded, after all this, of the start of the Commonwealth Bank Cup, one of Australia's longest running school sport competitions. Its birth resulted from an auction night at Easts Leagues Club in Bondi Junction. I had donated my Socceroo shirt for the fundraising. John Singleton was the auctioneer. Singo has a tremendous wit and a keen ability to portray himself as the quintessential Aussie bloke. A larrikin by nature as well as by manufacture, he is sharp, entertaining, successful, influential and connected. As auctioneer, Singleton was in charge of the memorabilia. There were rugby league jerseys, Wallaby jumpers and so on—an impressive collection that promised to raise a few bob. Amidst it all was my shirt. It was an ordinary piece of clothing too, although what it represented was invaluable. In these modern merchandising times you wouldn't expect it to attract the young and/or fashion conscious. You wouldn't expect it to be a huge seller. The designer dimples in the fabric made it appear moth-eaten but, in truth, it was in great condition. Singo picked up my shirt and began taking bids, his manner artistically dismissive. A bid came from the crowd—six hundred dollars. Singo, eyes raised and brow furrowed, cleared his ears, which he thought must have been deceiving him, before retorting that this bloke must have been joking. Joking he certainly wasn't. The bidding continued until it reached its peak at eight hundred dollars. My Socceroo shirt fetched the highest price at auction that night!

The incident caused much mirth. Singo was in his element and he milked it for everything he could. He, so representative of the community, was genuinely dumbfounded that there was a market for anything soccer. In meeting the buyer, Dennis Merchant, I discovered an advertising executive, one of whose clients was the Commonwealth Bank. He wanted to help soccer out and I directed his interest towards New South Wales Combined High Schools football. We established the Commonwealth Bank Cup and over the fifteen years it has been in existence, sponsorship in the vicinity of one-and-a-half million dollars has been injected into school soccer. It is the largest competition of its kind in the southern hemisphere. I was involved in travelling around to watch the games and to promote the competition. One such visit to a match at Bankstown where a breathtaking goal was scored sticks out in my mind. I asked a teacher in attendance the name of the scorer. 'Waugh' was his response. I can't recall if it was Steve or Mark, both of whom were splendid footballers, but it is extremely lucky for cricket, and a loss for soccer, that they chose to pursue the 'baggy green'.

For Australia to reach its football potential there are, in my mind, four challenges. The first is, as I've stated, to find and appoint a technical director who is active in the areas I have suggested. This is an immediate imperative. The second challenge concerns our national professional club competition. It requires urgent and radical surgery. The national league is the conduit to the third and fourth challenges; formal access to Asia and the growth and development of an Australian football culture. From here the world is our oyster.

Those in powerful positions need to embrace the game, or they will be replaced by another generation more conversant with and sympathetic to football. I feel there is a degree of inevitability about this. His Excellency Marcos Cortes, Brazilian Ambassador, explained at my fiftieth birthday celebrations that upon his arrival in Australia he wondered if our country had a problem with either language and/or our understanding of anatomy because the sports we commonly call football—rugby league, rugby union and Aussie Rules—are, in fact, played mainly with the hands, rather than feet. It is a common experience for many who come to Australia to question the fact that we have to call the world game of football 'soccer' to avoid confusion. This will change over time. The culture will develop and, as it does, the demands on those running soccer in Australia will be such that accountability and performance will be demanded. As the culture grows and the organisation of the game improves, the quality and size of both the playing and administrative talent pools will also increase. We will know when we are there, or nearly there, because the world will want to know us. The results will follow and Australia will be performing proudly, taking the world on at its own game and, knowing Australia, very probably winning.

Epilogue

⚽ IN 1988 THE St George soccer club held a tribute night for me in honour of my induction, alongside two hundred other Australian sporting people, into the Bicentennial Hall of Fame. The Hall of Fame is based at the Melbourne Cricket Ground and was established to recognise the greatest Australian sports stars throughout the nation's first two hundred years of European settlement. Being included in the Hall of Fame was one of the most significant and important acknowledgments I have ever received because of the great names that I was placed alongside. I will always remember the tribute night held for me at the St George club as a special night because of a speech made by my good friend and SBS soccer colleague Les Murray. I was so humbled by Les's words that I later asked him if I could keep his speaking notes. I have included an extract below.

> I have known Johnny for forty years after first meeting him at St George training. What I didn't realise then was that he would, in a sense, become a freak in Australian football. Not

because he excelled in a team of twelve year olds at the age of five. Not because he became his club captain at nineteen, national team vice-captain at twenty-one and Australian captain at twenty-three. Nor because he made a courageous comeback from a horrendous injury, which had him written off by doctors, coaches and fans alike. He is a freak because he is the true-blue soccer hero, in a country where soccer heroes are never true-blue. In our confusing Tower of Babel, where the soccer culture is entirely imported, he is the native who puts us to shame in his love and devotion to the game. When he played he played, when he coached he coached, when he writes he writes and when he talks he talks as if he was brought up not on Bradman, Churchill or Gasnier but on Pelé, Puskas and Platini. We don't know whether he was born inside the soccer prism or whether he was moulded so by circumstance, but it is certain that his soccer life, which spans some fifty years, is riddled by a series of events meant, it seems, by divine fate, to keep him on the football park.

Towards the end of his speech Les referred to my role in bringing out to Australia the United States club side, the New York Cosmos, and how their match against the Australian team demonstrated the overwhelming support of the Australian soccer community for the game.

The visit of the New York Cosmos, where gates were broken down and estimates of the crowd range from 80,000 upwards, proved conclusively what many of us up until then had only wanted to believe; that there are more than enough soccer fans in this country if you give them what they want. Johnny Warren did that for the past five decades, he is the singular outstanding example of someone putting all he has back into the game. It is certain that Johnny Warren got a lot out of the game, it is even more certain that the game got even more out of him.

It is true that I have got so much out of the game. The best things about football are its experiences. There is no market for these experiences; they cannot be bought. They are available to everyone who partakes of the football communion. Irrespective of the level of play, football unites its people with a bond that can neither be manufactured nor replicated. Playing football and meeting its people enriches the soul, or at least it has mine. Reflecting on my life in and around football has made this very clear to me. For while I have had the fortune to play football at the highest level and make a living from the game, my real satisfaction has come from meeting football's people. When I am asked to recall the great games or great victories of my career, invariably three events come to mind.

In 1975 Victor Fernandez, Atti Abonyi and I were invited by some soccer fans from Lightning Ridge—a town in far north-western New South Wales better known for its opals than for its football—to make a guest appearance for their team in a match there. Lightning Ridge, typical of mining areas, has a largely transient population and there was a broad cross-section of people living there. The Lightning Ridge football team was therefore made up of an interesting collection of players.

Upon arrival at the town we noticed the streets had been decorated with welcoming banners. Everyone seemed pleased to see us. We found out we were playing another far north-western team. We were also informed that the entire town—miners basically—had put their money on Lightning Ridge to win the game.

Victor and Atti played up front and I decided to play at the back to help organise the team during the game. The bulk of our team was made up of local miners, uncompromising individuals, who had little obvious feel for the game. While Vic and Atti were 'fannying about' (football vernacular for being fancy and ineffective, performing tricks and showing off without exerting yourself for the good of the team) I was shoring up the team with the rapidly increasing realisation that our opponents weren't all that bad and that if we weren't careful, we would be in for some trouble. Worse than that, our goal was under siege. It was like the Alamo back there. I was working harder than a one-legged man in a bum-kicking competition. Meanwhile, Vic and Atti were contentedly 'fannying about' up front.

By half-time we were down 1–0. The match had quickly descended from a fun outing to a very tough day. Vic and Atti were having a right old time, but I was worrying that if we lost, with all the town's money backing us, we might not make it out alive. I had to take my two mates aside during the break and in the nicest and most appropriate football terms, tell them to pull their fingers out. Thankfully, in the second half, both played more seriously and when the game ended we had managed to win 2–1. I have never experienced greater relief. The people of Lightning Ridge were happy; their hip pockets duly satisfied. After customary post-match country functions—a couple of tinnies with the sausage sizzle—we left. Lightning Ridge hasn't experienced J. Warren since, although the memory of that match and some of the characters we met there still warms my heart.

Another of my great games happened after the FIFA coaching course I attended in Malaysia. I was in Singapore and bumped into two Australian army officers, Warrant Officer Bruce Glossop and Lieutenant/Warrant Officer Tommy Moyes, both of whom I had met during Socceroo tours in Vietnam. Bruce had been posted there and Tommy was Master of the visiting army vessel (AV) *John Monash*. Tommy told me that there was a big soccer match coming up between the troops from the AV *John Monash* and the English frigate HMS *Yarmouth*. Both ships' companies decided that an Ashes style soccer match was in order. Most of the Australians came from Aussie Rules and rugby backgrounds and both Tommy and Bruce were worried that the footballing Poms would be too good. They asked if I would play to give them a much-needed hand.

At the time I was still rehabilitating from my knee injury. I hadn't played football for eighteen months. I was concerned about playing but felt a debt of gratitude to the boys from the Vietnam days and, anyway, I fancied a chance to have a crack at the Poms. The match-day tropical heat was stifling and I knew the English would find it more of an issue than our lads. I played at the back to organise the defence. I forewarned our keeper that the Poms would launch high balls into the box from the wings and that he shouldn't worry because, being an Aussie Rules player, all he had to do was come out and 'mark' everything that came by. 'Like picking cherries for you,' I told him. Also, thanks to Aussie Rules, the boys knew how to man-to-man defend, so all they had to do was be physical, stay with their man and eventually, with the heat, we would wear down our 'Hooray Henry' opponents. Sure enough, with our goal still intact, we pinched a goal right at the death, to win 1–0. For our lads it was like winning the World Cup. We Australians had beaten the Poms at soccer. The lads couldn't believe it and were completely jubilant. I was overjoyed to have been part of it all. It is one of my life's great experiences. An informal setting with dinky di Aussies; diggers taking on the mother country and winning. There was much cheering and drinking and singing after the match and I will never ever forget that day.

The third experience that comes to mind as a highlight of my life in football happened in Canberra. At the conclusion of my Canberra City days, my good friend Charlie Perkins, who was assembling a team to play in the ACT sixth division, telephoned me to sign me up. I agreed to a free transfer and decided to get the boots out of the kit bag for one last time. The time that followed with the Canberra City Old Boys turned out to be one of the most enjoyable seasons I have ever had. The combined age of the team came to five hundred and ninety-five, yet we still won the league and cup double. I had great fun playing with my old mates and showing some of the youngsters that we weren't completely past it. Some of the other teams must have been completely shocked to have been beaten by the geriatrics. During that 1986 season, the Canberra City Old Boys played twenty-nine games, scoring one hundred and forty-nine goals in the process and losing only once. I will always appreciate the friendship of all those wonderful Canberra City Old Boys—Keni Kawaleva, Mick Black, Danny Moulis, Ivan Gruicic, Roy Stark, Charlie Perkins, Steve Doszpot, Theo Moulis, Steve Matheson, Dom Catanzaritti, Herb Klemperer, Norm Sawyer, John Hawkins, Chris Janisewski, Eric and Bill Vandervlist, Mike Evans, Loc Bui, Neville Perkins, Ross Dobson, Tony Rita and Joe Pelle.

The season proved to me that playing soccer is more than World Cups and national soccer leagues. The game is about the entire football community, whether that is a Rio *favela*, or Real Madrid and Barcelona, or Jamberoo Pub or Canberra City Old Boys. The game is a unifying power. The feelings and experiences that are shared are common to all players. The feeling of scoring a goal, dribbling past an opponent, executing a perfect pass excite all footballers. Perhaps because of the shared joy of the game, football binds people outside the football pitch. The football family is warm and open. It embraces everyone who loves football. Membership to the football family does not depend on ability but rather on devotion and camaraderie, reinforced by a shared respect for this most beautiful, and basic, game. It is a simple game and people love it. Probably the most poignant theme throughout football is that its greatest players are also the most down-to-earth people. Football people, real football people, will do anything, anytime for other football people. That is community at work.

Cover photo: Johnny Warren in 1964 playing Pan Hellenic at the old Sydney Sports Ground. His Pan Hellenic opponent is George McCulloch, whose son Tommy captained Australia at the 1983 World Youth Championships in Mexico.

Back photo: Former Scotland and Glasgow Celtic goalkeeper Frank Haffey celebrates St George's 1967 5–2 grand final win over arch-rivals Apia at the Sydney Sports Ground by spectacularly balancing on the crossbar and waving to St George fans.

Every effort has been made to identify copyright holders of pictures and extracts in this book. The publishers would be pleased to hear from copyright holders who have not been acknowledged.